MOTHERLANDS

MOTHERLANDS

Amaryllis Gacioppo

BLOOMSBURY PUBLISHING
LONDON · OXFORD · NEW YORK · NEW DELHI · SYDNEY

BLOOMSBURY PUBLISHING
Bloomsbury Publishing Plc
50 Bedford Square, London, WC1B 3DP, UK
29 Earlsfort Terrace, Dublin 2, Ireland

BLOOMSBURY, BLOOMSBURY PUBLISHING and the Diana logo are
trademarks of Bloomsbury Publishing Plc

First published in Great Britain 2022

A catalogue record for this book is available from the British Library

ISBN: HB: 978-1-5266-2276-1; TPB: 978-1-5266-2275-4; EBOOK: 978-1-5266-2277-8

2 4 6 8 10 9 7 5 3 1

Typeset by Newgen KnowledgeWorks Pvt. Ltd., Chennai, India
Printed and bound in Great Britain by CPI Group (UK) Ltd, Croydon CR0 4YY

To find out more about our authors and books visit www.bloomsbury.com
and sign up for our newsletters

For Annalisa Gueli

Contents

Home

The experience of returning to my mother's city was different from what I had expected. Growing up in Australia, Palermo existed in my mind as a kind of spectral theatre. I had nose-bleed seats in this theatre, the curtains opened and closed on disparate scenes that jumped forward and backward through time. It was the stage of many of our family stories, and its setting was tied up with any notion I had of a family history. It was, to borrow a phrase from André Aciman, my 'soul home'. By which I mean that it was not the city in which I was born, but it was the city that I saw when I glanced back over my shoulder. It was my origin, a place that I returned to rather than visited.

The idea of the originary home is embedded in our global cultural and psychological framework. The world's religions and cultures contain different origin theories at their cores. From Freud's theory that the first human desire is to return to the womb, to the Biblical first home of Eden from which humanity was expelled, to Odysseus's Ithaca, home is both the origin from which we have been expelled and, if we have behaved ourselves, the promised land which awaits us.

When I was three, my parents moved from Sydney to a small coastal town ten hours north of the city. Brief snatches of the trip return to me: being placed into the backseat of my parents' old Renault Fuego with a trailer of our belongings hooked to the back of the car; the smell of petrol and sticky ocean air when we stopped to fill up at a station on the coastal highway; the swirling sensation of car sickness in my stomach made worse by the stuffy heat of the car; pulling into the driveway of our new home. In each memory I am crying, which leads me to believe that I cried the whole drive there. I have taken this drive from our town to Sydney countless times since, and in the intervening years it has become unrecognisable. What once used to be a winding ten-hour journey along unbroken coasts and through sleepy town centres is now a streamlined eight hours down a sleek highway.

Our new house was in an area that was just beginning to be developed; our few neighbours were made up of either young families or retirees, and the neighbourhood was a chessboard of zoned-off plots of land and the skeletal frames of future houses. Over the years, the town evolved at the same rate as the drive to Sydney. The landscapes of my youth − the rainforest remnants, the macadamia farms, the green valleys, the abandoned drive-in − all disappeared and were replaced by neat brick bungalows with terracotta roofs. My mother liked to seek out open houses so that she could compare them to our home. With her practised air of a potential buyer, she would tour the rooms, all pungent with the smell of new paint and fresh carpet. These newer houses all seemed to be chosen from six or seven prefabricated open-plan designs. In that subtropical climate, it was always sunny, and you could smell optimism in the air: every open house represented a new beginning. The residents' gazes were firmly directed towards the future.

Inside our home, it was a different story; all our family stories took place in Italy, all our heirlooms had been shipped over in the white travel trunks that followed my mother to Australia, as did our family recipes and the language we spoke. Our walls were covered in sepia-toned photographs of people I didn't recognise, the streetscapes and landscapes behind them starkly different from the world outside our home.

In Italian, there is no direct translation for 'home'. There is *casa*, literally meaning 'house', but used also for one's apartment, country, origin, town, city. There is no separation, as we have in English, between 'house' and 'home'. All languages have telling gaps or untranslatable terms that reveal something about their culture. A culture that has no word for a certain emotion evidently has had less need to articulate that emotion. For example, in Italian, there are two ways to say 'I love you': *ti amo*, which is reserved for the expression of romantic love between lovers, and the much more freely used *ti voglio bene*, which expresses the platonic love between family members and friends. The same goes for the absence of a distinction between house and home in Italian; in Italy, there is no way to articulate that a house – one's residence – might not also be a home. Correspondingly, there is also no direct translation for 'homeland' in Italian. The closest would be *patria* (fatherland), *madrepatria* (motherland) or *terra madre* (motherland again). Origins are often associated with mothers: Mother Russia, or Bharat Mata (Mother India). Personifying a country as a mother also holds empirical connotations – the British Motherland. Or 'metropolis', from the Greek: mother city. The mother is the root, the beginning.

My desire to know Palermo was a desire to possess it. Until I returned for the first time as an adult after a decade-long absence, in my early twenties, I took for granted that I did indeed possess all the sites of my family's past. My parents, my brother and I had made the drive down to Reggio Calabria from Rome, and then boarded the *traghetto* that ferries passengers and their vehicles from Italy's mainland to Messina, a city on the easternmost tip of the island, from where the toe of Italy's boot can be seen. From there it is a three-hour drive west to Palermo, Sicily's capital, and my mother's city. In the months before the trip, I had referred to it as my homecoming. I would recognize the cobblestone streets and Baroque buildings, not just from childhood memories, but from an innate place within me. Somehow, I would know how to get around the city, my Sicilian blood bestowing me with an internal compass. The gentle ripples of the Tyrrhenian Sea would swaddle my body like a baptism, and when the hot winds of the sirocco whipped my face with the red dust of the Sahara, it would feel like home.

The best way to describe how I felt when actually confronted with the real-life city, driving into Palermo's smoggy anarchy of traffic, is by using an Italian word, *spaesamento*. The Zingarelli dictionary defines its root word, *spaesato*, as 'the feeling of discomfort and awkwardness due to being among strangers, or people who are too different from oneself, or in an unfamiliar environment'. Used in common speech to describe the feeling of being lost, the term *spaesamento* (the suffix of 'mento' in Italian corresponds to 'ness' in English, as in 'sadness') is also often used in Italian as a translation of Freud's concept of the *unheimlich*. The German *unheimlich* − literally, the unhomely − is referred to in English as 'the uncanny': the unsettling sensation of finding the unfamiliar in the familiar, or vice versa. But *spaesamento* connotes more than this. Within *spaesato*, we have the root Italian word for country, *paese*, and the 's' prefix, which corresponds to the English 'dis', as in 'disappear', and 'un' as in 'undone.' Literally, to feel *spaesato* is to feel un-countried or un-homed. It suggests a dispersal of the self, a confused state of inner unmooring.

I see now that there were two Palermos, which I had conflated − the one that existed in my mind, and the one I encountered. More than this, I associated time with geography − some places held the past, and some held the present and the future.

Depending on the map, Palermo resembles the head of a dog, an ant-eater, a wailing woman. The port is undoubtedly a crooked grin. Topographic maps of the city drawn by Matteo Florimi circa 1580 and G. Brown and F. Hogenberg in 1581 reveal an urban patchwork in the centre dissected by one off-centre thoroughfare that runs from the outer limit of the city directly down to the port, and a haphazard tangle of streets throughout. The maps show the city walls, beyond which the mountains were populated with agriculture. The walls trace the curve of the city and mountains, an off-kilter rectangle with turrets that jut out, like spades on a playing card. The port curls into the city. The mountains, cradling the city. Palermo's geological features determined its name, which originally came from the Greek '*Panormos*', meaning 'all port'.

A map is a way of colonising physical space. We shrink terrain down to scale to create the impression that, looking down at it from a godly perspective, we have some control over it. Still, I can't seem to wrap my head around the city in which my mother was born, even when it's flattened and printed on a page. Even represented in a book, Palermo seems as untameable and chaotic as it does when one is standing in one of its streets in a sea of its citizens, motorists weaving their way around its roads with one hand perpetually pressing down on their horns, or else gesticulating at other cars and motor scooters, cigarettes clamped in teeth, everyone ignoring any kind of rule that might attempt to govern the road. Zooming out and gazing at the topography of Palermo on the page, I can almost see the roads pulsing.

Recently my mother and I were discussing the concept of home and where it is located for each of us. We decided that home was a physical place which claims a reassuring ownership over us. My mother admitted that the last time she felt this ownership was on via la Farina in Palermo. In her mind, the city had remained her home throughout my childhood. She had come to Australia on what was supposed to be a six-week holiday, met my father, who had migrated to Australia from Sicily twenty years prior, and married him three months later. From when I was born in Sydney until I had my fourth birthday in that apartment on via La Farina, we visited a few times, but we didn't return until I was eleven. By this point my maternal grandmother, Nonna Annalisa, had sold the apartment on via La Farina and bought a villa in Mondello, Palermo's beachside borough, which housed my aunt, uncle and two cousins. Despite having left her childhood home fifteen years prior, my mother told me that this was the moment when she felt Palermo truly ceased to be her home. Up until then, the Palermo apartment was her centre, her fixed origin.

When I was lost in Palermo, I walked to my mother's old palazzo on via La Farina. La Farina is in the centre of Palermo, a crossroad of via della Libertà. My mother's sister, Zia Esmeralda, tells me the palazzo is now full of lawyer's offices. Now people get divorces and make up wills in the rooms in which my mother grew up. I stood outside, across the street from the butter-coloured building. I tried to imagine my mother flicking ash onto the street while leaning over the balcony railing, tried to see her ducking in and out to answer her mother or a phone call. I was here, metres from what I had presumed to be the centre, and yet, I felt so far away.

The trip was an uncanny homecoming. Certain things that I thought would feel familiar were not, and yet in unexpected moments I experienced rushes of familiarity: a sensation of seeing and being seen by the city. Sights or smells could trigger it: the waft of bread baking in a *fornaio* recalled a trip to Favignana, a small Sicilian island, taken when I was eleven, or a mother bundled up a sniffling child, and I would think *I know this, I've been here.* Perhaps because it matched some scene or background in a photo back in my parents' home, or imitated some story my grandmother had told me. It was a similar sensation to that of travelling to a city in which one's favourite book is set – the sense of encountering fiction in reality, fiction that has affected one's life in a real way, and having that familiarity confirmed. Within that moment, I think, of recognising and feeling recognised by one's surroundings, is a sense of belonging.

In spite of my occasional bouts of alienation, I nonetheless felt as though Palermo belonged to me, like a never-met birth parent. When I was young, I had pictured elegant dinners, my mother and her siblings as children clutching silver cutlery in their hands, heavy and gleaming, and parties in the apartments of family friends. In my mind the streets were full of criminals masked by the foot traffic, swiftly snatching the gold chains from women's necks, sucking the rings off their fingers, tearing earrings from lobes.

This image I had of Palermo was largely due to my mother. If we were out to eat at a café in Australia and I hooked my bag over my chair, for example, she would point out how I could never live in an Italian city: nobody in Palermo would ever do that. In Palermo women would leave the house with their jewellery in their pockets and put it on at the door of their destinations. Or if my brother and I didn't want to wear our shoes to the supermarket (going barefoot was common in our small Australian town), she would remind us that in Palermo, kids wore their shoes all the time, lest they stepped on a syringe. When I looked in my mother's wardrobe, I found vintage furs and shirts made of lace; in her jewellery box there were pearls and gold rings. Our family seemed rooted there, and this rootedness both attracted me and made me feel trapped. Naively, I had assumed that Palermo would remain in stasis during my long absence – after all, that is how my mother spoke of it, convinced that the social and cultural customs of a 1980s Italy would be the same thirty years later.

When I was growing up, my mother would tell me about Palermo, and her mother – Nonna Annalisa – would tell me about Benghazi and Turin. My grandmother's stories began with her mother: my great-grandmother Rita, who at twenty-nine left her home in Turin, a city at the foot of the Italian Alps, for Libya. At this time Libya was an Italian colony, seized during the European Scramble for Africa. Here she met my great-grandfather Salvatore and had my Nonna Annalisa. My grandmother spent her childhood in Benghazi. Like Palermo, it is a coastal city founded by the Greeks that has since undergone a series of colonisations, by the Romans, the Byzantines, the Phoenicians, the Ottomans and finally the Italians. Each colonisation left its imprint on the cityscape; there is still a hunk of Ancient Greek wall, Roman dwellings, a Byzantine church. The Italians constructed a *lungomare*: a seaside promenade that still skirts Benghazi's downtown area. Looking at old photographs and postcards, certain places could be mistaken for Palermo. The streets are lined with palm trees and the buildings are all white in colour, as though they have been bleached by the Mediterranean sun. Moorish arches adorn buildings, colonnades provide shelter in a maze of narrow souks and squares, Arab minarets and domes punctuate the skyline, and the neoclassical Italianate buildings along the seafront look like a Cinecittà film set. Much of this – the Benghazi my grandmother pictures when she recalls her childhood – no longer exists, having either been bombed by the Allies and then the Axis forces during the Second World War, or else wiped out by Gaddafi when he seized control of Libya in the sixties.

My grandmother left Benghazi and was sent by her parents to Turin at the outbreak of the Second World War. Separated from her parents, she was moved first to her grandmother's home in Turin, then to a family friend's house, then to an Alpine boarding school, and then to her aunt's apartment in the city centre. She was reunited with her parents in 1943, in Rome.

After the war was over, Salvatore was offered bureaucratic jobs in Rome and Palermo. He wanted to go to Palermo, and Rita preferred to stay in Rome, so they enlisted Annalisa as tie-breaker. I never thought to ask my grandmother why she chose Palermo over Rome. I had always assumed that she wanted to be as far away from her wartime experiences as possible. Later, when I was in Palermo, I thought that perhaps it was because the city was closer to the Benghazi of her youth, both geographically and culturally. Historically the point at which the East and the West meet, Palermo is culturally more a Mediterranean city than a European one. The islands and countries that ring the Mediterranean share a deep history of colonisation and cultural cross-pollination, and both Sicily's fertile terrain and its strategic location as the gateway to Europe made it an essential conquest for empires dating back thousands of years. Of these colonisations, the Arab Empire made one of the most lasting impressions on Sicily and Palermo. During this time, Sicily was established as an Arab Emirate, with Palermo as its capital. The Arabs transformed the city from a strategic foothold into an actual urban centre. They built roads and planted date palms and citrus groves in the surrounding hills. They filled the city with mosques and souks, four of which wound outwards from the centre and down labyrinthine streets and alleyways.

They still exist today as open-air markets, and as I made my way through Mercato del Capo one morning a few years ago,

I watched as fishmongers hosed guts off pavements and hoisted swordfish onto trays, slotting tuna and salmon into neat rows with lit cigarettes dangling from their mouths. Fruit vendors yelled the prices of their produce beneath white sheets and underwear hung from balconies. One stall had a whole lamb for sale, shorn and halved, strung up so that you could see its gutted insides, its spine, its liver and heart and spleen swinging from its neck in different shades of purple and red. Whole octopuses and squids reclined on beds of ice, and the spice merchants were old men in caps sleepy-eyed on stools, with scales and orange, red and green mounds in front of them. They weighed packages of dates and dried figs and pine nuts. Green and black olives in vats. People clustered around vendors in aprons selling fried things in paper cones. Clouds of steam wafted from windows and women stepped out of the *foccacerie* with fresh bread wrapped in paper tucked under their arms. Fruit gleamed like jewels: strawberries and mulberries and persimmons and prickly pears. The cobblestones were wet with fish guts and melted ice, and it smelled like steam rising from bread and the sea. The quality of the sun here was different from how it was, as the Sicilians say, 'on the continent'.

In Palermo she studied law, political science and music; married, had three children (my mother the first of them) and left her husband by the age of thirty. She could just as easily have chosen to stay in Rome, where she would have lived a different life – one in which her husband wasn't a drunk and a gambler, but a different man with whom she would have had another host of children. Men were largely absent from my mother's youth. When she was four, she and her parents lived with her father's family. The marriage between her parents was supposed to be a fortuitous match; he came from a 'good' family – old money, well educated. My grandmother depended financially on her in-laws; her husband, a spoiled only child, was happy to remain so and spend his family's wealth on follies. One day, finding her purse emptied out by her absent husband, she asked her mother-in-law for money to buy formula for the hungry baby, my Zia Esmeralda. Her mother-in-law refused; her money was reserved for her son's wine consumption, and she advised my grandmother to tend to her own children. My grandmother packed her bags, and that night she left her husband and returned with her children to her own parents' home.

It was my mother who told me this story, not my grandmother, who hardly ever spoke of her ex-husband and gave the impression that she wouldn't have left him if not for the sake of her children. I imagine that the decision came after a long period of feeling not-home in her husband's family home, and her mother-in-law's words only confirmed that she and her children did not belong there. My mother recalls that her maternal grandparents, Salvatore and Rita, who then lived in the apartment on via La Farina, put my grandmother, my mother and her two siblings in my grandmother's old bedroom. I suppose this was a subtle effort not to make them feel too at home, because after a few months, once they realised their daughter would not be returning to her husband, they surrendered other bedrooms in the apartment to the children. This was 1960. Divorce would not be legal for another decade, and it was unheard-of for women to leave their husbands. For the rest of their youth, my grandmother would tell her children that they had to be vigilant about the image they presented to Palermo society. In their social circles, they were watched more closely than others, and any mistake they made would be attributed to my grandmother.

Walking through the streets of Palermo, I thought about how the city would have looked back when my mother and my grandmother lived there. When my grandmother arrived, it was a ravaged city. During the Second World War, Sicily was the target of 'Operation Husky', an Allied military campaign to capture the island. The campaign deployed what is called an amphibious assault: a combination of air raids, ground troops and naval attacks. Palermo was so devastated by the bombings that more than 200,000 dwellings in the province were destroyed or damaged, and, as a result, many were left no choice but to live in shantytowns and, in some cases, caves. Even now, many buildings still boast bullet holes, while others are missing entire walls.

When my mother was coming of age in the seventies and eighties, Italy was going through its *anni di piombo*: years of lead. This term refers to the chaotic thirty-year period of social and political turmoil that lasted from the late sixties until the late eighties. It was a time marked by mass protests, bombings, political abductions and assassinations. It was a time when the car bombings and assassinations of prosecutors and judges regularly covered the front pages of newspapers, such as the murders of the famed antimafia magistrates Paolo Borsellino and Giovanni Falcone in 1992. Art Nouveau villas, historic hamlets and the city's once-famously lush gardens and citrus orchards were razed and replaced by ugly apartment buildings and concrete. These shoddy post-war constructions were so cheaply built that many are now falling to pieces, collapsing in on themselves like paper houses. Palermo is a city that bears its history like an open wound. Strangely enough, seeing all these markers of the past in the city only seemed to highlight how much time had passed. They were ruins, burial sites, memorials. They emphasised the fact that the past was dead, long-gone.

The English word 'home' derives from the Old English *hám*, which itself comes from the Proto-Germanic *haimaz*, meaning home or village. Thanks to its Germanic influences, English has another word that Italian does not: homesickness, a calque of the German *heimweh* (literally 'home-woe'). The closest term that Italian has to homesickness is '*nostalgia di casa*'. The term 'nostalgia', coined in 1688 by Swiss medical student Johannes Hofer, derives from the Greek *nostos*, meaning 'home', and *algos*, meaning 'pain', which derives from Algea, used in Ancient Greek mythology to personify sorrow and grief. Hofer proposed entering this state as a medical diagnosis, under the new scientific term 'nostalgia'. Missing home could literally kill you, and symptoms included fever, indigestion, fainting spells, insomnia, anxiety, loss of appetite and death. These were all symptoms that had been reported to Hofer by the Swiss mercenaries he treated, many of whom actually did die while yearning for their Alpine villages, surrounded by foreign landscapes and tongues. Up until the early twentieth century, 'nostalgia' was interchangeable with 'homesickness'. However, in the last hundred years the meaning of nostalgia has shifted from describing a specific yearning for home to something perhaps closer to the Portuguese *saudade*: an emotional state of bittersweet longing for the past.

When I was in my early twenties, my grandmother started to get sick. It started when she couldn't drive anymore. She lived in Australia now, not Italy, in an area where one couldn't walk places. She didn't speak English, and needed my mother to translate if she wanted to socialise outside our home. As the number of our English-speaking relatives grew, she could no longer participate in discussions at family gatherings, and I watched her in her throne at the head of the table, eating glumly. I wondered if she knew, when she moved to Australia five years before, that she would never return to Italy and the extent of what that meant. This is a woman who has left many homes in her life without looking back. Before her final move to Australia, she had left Benghazi, Turin, Rome, and then her husband's home. The final move was to Australia, the furthest away, and perhaps the one that hit her the hardest. Most cruelly for someone who was once a great storyteller, strokes had razed her ability to recount the stories of our family's past. Speaking to her when I called home, I listened to the guttural sputterings of her voice as she attempted to give form to the words that filled her mind.

As my grandmother's health worsened, I began to notice symptoms of my own: chest pangs, migraines, anxiety, unexplained crying, an unsettling feeling of abstract yearning. I had experienced this before, particularly when I was young, and it was time to go to bed at childhood sleepovers – I was homesick. Not for my parents' house, nor for a specific location, but – as I realized in Palermo – for the past. The situation felt desperate to me, I suppose because throughout my childhood, my grandmother was my most constant tie to Italy, to my family history, to an idea of roots and home. It was in Palermo, in those moments of unfamiliarity, that I was struck most acutely by how much time had passed, to the point that it seemed irretrievable – a sensation I can only compare to standing on the precipice of a gaping crater. My connection to the city felt so circumstantial.

The concept of home is essential in constructing a sense of who we are, which is why those who find their cultural identities at a remove from their surroundings – migrants and exiles, for example – often cultivate an idea of homeland. This origin story is a way of explaining to ourselves who we are, where we came from, and how we arrived. We might not belong here, but we belong *somewhere*. Once a home becomes a homeland, however, we can't return to it. Homeland is a country that is located in the past. This may be because we were forced to leave it, or it was destroyed. Perhaps we were away for too long, and time has rendered the home that we remember unrecognisable.

My grandmother and I have always shared an intimate bond. We have always understood one another, perhaps in part because there are quite a few parallels in our biographies. Both of us are the product of happenstance. Both of us are the first in our family lines to be born in our countries of birth. Both of us were born in colonised countries, onto earth that had been stolen. Neither of us had any history in the places in which we spent our youths. Questions dogged me when I was young, and still do. What claim do I have to the place I call my country? What is a homeland? What is a home? I have two passports: two pieces of paper that declare me a dual national, a person with two homes. And little claim to either. What determines the granting of a passport, other than politics and paperwork? After that visit to Palermo, my conception of time – the past and the present – as a geographic dichotomy ruptured. Where before there were clear borders, now everything was connected. People who have experienced the dislocation of leaving one home for another know that culture and language are not external or independent of us. Rather, they are the mediums through which we live. To lose a mother tongue or an inherited culture is to become a stranger to something innate within us. We lose the ability not only to articulate, but to speak to a part of ourselves. We dissolve our ties to our histories, and sometimes those close to us. My mother occasionally works as an interpreter for hospital patients, and the majority of her clients are migrants who, in their final years of life, have reverted back to Italian, their first language. This is common in sufferers of Alzheimer's disease. In many cases their adult children only speak English, and find themselves no longer able to communicate with their parents. For the children, it's a particularly brutal instance of the *unheimlich*. Finding the unfamiliar – the unhomely – in our first homes, our truest origins: our mothers.

A Fata Morgana is a type of mirage that appears on coastal horizons. Have you ever gazed at the ocean and seen a bridge stretching across the water, the outline of a sailboat bobbing over waves, or the craggy shore of another island, knowing that there should be nothing? A visual trick, a Fata Morgana happens when air of different temperatures is compressed, creating a lens-like duct in the atmosphere that refracts light in a way that produces these visions. Fata Morgana have been reported to appear as ghostly ships, islands, bridges, or castles floating above the shoreline. It is the Italian name for Morgan le Fay, the sorceress and half-sister to King Arthur, who takes him to Avalon. Sicilian folklore has her residing in a crystal castle at the bottom of the strait. According to legend, she is the mistress of the sirens that populate the sea surrounding Sicily, and the conjurer of these shifting visions that deceive the eyes of those who gaze across these waters.

The indistinct sites of our family history that I imagined were like the floating castles of Fata Morgana. I felt the need to look closer.

Turin

On the early morning train from Bologna to Turin I surveyed the countryside as it flickered past my window – a smattering of trees, small concrete buildings and yellow squares of farmland. The landscape in northern Italy isn't dramatic and rugged like Sicily, or romantic and lush like Tuscany. The Pianura Padana is an unbroken flatland plain that stretches from the Apennine Mountains in the South to the western Italian Alps in the North and to the northern part of the Adriatic coast. It sits atop the Po River Basin, covering a network of ancient hidden canyons formed by a prehistoric collision of African and Eurasian tectonic plates. It is also Italy's industrial belt – drab, grey, thick with fog, humid and swampy, mostly flat, dotted with factories. The air was thick and dusty here, and I'd been coughing up brown phlegm for months.

At the time, I was living in Bologna, a university city and the capital of Italy's Emilia-Romagna region. I was going to make my first visit to Turin. Throughout my childhood, when we made trips to Italy, we stayed exclusively in Sicily, where my parents had grown up. Turin was at the opposite end of the peninsula, at the foot of the Italian Alps. All I knew of Turin was derived from my grandmother's stories about her wartime youth there, of her schooling at an Alpine college, and of air raids and city-wide blackouts. My mother had told me it was an industrial city of vehicle manufacturers: Fiat, Lancia, IVECO. These were the city's largest employers, and during the nineties it was said that after these workers returned home from work at five, the city was silent by six. It was then known as one point

of Italy's *triangolo industriale*, made up of the northern cities of
Turin, Milan and Genoa (now it's said to be Milan, Bologna and
Treviso). As a kid, I perceived it as the opposite of the South: no
socialising or fun, people eating dinner early and staying cooped
up at home. My plan was to arrive, place my luggage in a locker
at the station, and attempt a kind of pilgrimage, by recreating
the walk that a young Annalisa took from her aunt's apartment
in the city to Turin's cathedral every day to shelter from air raids.
After that, I would be taking the train to a small town half an
hour out of the city where my Piedmontese relatives lived.

Since that first trip, I have returned to Turin many times from
different locations and by different modes of transport. Once,
I took a bus that sped down the *autostrada* and dropped me on
the industrial outskirts. Another time, I flew in from London on
my way back to Bologna from Australia. Italy announced itself
with the violet ripples and ridges of the Italian Alps beneath
the plane, finely lined with white snow. I had the same flood
of feeling I have always had upon crossing a border into Italy, a
bodily reaction that invariably makes me cry. As a rule, though,
I have long preferred the train for getting around. The first
time I took an intercity train was in Australia, from Sydney to
my hometown. It was an overnight clunker, with torn vinyl
seats in school-bus blue that took twelve hours for what was
an eight-hour trip in a car. Unsurprisingly, that train service
has since been abandoned, and large tracts of the tracks pulled
up. Five years later, I was introduced to the real beauty of train
travel as I caught overnight and all-day trains through Europe,
those ones with pull-out beds and meal cars that sold bottles
of wine to passengers. In Italy, the cars of the classic intercity
trains are divided into six-person cabins that become temporary
communities.

It's not just the opportunity to chat with strangers or the time
to think that draws me to train travel. It's also the way it makes
time tangible.

As the train passed squares of green and yellow fields,
farmhouses, barns, abandoned factories, I saw an old woman

shaking a tablecloth free of crumbs out of her front door, not bothering to glance at the passing train, an occurrence she was evidently used to. We were experiencing time differently, she and I: for the next couple of hours, time existed for me solely on that train, a temporary dimension, both sped up and suspended, and measured by land crossed.

Walk out of Porta Nuova train station onto Piazza Carlo Felice. Turn right and walk the wrong way for a block

The wide tree-lined boulevards of Turin were overwhelming after the narrow medieval streets of Bologna. The oldest, such as corso Francia, cut across the city, with a seemingly endless line of London plane trees planted at precisely equal distances from one another, bordered by stately buildings. It wasn't the Italy that I had come to expect, of sunset-coloured buildings and washing hanging from windows, of winding narrow streets, or café terraces filled with families and old men reading newspapers.

Turin isn't the Italy reproduced on postcards, and its inhabitants are not the kind caricatured in advertisements and films. Turin's topography is so ordered that the nineteenth-century Italian writer Edmondo de Amicis wrote in his Baedeker-style guide, *Torino 1880*, that it was as though the city had been 'built on top of an immense chessboard'. The city's boulevards predate Haussmann's Paris by some sixty years, having been designed and built by the Savoy dynasty in 1808. Criticisms of Haussmann's modernisation of Paris – that the wide boulevards made suppressing civilian uprisings easier for the military – are germane. Straight tracts of road made it easier for troops to barrel through, and in a wide, open space it is difficult to create a barricade or dive into a nearby building when it is set so far back from the street.

Haussmann was very likely influenced by Turin's cityscape. Turin was the capital of the Savoy dynasty's Kingdom of Sardinia, and its military centre, where de Amicis describes meeting 'a sentry at every step'. These are cities that *want* you to feel overwhelmed. Empires favour neoclassical architectural styles because they make people feel small by comparison. Their purpose is to elevate the State into a monolith to discourage civilian revolt. For me at least, this kind of architecture achieves its purpose. There was no sense of owning the city, or feeling at home within it, like in Bologna or Palermo, cities in which one can walk down the middle of the street, or lounge on church or theatre steps, or on the ground in the middle of a piazza with a bottle of beer and a pizza. The city invited me to hurry along with my business and retreat to more homely surroundings.

After the Risorgimento in 1861 unified most of the country, Turin became Italy's first capital (it lost this status to Florence in 1864, which caused mass riots). Elizabeth Missing Sewell, the English author of young adult novels espousing Anglican values, travelled through Italy a few months after it became a constitutional monarchy. She wrote her impressions of Turin, which she had previously heard criticised as being a very 'modern' city, and 'therefore, quite uninteresting', in the 1862 text *Impressions of Rome, Florence and Turin*. On the contrary, however, once there, she sentimentally pronounced Turin to be the 'very heart ... the life-blood of Italy'. The new Kingdom of Italy at that point subsumed the Kingdom of the Two Sicilies, The Kingdom of Sardinia, and Lombardy, which had been under the rule of the Austrian Empire. Venetia (still under Austrian rule) and the Papal States (ruled by a Pope King) wouldn't be won until 1866 and 1870 respectively. According to Sewell, one could not set foot in Turin without emerging a believer in Italian independence from Austrian oppression. Despite being modern, the spirit of Turin was that of a 'grave and heart-stirring antiquity'. She likened the cityscape to Paris, with its numerous arcades, 'handsome piazzas', ample boutiques, straight roads, elegant hotels, Baroque apartment buildings and 'pleasant public walks'.

My great-grandmother was born a few decades later, in 1895. Named Margherita 'Rita' Bertone, she was her parents' first child. Her biological father died shortly after her birth, and her mother soon remarried her late husband's cousin, who became Rita's stepfather, and with whom her mother had her younger sister Carolina ('Lina'), and a brother Francesco ('Francie') who was a '*ragazzo del '99*' – one among the swath of Italian youths born in 1899 who were conscripted to the war on or prior to their eighteenth birthdays (thanks to a grenade explosion, he returned from the war completely deaf). The siblings grew up splitting time between their two family homes in Turin and Chivasso, a village in the foothills of the Alps, until Rita's stepfather's death. A few months later, she sailed to Libya on her own, while Lina took an office job in the city and her own apartment on via Cibrario. Turin, and her departure from it, was the origin story to all our family stories. Lone Eve leaves Eden to embark on her own odyssey. In our family stories, adulthood was always marked by a geographical move: Rita to Libya, Annalisa to Sicily, my mother to Australia.

Turn around and walk the opposite way down via XX Settembre

Landscapes are the context in which human history unfolds, and walking is a way to read and revisit these stories. A pilgrimage is taken with the hope of attaining some religious or spiritual fulfilment, and so the footsteps followed are often those of a saint. Christians embark on trips to the Holy Land, Muslims to Mecca, Jews to the Wailing Wall, Zoroastrians to the ruins of fire temples, Hindu pilgrims trek to the cave-temple of Amarnath, and Buddhists travel to Bodh Gaya. Many pilgrimages require that the pilgrims journey there in a particular way – in Palermo, for example, the traditional way for a pilgrim to pay a visit to the sanctuary of the city's patron saint, Rosalia, at the apex of Monte Pellegrino (Pilgrim's Mountain), is to hike up the mountain on their knees before entering the deep cave shrine.

In Western Europe alone, there are over six thousand pilgrimage sites, collectively drawing over a hundred million pilgrims each year. Of these, 66 per cent are devoted to the Virgin Mary, 7.5 per cent to Jesus Christ, and the remainder to various apostles and saints. Whether or not a pilgrim is religious, most undertake the pilgrimage with the hope of attaining some kind of spiritual transformation or inner enlightenment, or at least a sense of returning to oneself. I once met a couple who had walked the month-long Camino de Santiago, from Jean Pied de Port in France to Santiago de Compostela in Spain four times, and I had another friend who had made the trek twice. While all were atheists, each claimed to have experienced a spiritual awakening with each trip; each time they were able to see themselves and their lives more clearly, and came away with a sense of renewal. It's not just saints, though, that can provide us with spiritual meaning – many seek this sensation by retracing Leopold Bloom's route through Dublin, following in Hemingway's footsteps through Paris, or tracing the path of an ancestor through the city they lived in.

I had hoped that the simple act of being in and walking through my great-grandmother's city would trigger a kind of awakening, or at least help me feel closer to her. She had died long before I was born, and yet she had been a major figure in my life, an almost mythological being whose presence was palpable in all our family stories. When my mother recounted Italian history to me, Rita was always a main character in my mind. I knew, for example, that she had lived through both world wars. She was an adolescent when the First World War broke out, and a young adult when the culmination of that war blossomed into political turmoil in Italy, and especially in Turin, which had historically been a political battleground. The outbreak of the First World War intensified the already stark class and political divisions in Turin society. There was already widespread hostility towards the military, which had manifested in protests against the Italian invasion of Libya in 1911.

As a result of the war, seventy thousand refugees arrived in Turin and local industries collapsed, leading to mass unemployment, food shortages, and protests. Conversely though, the city profited, becoming a primary producer of weapons and military equipment, but only the wealthy benefitted from the subsequent economic growth. With the end of the First World War, conditions worsened in Turin and throughout Italy. Land ravaged by war, a population in political turmoil, and economic unrest left the Kingdom of Italy devastated. Turin's industry had come to depend on the war, and now it was left with a product – weaponry – for which there was no longer a demand. Companies underwent mass layoffs, like Fiat, who fired eight thousand of its workers.

It's not surprising, then, that Turin became the crucible for Italy's most intense political warring and uprisings. The Socialist Party had been gaining mass popularity since the turn of the century, and city-wide workers' strikes and protests became commonplace in the years leading up to 1920. There was infighting, however, between the reformist and the more radical communist factions that had formed within the party. In 1919,

Mussolini, who had been thrown out of the Socialist Party for supporting the war, founded the Fascist movement in Milan. The two years, from 1919 to 1920, which became known as the *Biennio Rosso*, saw mass strikes and riots, occupations of factories and seizures of farms. Later, the previously marginalised Fascists subjected the city to the so-called '1922 Turin Massacre', a three-day event that took place from 18 to 20 December. Fascist gangs known as *squadristi* donned black shirts and roamed the city, instigating street violence in working-class quarters, attacks on suspected communists and subversives, and raids on socialist and union offices.

It was with the help of the *squadristi* that Mussolini took control of Italy. As the civil violence escalated and the *squadristi* seized more and more control, the plan for a coup formed. In late October 1922, Mussolini's Blackshirt troops gathered outside Rome, in effect taking the city hostage. The Prime Minister at the time, Luigi Facta, had requested that King Victor Emmanuel III call the military to protect the city, but he refused (there is disagreement as to why – some think that he was afraid of a civil war, and others think that he was afraid of losing his throne). Instead, the King asked Mussolini to form a national government, and the next day he and the *squadristi* staged their 'March on Rome', a massive parade to celebrate the surrender of the authorities and the Fascist rise to power. Mussolini later won the general election in April 1924. In May 1924, the Italian Socialist leader Giacomo Matteotti publicly denounced Mussolini in the Italian Parliament, accusing him of rigging the elections. In June 1924, six Fascist *squadristi* assassinated him, hastily burying his body outside Rome. It soon became clear that Italy was now a dictatorship, as Mussolini abolished the democratic system. He banned opposition parties and the free press. He abolished non-fascist trade unions. He made use of spies and secret police to detect dissenters.

I had decided to attempt to replicate the walk my grandmother Annalisa took because I saw in it – or wished to confer on it – a kind of spirituality. I hoped to overlay her footsteps with my own, to trigger a kind of temporal magic. Undertaking a pilgrimage requires the pilgrim to believe three things: that there are larger forces than themselves in the world, that it is possible for a human to harness these forces, and that there are certain places in which these forces are more concentrated and accessible. These forces don't have to be godly – they can also be powers of memory or meaning or association. There are times, for example, when you walk through a city or town you once lived in, and a certain scent or sight will incite a jolt of overwhelming memory so total that it feels like travelling back in time. It feels as though rather than being lost to a vanquished past, moments can be returned to in the places where they occurred. Something of ourselves has been left behind in these places, will go on living there even after we've left, will await our return.

When I return to the town I grew up in, I recall it as it was during my childhood, superimposing my memory over the present, unsure of which reality holds greater importance. Likewise, when I visit a famous city, I don't just see it through the lens of the films that have been set there, I seek out the places in which memorable scenes have occurred. Looking at the Trevi Fountain and imagining Anita Ekberg wading in it somehow enriches the experience. Or else I try to recreate an imagined past, walking through the Left Bank to Gertrude Stein's old house, pretending I'm Hemingway. It's the same when I visit the cities where my ancestors lived. As I navigate the streets, my mind murmurs like a persistent song: *she too walked this path, she too gazed at that building, listened to that river.*

When my grandmother was nine, her parents sent her away from Libya to her grandmother's house, on her own, to escape the daily bombings in Benghazi. However, soon after she arrived, Turin became a military target in the Second World War. Aerial bombings gradually intensified following the summer of 1940. In the first two years of the war, Turin experienced fourteen bombardments, mostly nocturnal. After 1942, the incursions intensified in size and frequency. These bombings killed and injured thousands of civilians and destroyed a third of the city's buildings. Being hungry and cold became daily realities, since rations were scarce and an electricity shortage prevented homes from being heated during Piedmont's bitter winters. The historians Geoffrey Symcox and Anthony Cardoza estimate that, in 1942, 40 per cent of families in Turin suffered from some form of malnutrition. These conditions caused so many people to abandon the city that, by July 1943, Turin's population had been halved. Yet in our family photos, which feature pastoral Piedmontese landscapes, little is given away. I search smiles for tensity or tightness, the forced corner of a grin that might betray a grimace, and I am struck by the inadequacy of photos in recording the realities of a life.

I'm not sure exactly what I expected to find in this city, other than a sense of recognition. A homecoming. It had been present throughout my life only via phone calls to my family's home in Australia: disembodied voices asking for my mother, the receiver handed over, my mother's happy exclamations. I hoped to hear the other end of these phone calls to and from Italy. I suppose I wanted to see those years when my grandmother lived in Turin during the war, I wanted to meet my great-grandmother Rita, and visiting the places where she spent her life seemed the closest I could get to her. In other words, I wanted insight into my family history, and I had a vague idea that if I travelled to the city where part of it happened, I would see it play out in front of me like a performance in the streets.

Cross the road and take a slight right onto corso Vittorio Emanuele II

I have returned to Turin many times and by many different means, but each time is the same, or maybe it's that my memory has superimposed them all, one on top of the other. I haul my suitcase off the train in Porta Nuova station, coming directly from Bologna or Trieste, or from the airport or some bus stop on the industrial periphery. As the mess of people clears and settles like a dust cloud, my relative, the wife of my grandmother's cousin, emerges in the near distance, or perhaps I'm meeting her later, and I drag my suitcase to the left-luggage. When I emerge on the busy street in front of the station, the roar of the traffic is always overwhelming. The fact of being in Turin hasn't caught up with me yet. I feel like I'm sleepwalking.

One of my favourite homecoming scenes in literature is Odysseus's return to his island home of Ithaca. He has been gone for twenty years, having left as a young man with a wife and a newborn child, and returns in middle age, ravaged by war and half a lifetime at sea. His son, Telemachus, is the same age Odysseus was when he left Ithaca, and his home is filled with a hundred young suitors from Ithaca's nobility, all of whom want to marry his wife Penelope and are laying waste to his fortune as they wait for her to choose one of them. When we meet Odysseus, he is halfway through his journey home. His crew is dead, and he has been shipwrecked on the goddess Circe's island, where he has lived as her lover for over a year. Despite her promises of an immortal life of leisure, he is whiling away the days, moaning at the ocean. He has grown tired of Circe and he yearns for his rugged homeland of Ithaca, but there will be another ten years of roaming the seas and strange lands before he reaches it. He finally does reach home, in one of the most anticlimactic homecoming scenes in literature, not least because it happens not when one would expect, at the end of the story, but just over halfway through it.

One would think that Odysseus's return to Ithaca after a twenty-year absence would be a momentous, moving event, but strangely he sleeps through the whole thing. The Phaeacians, a seafaring people who deliver him home on their ship, reach the island's shore and carry him, bundled in blankets like a baby, from their ship to the sand. When he eventually wakes up, he doesn't recognise his native land, which the goddess Athena has plunged into a thick mist. He doesn't recognise 'The friendly harbours and the winding paths / and leafy trees.' He panics, convinced that the Phaeacians have brought him to the wrong place, worried that the strange inhabitants will steal his belongings. He paces the shoreline beside a rough sea, 'hunched up / with homesickness and sobbing in his grief.' It is only when Athena comes and informs him of where he is that he feels relief.

But he isn't welcomed back with open arms. First, he must defeat the suitors who are ready to kill him should he return, and he must find out whether his wife Penelope has remained faithful to him after all this time. Athena disguises him as a beggar and, along with the help of his son, he slaughters the suitors in a gruesome scene. Still, even after this, his troubles aren't over. Only a few of his slaves have remained loyal to him and the poem ends with Ithaca on the brink of civil war, with Odysseus and his son against the grief-stricken and enraged noble families whose sons he has murdered. Coming home is never what we think it will be.

The Odyssey comes from an oral tradition of storytelling, used, much like family storytelling, as a way of remembering things that happened before the listeners were born. These real events were peppered with magical elements and characters: gods and goddesses, mythical creatures, personified winds. They contained lessons that reminded the listeners of their society's values, such as hospitality, being a good guest, and subservience to the gods, like when Odysseus's men steal and slaughter the sun god Helios's cows and end up drowning at sea. Family myths and stories work in a similar way: they may feature fantastical elements, and their purpose is to shape us and illustrate our values. They teach us how to be. *The Odyssey* was told in Ancient Greece, a civilisation that had begun to create colonies across the Mediterranean, in Libya, southern France, the Italian peninsula and Sicily, forming what is known as Magna Graecia. In a story like *The Odyssey*, where the hero never fails to lose sight of and fight for his homeland, despite a twenty-year absence, the listener – who may be a Greek-speaker living in a Sicilian or Libyan colony – is reminded not just of the ties that bind them to their Greek motherland, but also of their Greek values, and the consequences of failing to maintain control over their colonies and culture.

Family stories, those passed down over generations, tend to function in a similar way. They separate your family from other families. They bind the members of a family together, helping them define a shared identity. They confer values and advise us as to how we go about surviving in the world. They tell us what the rules are. These kinds of generational family myths tend to cast a positive glow over our ancestors, portraying them – and therefore us – as unique and good. People don't generally go around sharing their suspicion that their ancestor was a Nazi or a fascist, after all.

My own mother would tell me about a great-great-great uncle who was a political revolutionary, a member of the *Carbonari*, the secret society who would meet in underground bunkers, plotting to launch the coup that would overthrow the empires colonising Italy and unify the country. Or my great-grandfather – who was not a fascist, she took pains to stress – and who smuggled secret photos from Libya to Italy, risking his life. She suspected him of having been part of the Resistance against the Nazis and Fascists in Rome. Many of my mother's stories told of political and intellectual achievements that were intended to assure me that the member in question was not a fascist (I assume this is common in left-leaning Italian and German households – the ancestors who didn't do anything, or did very little to resist, but at their core *did not believe*).

We talk about ancestors as though we know them and their thoughts intimately. My mother and her siblings speak with authority on their grandparents and great-grandparents, even when they all disagree. While my mother is adamant, for example, that my great-grandparents were against fascism, my aunt, who tends not to trouble too much with the past, asks: who cares?

This kind of generational storytelling is not a new practice. Genealogical sagas have been written for centuries across Europe. The difference now is that once, sagas were chronicles of noble names and deeds, created with the goal of legitimizing the heightened status of powerful families. Now, the practice is a bourgeois occupation. Many families have their own amateur historian who scours county registers and ancestry websites for figures of interest or virtue in their lineage. In my own family, it's common for anecdotes to refer to members reaching back to the Risorgimento and further – my grandfather often touted his descent from minor Spanish nobility.

Turn right onto corso Inghilterra

Rita and Salvatore remained in Libya until the Allies took the country in 1942, while Annalisa was sent away to Turin soon after the outbreak of the Second World War, in 1940. Originally, Rita was supposed to accompany her daughter, who was suffering from a nervous condition due to the aerial bombings, but she decided to remain with her husband in Africa at the last minute. When she first arrived in Piedmont, Annalisa was sent to stay with her grandmother Anna in Turin. It seems grandmother and granddaughter did not get along, because the latter was soon sent to live with Rita's friend, a pharmacist in the same city. She was then sent to a convent school in the Alps. For the entire time that she was there − a year − she was bullied for having been born in Africa.

One day, one of her classmates claimed that she had followed him into the bathrooms to see him naked. The nuns took her to the chapel so that she could confess and repent, which she refused to do − she was adamant that the boy was lying. The nuns called her maternal grandmother, who came to the school to attempt to convince her that she must admit to this apparently perverted act. Still, she refused. In desperation, Zia Lina wrote to her sister Rita in Libya so that she might be able to convince Annalisa to tell the truth. Rita wrote to both the school and her family, insisting that her daughter wasn't a liar. Rita then demanded that they take Annalisa out of that school, and she went back to Turin to live with Zia Lina.

When I ask myself where my fascination with our family folklore came from, I must point the finger at my grandmother, an expert in transforming her own and our family's lives into mythology. My whole life long I heard about the achievements of the great women in our family, women turned to demi-gods and romantic characters. In passing down stories, we are aided by photos, jewellery, knickknacks, memories and recipes. When I was a child and she came to visit from Italy, I would move my bed into her room and be lulled to sleep by romanticised stories of her youth in Libya, Turin, Rome and Palermo. I truly believed that she had seen and done everything there was to be seen and done. I imagined that she had dined with Arabian royalty and ridden camels across the desert. Her gifts, brought back to me from her extensive travels, lined a shelf in my room: painted fans from Thailand, nesting dolls from Eastern Europe, petrified wood from California, maracas from Mexico, castanets from Spain, embroidered Japanese silk.

It is said that having children gives one a sense of continuity. It's a way of guaranteeing our existence in the future. Ancestry works in the opposite direction. It lends a sense of meaning and continuity to our lives by proving our existence in the past. Just as it's comforting to believe that we won't leave this world without a trace, so it is also comforting to believe that we didn't just drop into this world out of nowhere.

Cross corso Francia. Turn left onto via Cibrario. Look
for number 2. Spot via Cibrario, 4. Find via Cibrario,
6. Double back. Turn the corner back towards Piazza
Statuto. Find the entrance to via Cibrario, 2. Stare into
the glass double doors, consider walking in, at least to the
courtyard. Feel like a creep; don't

Gold plaques inside the foyer of the apartment building
announced a number of law offices and accounting firms. Tiles
led to stained-glass doors in the same pattern as the tiles. A small
chandelier hung from the domed ceiling. I tried to imagine
what it was like when my grandmother lived here, and she and
the inhabitants of the building scurried out of the building at
the same time each morning.

I began my pilgrimage on via Cibrario, in front of the
apartment building where Annalisa lived with her aunt, Zia Lina,
and from where they would make the trip each day at noon to
Turin Cathedral. Did they move in a pack? Did they speak to
one another or were they silent? Did the act of the walk become
routine, did the route become just a bridge in the song of the
day, or did it never lose its solemnity?

Smog puffed out in sickly-coloured clouds from the exhaust
pipes of the cars careening past in six lanes of traffic. The
familiar sounds of the city: honking car horns, the distant wails
of ambulance sirens, screeching tyres, yelling. The traffic ringed
a circular piazza presided over by an austere monument. The
building Annalisa had lived in was pink and Baroque, like all
the others around it. Across from it, an ugly furniture store. This
palazzo was a landmark of my family history, but visiting it did
not take me back like I expected it to.

Returning, like leaving, can be curiously anticlimactic, perhaps
because leaving is a loss that is difficult to digest, and returning
to the places we have left not only recalls this sense of loss, but
amplifies it. Odysseus was asleep when the Phaeacians returned
him to Ithaca, and it's no wonder – just like leaving, returning

is a traumatic experience. When he awakens on the shore of his homeland, Odysseus fails to recognise it, and later, when he is reunited with his wife, she fails to recognise *him*. The trauma of return produces a numbing sensation: an empty un-feeling that exposes your own displacement. Could this building provide the link to my family's past I was hoping for, or was the present – and my own presence – too imposing to ignore?

Family stories narrate events that we *want* to remember. When my grandmother's health began deteriorating, she started to tell me certain things as we played cards at her house, although if I asked more questions, pressed for too much detail, she would close up again. The first time a person bears witness to the breakdown of the human body, it is usually that of a grandparent. People seem to crumple in on themselves, and it's during this time that we think of everything that we've wanted to ask them. The past seemed to recede, along with her break down, into a kind of black hole.

Rita left Italy in 1925. Her stepfather died that same year, when she was twenty-nine, and I was told this was the catalyst for her moving to Libya. Rita's stepfather considered Rita as his own, and even treated the first husband's parents – his aunt and uncle – as his own. While the new couple had two more children, Rita remained his favourite child. Rita's mother preferred her two younger children. She doted on Lina, but endured a tumultuous relationship with Rita. After her stepfather's death, Rita had less reason to stay at home. My mother told me that one day Rita and her mother had a particularly explosive fight, which ended with mother telling daughter she was free to leave the family home. The next day Rita went out and took the national entrance exam to travel out to Libya as a schoolteacher, an exam in which (so the family story goes) she was placed first. Rita returned home a few weeks later with her acceptance letter, announcing to the shock of all that she was, in fact, leaving – to go as far away as a single Italian woman could respectably get in those days, North Africa.

Our family stories don't tend to contain too much of the political – they are often confined to the domestic sphere. I have no way of knowing how much the political and social situation of Italy affected Rita, if it did at all, or what she thought about it beyond how it affected her, and the people close to her. Growing up, a favourite pastime of mine was to pull out the thick photo albums lined up on a book shelf in our house. I would lay them across my lap and go over each photo in its plastic sleeve. The albums had white labels stuck on their spines to identify their contents, which were sorted either by place or person: *Africa, Piemonte, Sicilia, Viaggi (Inghilterra, Parigi), Viaggi (Dolomiti, Spagna, Yugoslavia)*.

The Piedmont albums don't seem to show any kind of hardship or warfare. Instead, they tell stories of parties in the city and picnics in the country. My great-grandmother and her sister pose in furs on a picturesque bridge, or they pose at home, perhaps on their way to a party, clutching long cigarette holders, feathers pluming from their headbands, wearing long beaded necklaces and the drop-waist dresses synonymous with twenties flappers. In others, they grin at the camera in bathing suits, seemingly ready to dive into a lake, and lounge by a picnic spread in a glade with some friends, all arranged like Manet's *Le Déjeuner sur l'herbe*.

Personal photographs offer a myopic glimpse of the past. They reflect nothing but the moment being captured, nothing beyond the frame. And yet I look and look, hoping to find a way in. I have looked at the photos so many times that I can close my eyes and reconstruct my favourites.

Spaces are the product of all the histories that they have hosted. I tried to picture how it would have been when they lived here. Most probably not more peaceful; the absence of cars would have been more than compensated for by the bombings, planes purring overhead, cries and shouts.

I made my way across the road with a crowd of pedestrians – construction workers, mothers with their children, African women carrying plastic shopping bags stuffed with fabric, impatient men in suits. We crossed onto Piazza Statuto, a giant green island ringed by traffic. This used to be a piazza, and technically still is in name. The noise of the traffic, however, and the smoke from car fumes, does not encourage loitering, which is the usual function of a piazza.

When Annalisa lived here it looked totally different. The *battaglia del grano* (Battle for Grain) was a Fascist economic policy that aimed to reduce wheat imports and make Italy self-sufficient. This led to *orti di guerra* ('war gardens'), a precursor to urban community gardens. The press reported that in Turin, every city piazza and public garden had been transformed into a fertile vegetable patch or miniature wheat field. A photo from Turin's city archive shows Piazza Statuto in 1942, blanketed by the tall stalks of sunflowers.

Coined by the French philosopher Jacques Derrida, the concept of hauntology suggests that we are never only in the present moment; rather, we are always comparing the present to the past, and anticipating the future. Thinking about it in terms of a song, you could say that we only ever hear a note, or chord, of the music at a time, and that this note, or chord, only makes sense if we consider it in relation to the notes that have preceded it and the notes that will follow. Because of this, our experience of the present is 'haunted', by everything that has happened in the past and that might happen in the future. Hauntology posits that our experience of being alive is haunted by the ghosts of the past and the future – ghosts because both the past and the future are absent from the present moment, but nonetheless exist within it. It's not that the past has happened – it's that it won't stop happening, over and over. A pilgrimage could be seen as a conscious invocation of haunting – a way of calling out to the ghosts of the past.

I had expected to feel something, standing at the entrance to the apartment building – a sense of profundity, or an awakening of some kind. I should have remembered some lost 'postmemory', a memory of my grandmother's passed down to me through DNA. I think I even half expected to glimpse the ghosts of

Annalisa and Zia Lina brushing past on their way out. But all I felt was flustered, and annoyed at the choked-up traffic. It was overwhelmingly underwhelming. Reflecting on and reading about Piazza Statuto musters more emotion than actually being there did. Perhaps if I were to return now it would be different. I had hoped that my discomfort there was the effect of an inherited memory, but in all honesty, I had to admit that the past never felt so inaccessible as it did in that moment.

Walk across Piazza Statuto. Turn on to via Garibaldi. Find a bench and take a seat. Watch the university students and tourists having aperitivo

It's difficult to feel as though one is coming home while attempting to cross six lanes of traffic. The marble footpaths in Turin are wide and sheltered by high-ceilinged stone porticoes. But the imperial boulevards, piazzas and Baroque buildings were too imposing, the pedestrians too quiet, and the sparseness of the streets made me feel as though I were walking through a museum. I stopped in one of the countless historic coffee houses. The stained-glass windows featured designs of pink roses, and the walls were covered with frecoes which ended in gold mouldings that bordered the domed ceilings. Further back were the tea rooms: patrons sat on high-backed gilt chairs upholstered with plush blue velvet, the air buzzing with their murmurs. At a long marble coffee bar, I ordered a coffee from one of the tuxedoed baristas. Behind him were mirrored shelves of spirits – vermouth, Campari, Aperol. The barista was curt, and I felt awkward and clammy and wondered whether he noticed. I couldn't take his eyes on me, downed the coffee, slid a euro over the counter and left. For some reason, in that moment I felt desperate with the desire to fit in, paranoid that something about my appearance telegraphed that I was out of place. More than anything, I did not want to seem like a tourist, which is exactly what I was.

The desire to feel welcomed upon arrival at our destination is universal. We want to feel like we're coming home, wherever we are, but even more so when we are coming to a place that we believe to actually be home. A very common type of pilgrimage is the one diasporic people make back to their homelands. This idea of a homeland from which they are absent both links and defines diasporic people. Historically, when migrants left their home countries, they faced a probability of never returning, and of staying in touch via long-awaited letters, or later through expensive international phone calls. Their sense of origin, culture and belonging to a distant homeland was passed down to future generations through family stories and anecdotes, recipes and heirlooms. Now their descendants can return to the 'old country' whenever they like, provided they have the money.

In *The Odyssey*, foreign guests are always welcomed with a banquet by their hosts, who wait to enquire about their guests' identities until after the meal is over. Each time, the guest is asked two questions, which can be boiled down to variations of 'Who are you?' and 'Where are you from?' In Homer's world, *who* one is can be directly answered by *where* one comes from. In today's world, this equation is not so neat, as increasing numbers of people count themselves as migrants or descendants of migrants, and might consider themselves to be from more than one place, or might never have left their homeland, but have found it to be dispossessed or in the process of dispossession.

Like many others around the globe who grow up immersed in the mythology of their family's homeland, I had based my idea of Turin upon photos and stories, and arrived in the city unconsciously expecting it to animate these images. I now realised that I had woven a fantasy out of the city, and perhaps what I wanted was a sense of continuity.

Continue down via Garibaldi

As I walked, I could hear the echo of my own footsteps slapping on the asphalt on the tree-cloaked boulevards. Despite the trees, everything was muted, grey, vast, the piazza at Palazzo Reale a flat cobblestone sea. Turin: city of order, cleanliness, politeness, quiet. Silence envelops Turin, even with the drone of the traffic. Satellite images of the city show a concrete network of buildings cut by straight lines of main roads. The thin blue snake of the Po curves down one side of it and beyond the urban border is a green and yellow quilt of farmed land. Long streets run as far as the sightline, lined with cream-coloured palazzi with rust-coloured roofs, and thick green lines of trees demarcate the boulevards. Unlike many other Italian cities that are structured like spiderwebs – main roads that dart out from a central piazza, intersected by the concentric circles of smaller streets – Turin's topography is on a grid, like Melbourne or New York. This is thanks to its origin as a Roman military fort, an origin which perhaps explains the air of discipline. Turin has a quiet grace, especially when you view its skyline, with the spire of the Mole Antonelliana rising above the Alps.

The iconic Mole (pronounced *maw-leh*) was originally commissioned by the Italian Jewish community of Turin in 1861 as a synagogue, to mark both their emancipation in 1848 and Turin's new status as the capital of Italy. They hired the renowned Italian Jewish architect Alessandro Antonelli, who was to design a synagogue that would represent the Jewish community of Turin's integration into civil society. Construction began in 1863, on a building that would accommodate up to fifteen hundred people in its synagogue, as well as administration offices, a school, and community services. In the original plan, the barrel-vaulted roof was to be forty-seven metres. By the time works were suspended six years later, the roof had risen to seventy metres and costs were spiralling. The Municipality of Turin bought the unfinished building from the Jewish community, who built their synagogue elsewhere in the city (which still exists today), and the building was eventually completed in 1889. Its height upon completion was 167.5 metres. It was given the name *Mole* (meaning a large building in Italian) *Antonelliana* (for its architect), although the German philosopher Friedrich Nietzsche, who had exclaimed that it was 'perhaps the most ingenious building ever constructed', christened it *Ecce Homo*.

For Nietzsche, Turin was a city in which there was much to love – its boulevards, its palaces, its classical buildings, archways and arcades reminded him of Paris. He moved there in the spring of 1888, on the advice of a friend, who promised that this city between the Alps and the Ligurian Sea, with its mild weather and dry air, would agree with his delicate constitution, prone to stomach upsets and migraines. He was forty-three, with a handful of Italian words in his arsenal, although he was quintessentially European, in the sense that he was a continental wanderer, having already lived in Sorrento, Genoa, Venice, Zurich, the Swiss Alps and Nice.

From his room on the top floor of a lodging house on via Carlo Alberto, Nietzsche looked out over Piazza Carlo Alberto, and on clear days he could see the snow-topped Alps. His migraines disappeared and he began sleeping through the night. He loved it from the start, as he wrote to his friend Köseliz, who had recommended he go there. In the letter, he praises Turin for its 'aristocratic tranquillity', proclaiming it to be 'a dignified and serious city'. He spent his days there – when he wasn't sick – walking, eating, and writing. In another letter to Köselitz, Nietzsche pronounced Turin 'the first place where I am possible!' He wrote *Ecce Homo* in three weeks. He had, evidently, come home.

He, too, commented on the solemn silence of the piazzas, which he found calming. And it's true – there is an innate coolness in the way the Torinesi conduct themselves, in the straight lines of the cityscape and the straight backs of the reserved baristas who regard you impassively in the coffee houses. The snow-topped Alps seem to lull the city into a serene state of being, and the Po snakes through, its only sound a hushed rushing of running water. The calm extends to the Piedmont countryside, in the illusory idleness of the rolling green fields, the soft sway of the corn fields, the sharpness of the mountain air, the violet and white cradle of the Alps in the distance. The origin of the name Piedmont is the Latin *Pedemontium* or *Pedemontis*, literally meaning 'at the foot of the mountain'.

Despite having found his 'place', Nietzsche's time of happiness there was limited. He is thought to have contracted syphilis over a decade before, and before long he began showing signs of neurological decay. Already in December of 1888, his letters betrayed his sense of alienation and an intense political rage against Germany. His handwriting became illegible. At a music concert, he burst into uncontrollable tears. He asked his landlords if they could decorate his room with frescoes, like a temple, so that it would be fit to receive the King and Queen of Italy. As legend has it (there are many different accounts), on the third of January 1889, Nietzsche witnessed a horse being flogged in the street. In protest, he flung himself around the horse's neck, fell to the ground, and lost consciousness. He had to be carried home. In the days that followed, he played piano at all hours of the night, pranced naked around his room, and wrote a flurry of notes to friends, signing off in some as 'Dionysus', and in other as '*der Gekreuzigte*' ('The Crucified One'). Worried, a friend came to Turin and took Nietzsche away, accompanying him to a psychiatric clinic in the Swiss city of Basel.

Despite Nietzsche's unfortunate end in Turin, reading him describe the city – one in which the streets were full of elegantly dressed pedestrians, the restaurant prices were low, the historic coffee houses were music-filled hotspots, the crisp mountain air was unmarred by the fumes of car exhausts, and the cacophony of traffic was absent from the urban soundscape – I couldn't help but wish I could see it as he did. I felt I should have inherited memories of the city, a sense of déjà vu that I could feel in my bones, but instead I felt a gnawing hollowness. Afterwards, I tried to find proof that my initial failure to feel welcomed by the city wasn't, in fact, such a failure. I collected criticisms. In a *New York Times* article, the artist Lara Favaretto comments that in Turin 'nothing happens, nothing happens, nothing happens'. It was described by Le Corbusier as the city with 'the most beautiful natural location in the world' (this is a mark against Turin, I hate Le Corbusier). It wasn't me, you see, it was *Turin*.

Nietzsche isn't the only writer to love the city – so did Cesare Pavese, a Turin native. Pavese is often quoted on it, describing Turin in his diaries as 'city of reverie, for her aristocratic perfection composed of elements new and ancient; city of rules, for her absolute absence of discord in the material and spiritual realms; city of passion, for her benevolent respect for idleness; city of irony, for her good taste in living; exemplary city, for her tumultuous calm'. In her essay 'Portrait of a Friend', written for Pavese, another Turinese writer, Natalia Ginzburg, describes returning to the city. She had grown up there, leaving to follow her husband into his imposed confinement in a village in Abruzzo. In her incarnation, Turin's avenues are filled with mist, the sun delivers weak light. The city smells of soot and exchoes with train whistles. It is 'grey, heavy, and unpoetic', which is what makes Pavese's poetry about the city so remarkable. Returning fills her with sadness, because in this city 'few things are still alive for us'. The Turin evoked by Ginzburg is timeless in the sense that time lies stagnant. 'There are no new movie houses', she notes, and 'the clock on the riding path has stopped, from time immemorial, at a quarter to eleven.' The very soul of the city, she seems to say, is melancholy.

Of course, the way in which she writes and sees the city, in this particular essay, is coloured by Pavese's recent passing. She portrays him as a figure who embodies Turin in such a way that he and the city are one and the same, inextricable partners in sadness. Pavese overdosed on barbiturates in a Turin hotel room in the August of 1950, after decades of thinking and writing about death and suicide. He was forty-one years old and his latest love affair, with the American actress Constance Dowling, had ended. According to Ginzburg, both Pavese and Turin are industrious, unsmiling, simultaneously productive and prone to idle daydreams. The city evokes his memory, and as she walks, Ginzburg recalls him stalking the streets or scribbling furiously in the corner tables of cafés.

August is an acutely melancholy month for most cities in Italy, during which locals flee to the South, to seaside or mountain homes. If one stays in the city during August, it feels like living in a Giorgio de Chirico painting: a vast urban desert, in which the thick heat creates the impression one is wading through a glimmering dreamscape (and in fact, de Chirico always touted a midsummer visit to Turin as the inspiration for his metaphysical painting style).

I turned down onto via Garibaldi. Open only to pedestrians, via Garibaldi was teeming with foot traffic – tourists, students, families from the country come for a day trip in the city. It was lined with chain stores and cafés, each with tables out the front piled high with food for *aperitivo* – cheeses, slices of melon, strawberries, cured meats, *pizzette*, rice and lentil salads, olives, potato chips, ringed *taralli* crackers. Fairy lights danced between the awnings. The pedestrian-only walkway is swamped with strollers on weekends. Via Garibaldi is perhaps Turin's most ancient street – it was originally built by the Romans, and leads from Piazza Statuto to Piazza Castello, which fronts the royal palace.

The Romans called it '*strata Civitatis Taurini*', a name which underlines its importance in the Roman settlement: *strata* means 'paved road' in Latin, while *civitatis* means 'of the state', and *Taurini* comes from the Roman name for Turin, *Julia Augusta Taurinorum* (which itself derives from the name of the original tribe that settled in the area). After the fall of the Roman Empire, the road deteriorated, and was reduced to a width of four metres. It was cramped and unpaved. Rather than the elegant palazzi that now line it, it boasted squat stone buildings – its old temples transformed into Christian churches. It remained Turin's area of commerce, however, and was the road taken by merchants crossing the city – lending it the nickname 'via Sant' Espedito': protector of merchants. Eventually it gained the new name of Contrada Dora Grossa, most probably due to its proximity to the original via Dora, which was transformed into a canal in the 1500s (in Piedmontese, the word *doira* refers to a narrow or small stream). During the Savoy rule in the 1700s, the *via* grew along with the rest of the city, becoming the main street of Turin. In 1730, footpaths were added to the street, making via Garibaldi what is now thought to be the first street featuring pedestrian-only space in Europe. During the Napoleonic occupation, it became known as rue du Mont-Cenise, but returned to its prior name in 1814, following the Treaty of Turin, which restored Savoy, Piedmont and Nice to the House of Savoy. Following Italy's unification, it was definitively renamed via Garibaldi, after the revolutionary who was instrumental in uniting the country.

It became pedestrian-only in 1979, long after Annalisa left the city, and so while I was certain that both Annalisa and Rita spent time here, knew this street well, I was aware that they each saw a different street to the one I was seeing. I found myself wondering, what does it mean to return when a street can throw off one name for another like a dress, when everything we know will surely be torn down and rebuilt?

Take a left off Garibaldi onto via Piave. Right on via del Carmine. Walk along Carmine until Piazza Savoia. Follow via della Consolata all the way to its conclusion, Piazza della Consolata. Turn right down vicolo della Consolata.
Left on via Santa Chiara. Continue down via della Basilica. Turn right down via Porta Palatina. Left at via IV Marzo. Turn left onto via XX Settembre. Cross Piazza San Giovanni. Enter the cathedral

According to 'the belongingness hypothesis' posited by the American psychologists Roy Baumeister and Mark Leary, the need to belong is a universal, fundamental human need, and to be deprived of it has negative effects. What Baumeister and Leary found, however, was that it doesn't matter where or to what or to whom we decide to belong – just that we feel a sense of belonging. This is, perhaps, part of what renders the idea of homeland so enticing. No matter where we are, where we don't fit in, or are rejected from, it is a place we can always refer to: we would belong if we were there.

The Greek *nostos* is mostly translated as 'home' when breaking down the etymology of 'nostalgia'. But *nostos* actually encapsulates many meanings, depending on the context. It can mean either home or homeland, but for the Ancient Greeks, it more accurately referred to homecoming. From Robert Beekes's *Etymological Dictionary of Greek*: 'to reach some place, return, get home.' *Nostos* was a common theme of Ancient Greek epic poetry, which followed a hero's journey home. *The Odyssey* is probably the most famous example of *nostos*. It is telling that, in Ancient Greek, home only exists in relation to one's absence from it. Perhaps there is something to the idea that we can only clearly see home – the loved corners of our houses, the ongoing chatter with those that people our daily lives, the streets we move through each day, the meals we make each night –once we are far away from it, like the way we can only perceive the borders of a country when we see it from the distance provided by a map.

Just as in Ancient Greek, the notion of absence from the place one belongs to is still wrapped up in the idea of homeland. This is true of many Italian ancestral pilgrims, who might find that the Italian they learned from their grandparents or parents is a regional dialect, or that the traditions they practise in their family haven't been practised in Italy since the sixties.

For second and third generations of the Italian diaspora, making a trip to Italy is seen as a necessary pilgrimage, a way of legitimizing one's Italianness. 'Returning' is as much about proving that one has an active, dynamic connection with the homeland as it is about seeing the homeland. On message boards on sites such as Ancestry. com and subreddits titled AncestryDNA and Genealogy, users from all over the world post selfies and theories as to where they might be from, based on their facial features ('I look stereotypically eastern European lol'), share or question their DNA results from companies such as 23andme ('can Italians be blonde?'), or ask others for advice on tracking down ancestral branches.

When I visited, and eventually moved to Italy, it helped that I spoke Italian, although I still felt an irrational fear that people could 'tell' I wasn't from 'around here'. More than that, I was out of sync. I didn't know the particular rhythms of the day, or the social customs, which were simultaneously more relaxed and stricter than what I was used to. These feelings eventually dissipated, but it took conscious work. I kept diaries recording my observations of traditions and etiquette. I learned not to run errands or try to make plans during the hours known as *dopo pranzo* (after lunch), which extended from 1 p.m. until 4 p.m., and during which everything was closed and the streets were empty. I learned that *pomeriggio* (afternoon) began after *dopo pranzo* and continued until 6 p.m. or 7 p.m., depending on the season, at which point *la sera* (evening) began, and one could make plans for *aperitivo*. Eating dinner before 9 p.m. was for uptight northerners and children. I learned that when new acquaintances invited you to 'drop by for dinner whenever you like', they actually expected you to drop by. It was a slow, thrilling homecoming.

I subconsciously felt that a successful move to Italy would count as proof that I belonged there. The return of the ancestral pilgrim is bound up in a complicated sense of entitlement. In Italy, this entitlement is encouraged on a bureaucratic level, where almost anyone with Italian heritage is guaranteed a passport. But exactly *what* ancestral pilgrims feel entitled to is a complex and varied matter.

Returning offers the opportunity to witness an imagined past, and to confront all the baggage of one's absence. Like Odysseus returning to Ithaca asleep, and finding the island unrecognisable, you scan crowds for faces and cityscapes for backdrops that resemble the ones you've seen in family photographs. In a 2006 sociological study about return migration, researchers Anastasia Christou and Russell King interviewed Greek American return migrants to Greece on how they find life in their ancestral country. The interviewees focus on Greece's shift from being a mostly homogenous country to its current state as a multicultural nation. One of them, living in Athens, complains that this wasn't the Greece that they had signed up for, the one that they remembered from childhood holidays to a small village, in which they knew all their neighbours and could sleep outdoors, leaving the front doors wide open. He complains that this has all changed: 'Greece has started to resemble America very much insofar as there are other races here now and living here, not that I am racist, I have nothing against those people, but I liked it back then when Greece was Greece.'

It's not just that contemporary Greece has failed to live up to the subject's romanticised childhood memories of summer beach holidays, it's also that the subject has confused their ancestral village with Athens, a metropolis in which it is safe to assume that people have always locked their doors. Other interview subjects who had negative reactions blame the migrant community for their feeling of foreignness in what they consider to be their own country, or for threatening the national identity of Greece. For others, Greece's modernisation and growing multiculturalism are proof that the country is losing its authenticity (although they don't stop to explain what they mean by authenticity). It's possible that the new migrant community reminds them of the time that has passed, and the fact that the Greece their parents left no longer exists. Furthermore, if belonging or citizenship is not conferred solely by blood, but by being part of a community, this challenges some diaspora members' feeling of ownership over a country in which they didn't grow up, and have little current knowledge of.

Ancestral pilgrims who have these kinds of negative reactions may feel affronted that their homeland doesn't match the one that they inherited from their grandparents. The presence of migrants in Greece might also make them feel inadequate, as the migrants (or children of migrants) are likely to have a greater knowledge of and claim to contemporary Greek culture. Ancestral pilgrims believe that heritage is conferred by blood, but the presence of migrants contradicts this idea by reminding one that home is the place in which we pay bills and taxes, buy groceries, clean our houses, and send our children to school. Most ancestral returns are driven by a search for belonging. It's when the return fails to deliver this feeling that they feel alienated all over again, and start pointing fingers. Not all the interview subjects feel this way, however – many see their families' experiences as migrants to the United States reflected back at them through their own in Greece. What the interview subjects were almost universally unprepared for, and what left them most disappointed, was that they too, due to their American upbringing and birth, were seen as 'foreigners'. It calls to mind an Israeli joke relayed by Elliott Oring in his book *Folk Groups and Folklore Genres*. In the joke, an old Romanian Jew who has lived in Israel for thirty-five years, reveals to his friend that he is returning to Romania. His friend, stunned, asks him why he would return to Romania, where he has no family and no friends. The Romanian Jew replies: 'At least in Romania I can die as a Jew. Here in Israel, I will die as a Romanian.'

I often think that my desire for Italy began with the Australian suburbs where I grew up. The suburban landscapes of my childhood seemed and still seem to me now to be hermetic, sealed off from geography or history. The place where I grew up was once all rainforest scrub, until it became farmland, and then that farmland began to be sectioned off and zoned as residential in the eighties. When I lived there, there was one last rainforest remnant, a *lieu de mémoire* of what the terrain had been before, but even this served only to emphasise the man-made nature of the environment, so easy was it for one to enter and leave this shrine to the 'natural habitat', the reality of which the residents did all they could to deny. To combat the forty-degree summer heat, the houses were cooled with air conditioners and turquoise pools, and the front gardens were painstakingly cultivated with roses rendered fragile by the subtropical heat in which they had no business to grow. I had always thought that roses were difficult to grow anywhere, that they pushed out of the earth thorny and sparse, and so I was stunned when I moved to Melbourne and saw fat bushes of them growing like weeds.

When I returned to Italy, it wasn't just a sense of placeness that I craved; it was to be in a place where I had business to grow, where the lifestyle didn't involve stifling the environment. When I think of Australia's population, small in comparison to its geographical size, I am astounded by the damage people can do. Nature was kept intact on a superficial level: just enough that one might see the beauty line of trees suggesting a forest behind their home. Our back garden seemed to extend out into bush, but walking through it was a disappointment – five minutes on foot brought you to a sad dribble of a creek and the edge of someone else's backyard. When an environment has to undergo such radical changes as to make it unrecognisable to make it liveable for humans, it begs the question of whether we have any rightful place there, especially considering the constant droughts during which no one could water their gardens or drink the tap water, the floods during summer wet seasons, the hail storms that left tennis ball-sized dents in everyone's cars, the bush fires that caused black slivers of ash to fall from the sky and reduced trees to ink drawings of themselves. Growing up through all this, the idea of Italy as a homeland, a rightful place, was a comfort.

Leave cathedral. Head down via Porta Palatina. Turn left onto via Antonio Bertola. Left again on via Roma. Keep walking down via Accademia delle Scienze until it becomes via Giuseppe Luigi Lagrange. The darkened streets seem so empty and hostile; their inhabitants stare blankly at you or else don't register your presence at all. Cross via Antonio Gramsci. Realise from the sudden proliferation of hotels that you are reaching the station. Carlo Felice Square Apt. Best Quality Hotel Gran Mogol. Starhotels Majestic. Turn right on corso Vittorio Emanuele II. Best Western Hotel Genio. Keep going along corso Vittorio Emanuele II until you hit the stairs leading up to the station on your left. Note that the steps and the piazza opposite, still teeming with people, nevertheless seem a different place to where you began your walk. Perhaps it's the twilight that alters it. But note that no place ever seems the same to you, even after a short absence.

When I was eleven my mother took me to see the family vault in the Agrigento region of Sicily. I only remember the sharp edges, the white concrete, the barred doors like those of a cell. With a key, she slid open the heavy metal bars and there, stuffed shoebox-like, was my lineage. In massive marble coffins, stacked one on top of the other like a macabre game of Jenga. Our voices echoed and the air became cool and hollow as though we were underground. I stood in the midst of bloodlines turning myself around and around, acquainting myself with the deceased. But none of the tombs had names on them, and she couldn't tell me who was housed there, just that these bodies in boxes had once borne our family names. I remember wondering where I would end up. In a couple of generations no one alive will remember me, which seems like a second death. Already, this has started happening to Rita. She is remembered by my grandmother, my mother and her siblings, but most of her great-grandchildren could not even tell you her name.

We can see time in changes: layers of dust, wrinkles in skin, the broadening of our bodies, the slackening of muscles, the thinning of carpet, the growth of plants, the decomposition of fruit. But is it a tangible thing, or have we just imposed an imperfect framework onto it? Is time actually subjective, with the ability to speed up and slow down? In André Aciman's essay 'Temporizing', he discusses a very particular way of processing time. A temporizer, according to Aciman, foregoes the present. The temporizer is constantly gazing back to relive a bygone present (the past), or else looking ahead to a future in which they may reflect back on the actual present they are in. If we consider this in terms of hauntology, we might think of such a person as willingly haunted, because they seek out the ghosts.

This constant looking forward and back is perceived by the temporizer as a way of extending or enriching the present, as Aciman writes that the temporizer 'firms up the present by experiencing it from a future as a moment in the past'. This is to say that the temporizer has a troubled relationship with time, in that they fear both it and the continual loss wrought by it, a loss that they are hyperaware of. It is a contradictory notion, but one that psychologically makes sense to the temporizer: that sidestepping the present, anticipating its loss while simultaneously attempting to dive back into a past-present (because the past isn't actually past for the temporizer – it is, in fact, more present than the present), then time can be avoided and the present just might be extended. They can't be vulnerable in real time, because the present moment is always suspended.

Of course, this method doesn't work. There is no halting of time. In attempting to grip onto the present, we effectively obliterate it. The present – and its events, emotions and lessons – only becomes accessible in reflection, when it is long over. The ancestral pilgrimage has a similar kind of time-play. While walking, the present is forsaken in service of attempting to both enter the past and create memories to look back on in the future. Another trait of the temporizer: we feel we must be prepared for whatever the present might bring, in order to experience it. Which means that we are never ready, and that we spend a lot of time training for a race that is already almost over, attempting to return to the past so that we may prepare for a present that is passing us by.

This fear of forgetting and being forgotten – isn't it just a metonym for fearing time, just as time is a metonym for fearing one's own mortality? What I mean is that these fears, of forgetting and being forgotten, of dying and of time, all refer to one another. What would time be if there weren't an end to things? What need would there be to remember if no one ever left, if we weren't aware of our own eventual leaving?

Haunting is the flip side of mourning. While mourning can be characterised as the slow process of letting go, haunting is the failure to withdraw, the refusal to give up the ghost. We cling to the past like it's an old boyfriend we can't shake.

Benghazi

'Nel giardino del mio padrino'

Rita (left, looking at camera), girl holding Annalisa, Salvatore, Benghazi, 1931

Here is my grandmother Annalisa as a new baby in the arms of a young girl. Rita, in black, grins at the camera, Salvatore looks on proudly, the family is surrounded by a lush garden. I know they are in Libya because that's what the caption tells me: 'In my godfather's garden.' Judging by the photo alone, however, they could be anywhere. Later Annalisa would grow up to look like her mother, and she too would end up in a country foreign to her.

When my grandmother first moved to Australia and bought the house on Coral Street, my mother objected to its distance from us. The house was a ten-minute drive away, while my mother had envisioned a little house down the street from ours, so that she could duck in and out on foot. But my grandmother has never ceded to anybody. She said she didn't like the small suburban subdivision that my parents lived in, which was serviced only by a measly strip mall of a supermarket, a post office, a Chinese restaurant and a combination pharmacy/sporting goods store. It was a subdivision first built in the eighties and while it wasn't exactly ugly, it was exceedingly unremarkable in the way that suburban subdivisions aim to be. I also think that maybe it was a way to assert her independence – she wasn't moving to Australia for us, she was saying. She just happened to want to live in the same place that we lived. She chose a house in the larger-but-still-tiny town five minutes' drive away.

It was a decision my mother continued to lament even after my grandmother moved in with her, but I'm not sure it would have made much of a difference in the end. The fact remained that my grandmother could not live alone anymore. Right before coming home for the summer, my parents had moved some of her furniture into the semi-detached suite at our home. They bought a hospital-grade bed where the mattress moves up and down if you press a button on a remote. They installed railings and a chair in the shower. They stocked the mini fridge with her favourite snacks and drinks.

It was a tropical summer, and the air in my grandmother's three-bedroom 1980s bungalow was so humid that walking from one room to another felt like wading through a hot swamp. My mother and I were cleaning out her home to make way for renters. We emptied out the built-in wardrobes, the bookshelves, and the antique desk with its roll-down top, the imposing oak cupboards and the credenza which she had shipped over from Palermo years earlier. We made 'donate' and 'keep' piles, poring over photographs and hidden treasures: antique jewellery of unknown origin, eighty-year-old postcards, turn-of-the-century portraits.

The shelves in the study were occupied by rows and rows of photo albums and leather-bound encyclopaedias in burgundy, navy and cream. There were hundreds of paperbacks and boxes of porcelain tea sets, silver serving platters and crystal martini glasses. There were the miniature treasures that my mother also shared a love of: glass-blown animals, tiny gold fans and furniture, brooches. In the guest bedroom were hand-embroidered white linens and my great-great aunt Lina's embroidered bloomers and slips. There were lace fans and a silk fan that had been hand-painted with a garden scene, upon which buzzed embroidered bumblebees the size of my pinkie fingernail. There was a collection of butter-soft kid gloves in white, cream, navy and black, and two pairs of hand-stitched white lace gloves. There was a heavy mother of pearl cigarette lighter, one that was meant to be displayed on a table. This belonged to my great-aunt, who kept silk cases of cigarettes of every brand in the drawers of her coffee table for guests. There were leather wallets still in their boxes, never used. There were small, tasselled playbills from the opera, and both her and her father's identity cards from the fifties. There were portraits of men and women whom neither I nor my mother knew, of children wearing white wigs and powdered faces and drawn-on moles for a costume party, of funeral processions in a small Sicilian town, of weddings in Turin.

There were the gifts I had given her from my own travels: the hand-painted vase from a flea market in Paris, the magnets from Las Vegas, the silk scarves from Spain. There were her father's three antique cameras: a folding Agfa from the twenties that looked like a miniature accordion, a Comet II from the fifties, and another Agfa Isola from the sixties. There were stacks of postcards that she and her mother had written over a fifty-year period: from Benghazi, from Rome, from Madrid and Budapest and Paris. There were the matador and flamenco dancers' costumes that she had ordered to be made in Seville for my mother and uncle and aunt when they were children, not so much costumes as miniature versions of the real thing.

My mother and I spent sweaty days deciding what to give away to the Salvation Army and downing paracetamol in a failing attempt to fight off the migraines that bloomed under our skulls every afternoon. It felt as though we were giving away not just my grandmother's life, but those of her parents, her ancestors. It was a history that she had painstakingly kept safe, and it was now left in the hands of the Salvation Army, her children and her grandchildren, who did not know how to keep precious things safe, who were constantly moving from one share house to another, from one city to another. The remains of her life, dispersed through the world like crematory ashes.

A few days ago, I began using one of the leather wallets she had left, and a passport-sized photograph of my grandmother fell out and floated through the air like a feather, where it landed at my feet. It was from ten years ago, when she was still able to travel, when she still had the need for a passport. It reminded me of how she was, how I'd known her for most of my life, and though it was only a decade ago, it felt like an eternity had passed between now and then.

It felt grubby, going through her things. We hung her framed university degrees in our house, displayed along with her fencer's mask and foil. Her piano went to my uncle. They were reminders that she had deliberately been an only daughter, one lavished with the same opportunities of an only son. We donated hundreds of Italian paperbacks, collections of dusty encyclopaedias, the ugly Schumacher urn that no one wanted, the white pair of Zia Lina's 1920s bloomers. My mother would pull things out, like the set of Art Deco martini glasses, making sure they were crystal by licking her finger and running it around the brim, showing me the signature cut into the bottom. Among the fine china sets, all signed, we counted seventy-two cups and saucers, fourteen teapots, fifteen sugar canisters, eighty spoons. They were from North Africa, China, Japan, Germany, England, Austria, Italy.

On the last day, after my mother and uncle and aunt had divided up the furniture (the original Louis XVI settee and armchairs, the piano, the carved mahogany china cabinet), my cousins and I made piles of what we wanted to keep, picking at her things like vultures – the bags of postcards, Rita's felt hats, Salvatore's collection of antique cameras.

I got the photo albums. There were six: five blue rectangular leather-bound albums and one maroon scrapbook. All the photos in the scrapbook are glued onto the thick black pages and scrawled with captions meant for someone who has enough context to decode them. The other photographs in the scrapbook are of card games and parties, cigar-smoking men, Salvatore and his friends posing together by the sea, half-torn portraits of women who are not my great-grandmother. It had been compiled by Salvatore during his bachelorhood in Libya. There was also a box, filled with loose black and white photographs. These were the photos he had smuggled back to Italy, and they depicted a different world to the one in the albums – there were photos of Berber tribes in the desert; of he and his friends dressed as women, their faces carefully made up; of them drinking in sand dunes; of him on camelback.

Two of the five blue albums were dedicated to photographs of Libya, beginning with my grandmother's birth. I had always thought of them as a window into this country that seemed so foreign to me, but their surfaces lay flat – more like walls than windows. No matter how much I looked at photos of Libya, an image of the place in which my grandmother grew up refused to form in my mind. Instead, I felt as though I was looking at blurred images through a viewfinder.

When I was a child, my grandmother would come to visit us in our sleepy town on Australia's eastern coast every summer. It seemed that the season began with her barging into our home. On her way to us she often stopped to visit a friend in Japan or Peru, and so she was always laden with treasures – glossy green maracas from Mexico for my brother, a piece of petrified trunk from Petaluma for me.

She blew in through the front door like a mythic wind from the northern hemisphere, wasting no time in unpacking her many suitcases – whose contents spilled throughout our home – and barking orders at my parents in the tone that had earned her nickname, *la generalessa*. My twin bed would be moved to the guest room, and I would fall asleep to the stories of her childhood. She would tell them until she was exhausted, when a rumbling snore would rupture a sentence. I've since forgotten many of the details of these stories, and what I do remember seems pointless to reproduce, could only matter to me. Still, these half-remembered stories remind me of her as she was before she became ill: the respect she commanded, her adventurous life and independence, her manner like that of a military general, and her love for me.

She was born in the Libyan town of Barce (now Al-Marj) in 1931. A short while after her birth, the family moved to Benghazi. My mental images of the city could be reduced to photographs in travel agencies. A whitewashed villa baking in the sun. The scent of olive trees gently swaying in the sea breeze. Mediterranean waves battering the coastline. The Libya that I pictured was completely divorced from the Libya that we see on the news now. I became aware of how little I knew about the place that I had been hearing about my entire life. I snatched up the albums greedily, convinced that they contained all the information I would need.

'Archi di fantasia'

Annalisa and playmate, Benghazi, 1936

In this photo, a favourite of mine, Annalisa is around seven or eight, loose dark curls caught in motion, her clothing casual and so modern-looking one might mistake the picture for being contemporary. There are other children around her, all of them, like my grandmother, arms raised and mouths agape in celebration. It's the kind of photo that you can almost hear. I have no context for it, but I like it for its suggestion of movement, of spontaneity. I have never seen or known my grandmother like this, caught in a moment of euphoria. I know that she was in Libya, judging by her age, and guess that perhaps it was a fascist event, although neither she nor the other girl in the photo are wearing the fascist children's uniforms that they were required to don at events. I feel like, looking at the photo, I am stealing this unguarded moment from her, just as the photographer did, and yet it remains a mystery to me.

Photography has many fathers. The first commercially available form of photography was the daguerreotype, which was invented by the French chemist and artist Louis Daguerre in 1839. The process was highly complicated and involved: polishing a silver plate to a mirror finish, applying a coat of iodine, treating it with the fumes of various chemicals, exposing the plate to a camera for however long as light dictated it was necessary, developing the image by holding it over a dish of heated mercury, then removing its coating in a hyposulphite bath, and finally washing it in distilled water. The effect was that the daguerreotype was a mirror image of the scene it captured, like when you hold writing up to a mirror and the letters are reversed. The process produced a single, unreproducible photograph on a heavy silver-plate.

This invention was quickly followed in 1841 by a different method for capturing images. The calotype was invented by the Englishman William Henry Fox Talbot. In this technique, a sheet of paper was covered with silver chloride and placed in a camera obscura. Once exposed to the light, the tones of the image captured on the paper were reversed, like a photographic negative. The negative was then pressed to another sheet of coated paper, where the positive image appeared. The difference was that calotypes produced a negative from which numerous positives could be produced, rather than just a singular daguerreotype.

In her 1977 essay collection, *On Photography*, Susan Sontag writes that the idea for inventing calotypes first came to Fox Talbot in 1833, while on the Grand Tour of Italy customary for the wealthy young men of that era. Fox Talbot was in Lake Como sketching the landscape, assisted in his drawing by a camera obscura, a device that projected images rather than captured them. Musing on the beauty of the nature scene projected by the camera obscura, he wondered whether it would be possible to make a device that would not just project an image, but capture it too. It's fitting that one of the first impulses for inventing photography was possession, a human disregard for the fact that what draws us to beauty is our inability to possess it, anything other than fleetingly. Calotype, the name for Fox Talbot's process, derives from the Greek words for beautiful, *kalos*, and *typos*, meaning an impression, image or sketch.

The term 'photograph' was first coined in 1834 by Hércules Florence, a French-born Brazilian painter and inventor, who referred to his developments regarding *photographie* in his diaries. The term is derived from the Greek words *photos*, meaning 'light', and *graphe*, which comes from the Greek *graphos*, meaning 'writing' or 'drawing'. Put together, the literal definition of photography is 'to write with light'. Although I have developed my own photographs before, I still don't understand how or why cameras or photographic processes work, other than what the term implies: that it is a process involving light.

However many processes or people were involved in its invention, the introduction of commercially available photography marked the conception of another world. Looking at photographs, we are offered glimpses into a shadow world that seems to echo our own. Sontag writes that since its invention in 1839, we have photographed almost everything that we deem to be important: public inaugurations and private milestones, wars and ceremonies, overseas holidays and pretty landscapes, the aftermath of disasters like Chernobyl and Manhattan in the wake of 9/11, our pets, what we made for dinner. As a result, we have accumulated a visual inventory of the last hundred and fifty years. History is now catalogued in state photo archives and museum retrospectives, family memory is stored in personal photo albums, while the work of certain photographers, such as Diane Arbus or Robert Mapplethorpe, captures the mood of entire decades. This explosion of visual documentation begs the question: do we remember or value the moments that go unrecorded?

Photographs represent not just a mirror to our past world, but a better, slicker, richer version of it. We don't want to time-travel to the real sixties, we want to jump into Richard Avedon's stylised version of the decade. We want to travel through the places depicted in Steve McCurry's photographs. We want to inhabit a world in which the composition of light is as artful as that of Brassaï's *Grand Central Terminal*. These worlds have become, with social media such as Instagram, as real as our own, or an extension of it: we once used to record our lives using photographs, now we live *through* photographs. Part of the appeal is surely that we can control the composition of light, distort our bodies into a flattering angle, choose to allow only the happy scenes of our lives to enter the new reality.

John Berger wrote that a photograph produces tensions which we sense when looking at it. These come from its unknowability, or our discovery of its unknowability. The unknowability is what is happening outside the frame – it's an acknowledgement of time and distance. It's an uncanny sensation, the photograph an uncanny object. Freud's concept of the uncanny means to find the unfamiliar within the familiar, and also its inverse: to find the familiar within the unfamiliar. Perhaps the reason I am so drawn to this photo is because my grandmother is so alien to me as a child. I cannot recognise her in this photo. Within that realisation, of time and distance, lies the photo's unknowability. As Berger says, it is 'the abyss between the moment recorded and the moment of looking.'

And yet, the photo could be uncanny in the opposite direction too: the familiar within the unfamiliar. Maybe on another level I am so drawn to this photo because even as my grandmother as a child is so alien to me, there is something I recognise. I wonder, did I make that same expression when I was a child?

Desert Road

Man (Salvatore?) on road, beginnings of a settlement somewhere in
Libya, 1926

I can't make out the scrawl on this one, only the year, and I'm
unsure of what I'm looking at – a road, a barren landscape, a
few squat buildings in the distance, a man. Terrain beginning to
be tamed.

Like most other African nations, the borders of Libya were
drawn in a room a sea and a continent away, by hands who gave
little thought to who those lines were separating and grouping
together. Those lines ignored both cultural and natural borders.
The country is divided by the Gulf of Sirte, a body of water at
the midpoint of Libya's northern Mediterranean coast where
the sea dips into the shoreline. Muddy salt marshes and smooth
salt flats smatter the gulf's coast.

The Sirte Basin stretches across for 480 kilometres and then
down from this coast, deep into the Sahara Desert. The basin is
a terrain of shrubby desert steppes, a barren lid on the fountains

of oil that lie beneath it. It is the main natural barrier that has historically separated the three regions of Libya, which Italy fused together to form one country. Tripolitania lies to the west with Tripoli as its capital city, Cyrenaica to the east, its capital Benghazi. The third region is Fezzan, to the southwest. Its historical capital, Sabha, is an oasis city, and the hometown of Muammar Gaddafi.

Libya's name was, like its borders, decided by outsiders elsewhere. The earliest recorded usage of the word from which 'Libya' derives, *Lebu*, comes from Ancient Egyptian inscriptions from the thirteenth century BCE, to describe either an individual Berber tribe or Berbers living west of the Nile. The Ancient Greeks then used the term to refer to the entirety of North Africa and the Berber people. It was the ancient Romans who first officially called it 'Libya'. After the Romans, the name was forgotten until the twentieth century, when the Italians began eyeing the country and revived their old name for it.

The Kingdom of Italy declared war on what is now Libya in 1911. It had been part of the Ottoman Empire for over three centuries, one of the few expanses of African soil not snatched up by European colonial powers. Parts of East Africa had been granted to Italy during the infamous Berlin Conference, a series of negotiations that went on between European powers from 1884 to 1885. Otherwise known as the 'Scramble for Africa', the negotiations involved matching up European powers to parcels of African land, resources and people, a bit like cutting up a sheet cake and deciding who gets the corner pieces and who is stuck with the middle.

Twelve representatives of the European powers met in Berlin, convened by the German chancellor Otto von Bismark: Belgium, Germany, France, Portugal, the Austro-Hungarian Empire, Denmark, Sweden–Norway, Spain, Great Britain, Russia, the Netherlands and Italy. They discussed the matter for several months, in a conference room with a large map of Africa hanging on the wall. Eventually they settled on the following arrangement: Belgium was given the authority to colonise the

Congo. France kept Morocco and most of West Africa. Britain got Egypt, Ghana, Kenya, Nigeria, South Africa and Uganda. Germany was given Namibia and Tanzania. Portugal now owned Angola and Mozambique. Spain received Equatorial Guinea. Italy was granted the rights to parts of East Africa – Somalia, Ethiopia and Eritrea. It was gifted Ottoman-occupied Libya in 1887, in an agreement with Germany that was secretly signed by von Bismark.

Looking at maps of Africa prior to the conference and a little over thirty years later, one imagines a scene of European bureaucrats wrangling over a plan of the African continent, scratching pencil lines and scrawling their names in the sections that would become theirs. In 1881, 10 per cent of Africa had been colonised by European powers (other parts were under Ottoman rule, like Libya and Egypt), and by 1914 nearly 90 per cent was under European dominion.

In 1892, the British Prime Minister at the time, Lord Salisbury, wrote:

> [We] have been engaged in drawing lines upon maps where no white man's foot ever trod; we have been giving away mountains and rivers and lakes to each other, only hindered by the small impediment that we never knew exactly where the mountains and rivers and lakes were.

The fact that Libya had once, centuries before, been a Roman province and the fact that it was so close to Italy's southern shore rendered it an attractive prospect for the politicians who dreamed of building a modern Italian empire. According to the Italian government at the time, seizing back the North African terrain that had been lost with the fall of the empire was the first step in ascending to their past heights, when Rome ruled the Mediterranean.

There were few, if any, concrete reasons to colonise. There were no natural resources – those subterranean fountains of oil in the Sirte Basin would not be struck until the 1950s.

But what Libya lacked in material it made up for in what it represented: hope. Hope that the young nation of Italy would become a great modern power on the international scene, as opposed to what it had been prior to Risorgimento: a parcel of city-states and passive territories belonging to other empires.

In other words, Italy needed to prove its whiteness, and whiteness meant domination. The whiteness of Italians, and southern Italians in particular, has historically been questioned, both outside of Italy and within it, not least because of the Arab heritage of the South. In Italian professor Lucia Re's article, 'Italians and the Invention of Race', she writes that prior to the Libyan War, Italian racism was directed in on itself. It hinged on degrees of whiteness and racism towards southern Italians. Thinkers of the time were obsessed with race and whiteness, and promoted the idea that northern and southern Italians belonged to two different ethnic groups: the Aryans (*Arii*) and the Afro-Mediterraneans (*Italici*) respectively. The Italian South was racially inferior, not truly white, and could only be improved with colonisation and racial mixing.

According to Re, the Risorgimento, rather than a real unification, was more like a colonisation of the South by the North. After Unification, the South became poorer than it had been before. Southern Italy at the time had a feudal class system in which wealthy landowners held almost all the land and therefore control of the sharecroppers and peasants who worked their estates for them. High taxes targeted these peasants, the natural resources of the South were exploited by northern companies, and the national government was doing nothing to change the feudal class system. The working classes were leaving en masse, for the 'new world'. Others remained and were beginning to agitate for land and voting rights. Colonising Libya could mean a new place for these people to go, one where they could own their own property. It would also help to form a national Italian identity by creating a new 'other' that Italians could not just define themselves against, but direct their racism towards.

On 26 September 1911, Italy sent an ultimatum to the Ottoman Sultan in Turkey, giving him twenty-four hours to agree to an Italian occupation of Tripolitania and Cyrenaica. The response from Turkey was conciliatory, offering 'economic concessions' to Italy but maintaining that the territory must remain within the Ottoman Empire. Nevertheless, four days later, the Italian Prime Minister, Giovanni Giolitti, declared war. That October, thirty-four thousand Italian troops took the urban centres of Tripoli, Benghazi, Homs and Tobruk. On 23 October, ten thousand armed Turks and Libyans attacked Italian lines in the Sciara Sciat oasis near Tripoli. They killed over five hundred Italian soldiers. Their bodies were found nailed to palm trees, with their eyelids stitched shut and their genitals cut off, thought to be retribution for sexual abuse of the local women. That same October, Italian troops retaliated by slaughtering at least a thousand Libyans. In the main squares of towns, gallows were erected, and anyone thought to be a rebel was publicly hanged. Hundreds of Libyan families were exiled and deported to camps on the Tremiti Islands off Italy's Adriatic coast. The camps were slum-like, overcrowded and filthy, and food was scarce. Not even a year later, a third of the population, mostly children and old people, was dead.

A little over a year after the beginning of what would be written in history books as the Italo-Turkish War, on 18 October 1912, the Ottomans and the Italians signed a peace treaty in Ouchy, Switzerland. The Ottomans agreed to withdraw their military personnel from Libya and the Italians agreed to give Rhodes and the rest of the Dodecanese Islands back to Turkey. Cyrenaica and Tripolitania were now internationally recognised as extensions of Italian soil. Just as the future of Africa was decided in a German conference room, so the future of Libya and the Dodecanese Islands was decided at a Swiss lakeside resort, when the weather would still have been nice enough to take a swim.

The cultural historian Barbara Spadaro writes that at t the time of Italy's invasion, the two coastal regions, Tripolitania and Cyrenaica, had more in common with their border countries than with each other (French-occupied Algeria and Tunisia, and British Egypt respectively). The Fezzan, the interior region that takes up the largest portion of the Sahara, was populated by Berber and Tuareg tribes that had had little contact with the Ottomans or the coastal cultures. Italy embarked on its colonisation of these territories with little knowledge of the local population, or even a clear idea of what Libya looked like. Shortly after Italy's 'conquest' of Libya, the Arab Revolt began. Among the mountain tribes of Cyrenaica, the Sanusi Order, a mystical Islamic sect, created an independent state led by Sayyid Ahmad al-Sharif and declared jihad on the Italians in 1913.

The war for control of these regions lasted for almost two decades, with the Italians gaining and losing control of various territories, not helped by the fact that half their troops were fighting in the First World War. The Sanusi were experts in guerrilla warfare, but, armed with horses and antique rifles left behind by the Ottomans, they were David to the Italians' Goliath, who had aircraft, armoured vehicles, machine guns, and chemical weapons in their arsenal.

'Poste Italiane'

Salvatore emerging from tent with barbed wire fence behind him,
Libya, 1923

My great-grandfather arrived in Tripoli in 1920, two years
before the March on Rome and two years after the First World
War had ended. He had come to Tripolitania from a family of
bureaucrats in a Sicilian town. His father had owned the local
post office, and once the postal service in Italy was nationalised,
the men in his family received comfortable government
positions. However, he was one of seven siblings, and his family
had little land, the greatest source of wealth in Sicily. The more
land one had, the wealthier one was, and the only way to get
at this land was to inherit it. Migration to Libya was a way to
sidestep this issue, and a way to create something new within
the confines of the Italian state. It made sense. He would always
be guaranteed an Italian government salary, especially in Libya,
where the salaries for the same jobs were much higher.

The First World War had left Sicily poorer than ever, and it
was, in many senses, excluded from the rest of Italy: the schools
were poorly funded, there was little infrastructure, and the island

75

was overrun with bandits. In the minds of mainland Italians, European civilisation did not extend to Sicily.

I can see why Libya was such an enticing prospect for Salvatore. He was offered a position as a government diplomat in the new colony, and his job entailed setting up postal outposts in military forts or the newly captured or founded villages and settlements. I assume this tent was the beginnings of one. His identity card from 1957 tells me that later, after the war, he was an *archivista capo* – 'chief archivist' – in Palermo. The photo is like a poster for the *mission civilisatrice*: here is the white man dressed in his European suit, here he is standing in the wild and dusty desert, here is his makeshift office, here are the humble beginnings of civilisation.

Sometimes I wonder whether he had a clear picture of the situation he was stepping into, whether he ever reflected on what his presence there meant.

A thorough and seemingly grassroots propaganda campaign to colonise Africa was launched by 'colonialists' in the late nineteenth century. According to the historian Claudio G. Segre, they 'consisted of a heterogeneous band of enthusiasts, middle class, for the most part . . . There were scholars and scientists, explorers and missionaries, journalists and travellers, bankers and businessmen, literary figures and adventurers.' They organised themselves into blocs and founded newspapers. During the months prior to the Italian invasion of Libya, a few journalists and politicians made brief trips to Tripolitania and Cyrenaica to put pressure on the government to invade what they referred to as the *terra promessa* (promised land). Their writings have no scientific value – actually, in many respects they are falsehoods.

However, their campaign was successful, both in that their publications were widely read and that they were part of the reason why Libya was invaded. By the time of invasion in 1911, the idea of colonising Libya was welcomed by the Italian people, regardless of their politics. Writer and future Fascist minister Enrico Corradini was one such 'traveller-propagandist'. He visited Libya a few months prior to invasion, writing a book called *L'ora di Tripoli* (1911). In the book, Corradini waxed poetic about the fertile abundance of Libyan earth, beneath which were surely mineral riches. The colonisation of Libya would help everyone in Italy, from rich to poor, from north to south. According to Corradini, rather than diverting resources and time away from the domestic 'southern question' towards expanding Italy, colonisation would *solve* this problem.

In a panegyric that sounds like a fever dream journey through the mountainous Jebel Akhdar and the Al-Marj plain, he describes the land as a 'green sea', one that is even lusher than the rolling meadows of his native Tuscany. The fields are filled with barley and wheat and earth so red and fine and stone-less that it looks like tobacco. There are forestfuls of olive trees, planted by the ancient Romans and now turned wild and native. There are verdant valleys and gorges and plains in which there remain ancient Roman wells dug into the red rock, which still bubble and gush with water.

Three years earlier, the area that he is describing had been pronounced unfit for extensive settlement by the International Territorial Organisation, due to lack of water sources. Addressing these anti-colonialists and 'sorts of geographers' directly, he writes that he can see the facts with his very own eyes: 'the olive tree, the forest, the water.' By this he means that he can see Ancient Rome in Africa – in the now-native olive trees, in the still-used wells, and in the happy faces of the Berber girls. What he is saying is that this land is the rightful inheritance of Italy, the modern incarnation of Ancient Rome.

My great-grandparents surely would have read articles and literature like this before their departures. Sailing across the Mediterranean, both Salvatore and Rita would have expected to be welcomed by green fields and lush vegetation. I sometimes wonder whether either of them was surprised by what they found.

In 1916, the Sanusi decided to open negotiations with the Italians. Two treaties resulted from the talks: the 1916 Agreement of al-Zuwaytina and the 1917 Agreement of Akrama. These agreements granted Italian sovereignty along the Cyrenaica coast and recognised the ruling Sanusi tribes' sovereignty in the hinterland. They allowed for free trade and Sanusi exemption from land taxes, and promised the Sanusi family salaries in exchange for disarmament.

When Mussolini took control of Italy in October 1922, he immediately rejected the brief peace – albeit fragile and poorly managed – that had been in place for the previous few years. Fascism revered violence, and Mussolini more than proved his devotion to it. In early 1923, what was referred to as the *riconquista* ('re-conquest') began. Italian sovereignty was mostly confined to the coast, and Mussolini wanted it extended over the entire territory, including the sparse desert regions.

Italy and Libya went to war again. In the field, the Italians had modern arms and twenty thousand men on their side, including Christian troops from Eritrea. They had aeroplanes, machine guns, and poison gas. Again, the Libyan guerrilla forces took the role of David; their troops rarely comprised more than a thousand. The historian Ronald Bruce St John writes that by 1924 Italy had (mostly) won the war. Most of the coastal areas and the countryside were subjugated. In 1928, the head of the Sanusi Order surrendered to the Italian commander of Cyrenaica. Northern Fezzan was already under Italian control. In January 1929, Tripolitania and Cyrenaica were united under one governor, Marshall Pietro Badoglio. Tripoli was the new capital of the officially christened Libya.

Looking at my great-grandparents' faces in the photographs, I try to intuit their frames of mind. What made them leave Italy? What did they think they would find? I can only guess, by trying to consume what they may have consumed about Libya before departing.

'a Barce con cavolo del nostro orto'

Rita and unknown woman, dead rabbit, cabbage, Barce, 1931

In these photos, we are at the entrance of a stone dwelling. The first shows two women: on the left is Rita, and on the right is an unknown woman, possibly a neighbour. She grips a dead rabbit by the throat. The date of the photograph, 29 March 1931, means that Rita is three months pregnant with my grandmother. They are in Barce, 'with cabbage from our garden'. When Rita's ship docked at the port in Tripoli in 1925, she was twenty-nine years old. She had left home for the first time.

She would have left from Genova, the closest transit hub to Turin, on a large cruise steamer. All the photos of emigrants in the Fondazione Paolo Cresci online archives show messes of an impossible number of people and luggage stacked haphazardly at the port beside the ship. I imagine her sailing away from Italy as the coast recedes into the distance, the smell of fishing trawlers and saltwater in the breeze, shunning the dense mess of people pushing and clutching the railing, waving handkerchiefs in farewell to their loved ones. She waves a handkerchief for no one. She gazes at the other passengers clamouring for one last look at Italy, and the idea that she has no ties, that she is beholden to nothing and no one for the first time in her life thrills her. She retreats to her windowless cabin and sits on her single bed and steels herself.

Nights, she doesn't sleep, but instead climbs up to the deck and stares into the glassy expanse of black sea, listens to it sloshing about and feels the beat of her heart. The world would have suddenly gotten bigger. When she stepped off the ship that first day, did she have regrets? Every time I am in a new country, I am always shocked that each place smells so different, that the air has a unique quality. As the passengers shuffled off the boat, their pace wobbly with sea legs, their clothes wrinkled and hair matted, did she feel lost? This was when Salvatore saw her, my grandmother would tell me, clad in black mourning clothes. I wonder if she intuited what lay in her future when they first locked eyes.

The story is a fabled one in my family: he had seen her when she stepped off the ship, and was attracted to her because he had a preference for ample women dressed in black. She was robust and in mourning, so she caught his eye. Right after he approached her and told her which outpost he was assigned to, she signed up to teach at the one furthest away from his, ensuring their two-year separation. Despite her seeming disinterest, they exchanged letters for two years, and were married the next time they met.

The Libya that I grew up hearing about was also romanticised, and so inadequate an education in the history and culture of the country that when I began researching, I realised I had barely any basic knowledge. I think this was in part because my grandmother viewed the landscape of her youth with nostalgia, in part because she was conscious of being the guardian of her own past, and in part because stories are, by their nature, fictitious. Family stories are fluid, altering to accomodate what the teller wants to communicate in the present. My mother, too, is guilty of this, something I have observed as the stories she tells gradually shift over time. These stories are not history, they narrate our family's past through the lens of the teller.

We tend to conflate 'history' and 'the past'. But I'm not so sure that they are the same thing. If history can be categorised as 'what happened', then perhaps the past is 'how we remember or think about what happened' or perhaps 'how we make sense of what happened'. It's not just family stories, either — it's all stories and histories. Photographs furnish these stories, they offer material evidence. Each time I read the story told in the photographs it alters, moving in and out of focus. It's as if, the clearer I try to see the images, the fainter they become.

Salvatore and camel

Salvatore on camel, Libya, 1926

In another one from his scrapbook, Salvatore reclines atop a camel adorned with tassels. It's the kind of photo he would have sent home to his family in Sicily. I picture a cluster of my ancestors huddled over the photo, passing it between them, marvelling at what would have been a snapshot into an unknown world, Salvatore in the midst of an exotic adventure that they could not begin to dream of. But this is all conjecture and doesn't really tell me anything. I would like to think that my great-grandfather had a respectful interest in learning about Libyan culture, but that would be wildly naïve. For in all the stories she related to me, my grandmother neglected to pass on any Libyan history, of which I suspect she had little knowledge. I wonder how many colonising Italians read up on the history of the territory they were taking over, if they went further than the exoticism displayed in this photo.

Alessandro Spina is the nom de plume of Basili Shafik Khouzam, a Libyan writer born in 1927 to a wealthy Maronite family of textile magnates from Syria. His father had moved to Benghazi when he was seventeen, back when it was a sleepy merchant port. At the outbreak of the Second World War, when he was twelve, his father sent him to Italy, where he remained until he was twenty-six. In Milan, Spina studied and began writing his first stories, which drew from his own life, history, and imagination. They featured a vast cast of characters, including Italian officers and settlers, slaves, sheikhs, aristocrats and Sanusi rebels.

In 1953, he returned to Benghazi to help his father run the family factory. At work, he would write in his father's office. Despite the twelve-hour working days, he managed to complete and publish the first collection of stories that he had begun in Italy, a novel titled *Tempo e Corruzione (Time and Decay)*, and the three novels that would become the first volume of his 'Benghazi trilogy', *I confini dell'ombra (The Confines of the Shadow)*. The first couple of instalments were met with critical acclaim, if not commercial success, in Italy. The first, *The Young Maronite*, was shortlisted for the Strega and Campiello prizes. Although the third instalment, a novel titled *The Nocturnal Visitor*, was completed in 1972, Spina held off on publishing it until 1979, due to the uncertain political landscape of Gaddafi's rule. In the intervening years following the coup, Spina's father's factory had been nationalised, and thousands of remaining Jewish and Italian settlers were expelled from the country. Dissidents were jailed, a number of Spina's friends among them.

Gaddafi was targeting writers. By the time Spina left Libya for Italy in 1980, he was under surveillance, and the manuscript for *The Nocturnal Visitor* was smuggled out of the country in the briefcase of the French consul. Spina followed his manuscript to Paris and then settled in his villa in Lombardy. It was here that he completed the last two volumes of his trilogy and several books of essays. The trilogy is the only work of its kind: an epic that traces the course of European colonisation in North Africa. It spans from November 1912, the beginning of the Italian invasion of Libya, through Italian colonisation, the rise and fall of Fascism and the aftermath of the Second World War, and runs up until after Libya has gained independence as a monarchy in the 1950s, when oil and natural gas were discovered there in 1964.

In his introduction to the English translation, Spina's translator, the poet André Naffis-Sahely, writes that Spina was touted as the 'Italian Joseph Conrad' and 'a twentieth-century Balzac'. Despite drawing respect among literary circles, Spina was still largely unknown to the Italian public. This may be in part because he shunned attention, refusing to grant interviews or make public appearances, and he insisted on publishing his books in limited print runs with small presses. It may also be because the Italian public wasn't interested in the subject matter – he had once been warned by the Italian writer Alberto Moravia that Italians were both ignorant of and uninterested in the truth of Italian colonialism.

By the twenty-first century, his books had gone out of print. Whatever the reason for this, in reissuing *The Confines of the Shadow*, Bertoletti attempted to rectify the situation. After years of trying to convince Spina to reissue his books, he finally succeeded in 2006. The works which make up the trilogy were collected and compiled into three volumes. This magnum opus was awarded Italy's most prestigious prize, the *Premio Bagutta*.

It resulted in just one radio interview, some rave reviews, and a conference given in his honour. Spina didn't attend the conference, let alone allow an author photograph. He returned to his former obscurity.

When Gaddafi ordered that all Italian monuments be torn down, Spina found himself exiled from the violent world of his youth. Naffis-Sahely writes that Spina wanted to show 'the inanity of the concept of conquest as well as the existential vacuum it inevitably leaves in its wake'. It's a collection made for a reader who has no knowledge of the history of either Benghazi or Libya, an Italian public ignorant of its country's history.

It was in reading Spina's fiction that my vision of Benghazi began to expand. In the books, Benghazi evolves from a small colonial backwater to a bustling city during the Second World War. In the markets of Spina's Benghazi, cross-legged local soothsayers border souks and market squares, with pamphlets displayed on the sandy ground before them. Members of the Italian aristocracy look out of their villa windows over a network of labyrinthine streets and alleys, covered souks, public squares and palm gardens. On one side lies the sea, on the other the sparse and dusty desert. Windows are perennially kept open to catch the sea breeze, closed only when the desert winds, such as the sirocco and the ghibli, whistle through the city. The sky is cloudless throughout the year, still as glass, disturbed only by short autumn storms. The sea glimmers in the eternal sunshine.

Class Pictures

Class photos, Rita on the right, Benghazi, year unknown

A class photo of the elementary school where she taught. All the children are grouped in front of the building, both Italian and Libyan. Rita rests her hands on their shoulders and gazes at the camera. Some of the children hold their arms up in the fascist *saluto romano*.

Another photo taken inside shows the teachers and the schoolchildren huddled around a large table, a mess of tiny faces. On the table are framed portraits of *il Duce*, and another portrait of Mussolini hangs on the wall behind them.

A decree in 1928 changed the Italian education policy in Libya, so that Libyan children were not permitted to continue schooling after the elementary level. They were taught to read by repeating phrases such as:

'I am happy to be subject to the Italian government.'
'The Duce loves children very much, even Arab children.'

In Knud Holmboe's book *Desert Encounter,* a Libyan schoolteacher tells him that their textbooks began with phrases such as:

'In the old days there was savagery and barbarism in this country, but now the Romans have returned . . .'

A term that comes up often in both imperial propaganda and travel writing from the colonial era is 'civilisation'. In historical study, civilisation is used to describe past societies, like the Aztecs or the Greeks. We refer to humankind as civilisation when we wonder what will wipe it out – a nuclear war perhaps, or, more and more likely, climate Armageddon. In Italy, its variants pop up regularly in everyday usage – people who are violent or lack manners are often referred to as 'uncivilised' or 'barbarians'.

The notion that some societies are civilised and some are primitive may not have been invented in the seventeenth century, but the language to articulate it was. The idea that humanity was on a forward trajectory, in which the conditions of a society gradually evolved, was an idea developed during the Enlightenment. The stages of this evolution, according to the *Ancient History Encyclopaedia*, were 'savagery, barbarism and, finally, civilization'. That European society was evidently on the last step of this advancement, and other societies based on nomadic hunter-gatherer structures were not, meant that European societies were culturally superior.

Anthropologists traditionally used the terms 'civilisation' and 'civilised society' to distinguish (often their own) 'culturally superior' societies from the 'primitive' societies that they observed. When we think of civilisation, we tend to think of current or past societies that have built or left behind architectural marvels – the Great Wall, or the Colosseum, or the Pyramids of Giza, or Angkor Wat, which is not in and of itself problematic (civilisation does mean 'a society made up of cities', after all). It becomes tricky, though, when we impose this meaning on the idea of *being* 'civilised', inferring that nomadic societies today or ancient cultures that did not leave behind concrete structures are, by definition, inferior or less 'complex'.

The idea that European society has advanced at a faster rate than others seems like a fairly modern invention, but it's not. It's not even unique to Europe. The idea of civilising other cultures is one that has always been a component of empire. We even see threads of this notion in *The Odyssey*. During the time of the epic, Greece had developed colonies in Libya, southern Italy and Sicily, southern France and along the coast of the Black Sea. *The Odyssey's* translator, Emily Wilson, writes in her introduction that Odysseus reveals the coloniser's frame of mind in his travels, particularly when surveying an uninhabited island adjacent to the island of the Cyclops (thought to represent Sicily). He points out the natural resources of the island, which the natives (presumably Sicilians) have failed to exploit, along with their lack of military defence:

Cyclopic people have no red-cheeked ships
and no shipwright among them who could build
boats, to enable them to row across

to other cities, as most other people do,
crossing the sea to visit one another.
With boats they could have turned this island into
a fertile colony, with proper harvests.
By the grey shore there lie well-watered meadows,
where vines would never fail. There is flat land
for ploughing, and abundant crops would grow
in the autumn; there is richness underground.

This – the idea that the natives are not advanced or civilised
enough to have the technology to build ships and cultivate the
fertile land within their dominion – is presented as a justification
for the Greeks to colonise them. It's a familiar argument.

We don't know much about how the Greeks asserted control
in their colonies, but they left proof of their existence strewn all
over and around Sicily, through the introduction of olives for oil
production and grape vines for wine. To this day, one can tour
the remnants of the temples they left behind.

Odysseus's maiming and robbing of Polyphemus the Cyclops
is again justified using all-too-familiar reasoning. Once docked
on the island, Odysseus commands his crew to discover whether
the inhabitants of the island are civilised people, who 'welcome
strangers' and worship the same gods that the Greeks do, or
whether they are 'wild, lawless aggressors'. (Of course, the idea
that the mark of a civilised people is that they welcome strangers
is convenient, because it also means that they leave themselves
open to being colonised.) What follows is an episode in which
Odysseus and his men are trapped in Polyphemus's cave while
attempting to rob him of his lambs. Odysseus tricks the cyclops,
blinding him by driving a spear into his eye, stealing his flock,
and taunting him while sailing away.

Afterwards, Odysseus is proud of himself. Polyphemus follows
a different religion, after all, and he lives by herding his beloved
animals rather than taming the land by planting crops, which
makes him lazy. He is suspicious of Odysseus and his men. He
eats a few. He also looks different to the Greeks, which makes

him ugly. These characteristics give Odysseus the right to abuse Polyphemus.

Again, we've heard these arguments before. The uncivilised don't plant crops, they don't know how to build things. They're not developed enough as a society to have their own governments or laws or proper customs. They can't defend themselves. They follow primitive faiths and they are violent. They eat things they shouldn't – humans, or cats and dogs, or bugs. They don't even know what is good for them – otherwise they would welcome us when we landed upon their shores.

This idea, that other societies were further behind than European societies, conveniently fits into the construct of colonisation as a civilising mission. The *mission civilisatrice* was a mantra of French colonial expansion. The American historian Harry Liebersohn writes that the notion of the civilising mission involved the stuffing of diverse groups and cultures into the categories of 'barbaric' and 'savage' – an action which understandably inspired revolt in the societies that it targeted. The civilising mission – which placed the colonising power as culturally and morally superior to those it proposed to colonise – positioned colonisation as a way to deliver the freedom, education, opportunity, hygiene practices and infrastructure that the backward society so desperately needed. In practice, what being civilised meant was: dressing in European clothing; speaking the tongue of the coloniser; ceasing one's (often nomadic) way of life, traditional livelihood, culture and language; undertaking whatever work served the imperial government (such as manual labour and servile positions); accepting that one was and would always be inferior to the colonisers; and paying taxes to the imperial state. For most of the world, 'becoming civilised' essentially translated into mimicking the habits of whoever was ruling, and morphing into whatever was most useful to them.

Becoming civilised has the tendency to dilute or wipe out the colonised country's native culture. This idea of civilising the unwashed masses is one that countries have turned on themselves, mostly during dictatorships. One only has to look at how language has been used by dictators and emperors: under Napoleon's empire, for example, being a French citizen held the condition of speaking French. In his book *Nations and Nationalism since 1780*, the historian Eric Hobsbawm writes that in 1789, only around 12 per cent of France's population spoke French correctly, and 50 per cent didn't speak French at all. Any languages besides French were banned from being spoken in public life, including schools, with severe punishments for infringements. The majority of the country at the time spoke the patois unique to their regions, which have now been deliberately eradicated for the most part.

Mussolini, too, outlawed the use of dialect in schools, and in all public offices. Under Fascism, surnames and place names were Italianised. Just as in Homer's Greece, in which non-Greek speakers were considered barbarians, so language becomes a way to decide who is civilised, educated or worthy of being a full citizen, and who is not.

In any case, the colonising governments in question didn't actually believe in civilising – it was a response to the progressive evolution of thinking among the people. The historian Kenneth Pomeranz writes that around the year 1800, Europeans and Americans began to believe 'the idea that civilised peoples should rule themselves' (something that never worried the ancient empires). This was because liberal governments had begun acknowledging the idea of universal human rights. Anyone to whom these rights were denied, or any society to which self-government was denied, must therefore be 'not fully human' or societally uncivilised (both of which amount to the same thing).

Governments now had to justify or mask their colonial ambitions as practically humanitarian missions. This resulted in the westward expansion of the United States into Mexico, termed 'an empire of liberty', and Napoleon's French expansion, described as delivering 'freedom'. It wasn't just limited to colonial expansion. The idea was so in vogue by the nineteenth century that even the unification of Italy brought with it the idea of civilising the 'primitive' South.

However questionable the idea of civilising was, it was always a mask for a state's imperial ambitions of power, and/or their desire for another country's resources. A big part of the Italian colonial propaganda campaign was the idea of bringing civilisation to the 'primitive' and 'backward' tribes of North Africa. The magazine *L'Italia Coloniale* published regular updates on the developments in the colonies. It reported on economic activities, tourism and development of infrastructure. There were articles and photographs of the newly built Italian–Arab female school of Benghazi, pictures of Italian schools around the world, Fascist and diplomatic representatives, sporting events. Others featured members of the Italian colonial elite participating in charitable activities and patriotic ceremonies. These images and articles delivered the impression that colonial society was organised and compassionate. They were meant to stoke the feeling among the bourgeoisie back home that Italy was a legitimate European nation, dedicated to the mission of civilising the world.

'Piccole italiane'

Salvatore, Annalisa, colleague, Benghazi, 1939

This photo shows my grandmother at about age eight between two men. At the left is her father, in a military Fascist uniform, on the right is another unknown man, wearing a simple grey suit with a white shirt and tie. Annalisa wears the Fascist uniform for *piccole italiane* or 'little Italian girls' in the colonies.

My grandmother had told me that every Saturday all the Italian children and adults in the colonies were required to congregate in the public forum for weekly exercise and Empire-worship. They sang songs and squatted with medicine balls. The uniform for girls consisted of hair in braids, a white beret, a white T-shirt with dark ribbing around the neck and arms, and a symbol on the white shirt that was tucked into a coloured skirt, which ended just above the knees.

In the photo, Annalisa has her arms crossed over her stomach. Her smile is embarrassed. On her right is the man who seems to be her father's friend; he holds one hand on his hip and gestures as if in mid-speech, or perhaps preparing to pose. He may be holding a cigarette.

There are hardly any photos in either the albums or the boxes of photos of Benghazi's city or streetscape. Most of the photographs taken after my grandmother was born depict domestic interiors or garden backgrounds. The rise of Fascism, however, can be tracked in the photographs. Children in uniforms, or official processions, or schools with portraits of *il Duce* in the background begin popping up.

These photographs don't tell me what my grandparents thought of the new regime, or how it was experienced by Libyans or working-class Italians. They don't allow me to hear the chatter of the Benghazi streets, or smell the specific scent of a coastal city. I can only imagine the combination of salt air and motor fumes and spices.

In his book, *Understanding a Photograph*, John Berger writes that 'a photograph, while recording what has been seen, always and by its nature refers to what is not seen. It isolates, preserves and presents a moment taken from a continuum'. A photograph is about moments, about time, about mortality – both that of the thing photographed and ourselves. A photograph refers to the moment captured and the moments surrounding its capture. Photographs may help to furnish our mental topography of a place or a time, but they are not enough to attain a true picture.

In Spina's Benghazi, men wear the red fezzes, baggy white pants and embroidered waistcoats of their traditional dress, while the women wear colourful tunics and gold jewellery or else wrap themselves in scratchy woollen robes that cover even their faces and heads, leaving a barely discernible opening to see out of. They stroll through the streets of the medina, which are lined with palm trees and whitewashed houses, and are canopied by a vast, cloudless sky. In the souks, vendors peddle intricate jewellery, precious stones, and vials of perfume. At the cafés, couscous is eaten and muddy Turkish coffee is drunk. It is a different Libya from the one depicted in the writings of Italian travellers before the invasion, who made it seem like the country was a vacant territory, void of the intricacies of modern culture.

Months before the initial 1911 invasion, the Italian playwright Domenico Tumiati was bound back to Italy from Ottoman Libya on a steamer, and he envisioned an Italian colony that would make use of the 'African riches', constructing railways and mines and plantations and 'Italian villas . . . surrounded by palms and our lovely women danc[ing] away the summer nights amidst a cloud of jasmine near the resurgent remains of Leptis'. Tumiati was one of the principal travellers in Cyrenaica and Tripolitania who pushed the idea of Libya as a *terra promessa*. He was actually one of the first to do so, having travelled there seven years before the initial invasion of 1911. In his travel diaries, *Nell'Africa Romana: Tripolitania*, published in 1911, he swore that olive groves, pastures and vineyards would grow wild in the desert.

In Milan, Spina visited the opera often with his mother, and this love of theatre influenced his writing. Throughout his work, Spina makes both stylistic and textual references to theatre, to show the superficiality of propaganda and civilisation. His novels and stories include scenes which are almost only dialogue. Some chapters in his novels are formatted like theatre scripts, and include stage setting and directions.

The dialogue and the narration make it hard to miss Spina's point. In long monologues, Spina's characters critique colonialism, civilisation, history, the notion of an ancestral legacy, and the nature of power. In his novel, *The Marriage of Omar*, the Countess Rosina informs her husband that his belief in the great project of civilisation is naïve. Civilisation is not the inevitable culmination of human evolution. It is simply the wielding of temporarily seized power by one group over another. Their civilisation will end much in the same way as everyone else's, as 'the rubble on which others will build another edifice once they've reconquered their freedom'.

This was the opposite of what Italian propagandists peddled. In his diaries, Tumiati describes the Roman ruins that scatter the landscape. There are wells, cisterns, tombs carved into rocks, towers and bridges, abandoned ancient amphitheatres in the middle of the desert, the remnants of seaports. There is an entire Roman city (Leptis Magna, the birthplace of the Roman Emperor Septimius Severus) half-buried in the sand. Built by 'our fathers', these ruins are proof that Rome is eternal, and Italy's right to Rome's former Mediterranean colonies is divine.

It's not only that Italians have a right to Libya, it's also that they have a duty to their heritage. Tumiati claims that the backwardness of the Romans' 'Arab successors', who live a 'wandering existence', is squandering all that the ancient Roman empire left behind. According to Tumiati, the Libyan people are primitive because they don't build structures that are made to last, and only produce what they need. They haven't built their own wells – they use those that were left behind by the Romans. He goes so far as to accuse the Libyans of taking columns and stones from Roman ruins to build mosques (never mind that it was the French who ransacked Leptis Magna for Versailles).

Spina's novel, *The Young Maronite*, reveals clues as to how exactly the Italians treated these same ruins that Tumiati so yearned for. The narrative follows an Italian captain and a *zaptié* (a Libyan officer in the Italian military), named Fathi, on an expedition through Cyrenaica. On their journey, they find the tips of statues emerging from the sand like icebergs – perhaps a stone fist or scalp. They find tombs and mosaics, evidence of empires long gone. In each tomb, a round hole is bored into its depths, large enough for the hand of a looter to slither in. When they arrive at Cyrene, an ancient Greek city, they find that it, too, has been raided, this time by corsair archaeologists, who lopped off the statues that once emerged from the ancient city and sold them off to European museums. When Fathi and Martello subsequently vanish, the Italian troops stationed at Cyrene use their disappearance as an excuse to raid the tombs further.

Libera

Annalisa and Libera, the family's housekeeper, Benghazi, 1932

Annalisa is a year old in this photo, taken in February 1932, and she's scowling at what would have been my great-grandfather's

Agfa folding camera. I wonder who took it, Rita or Salvatore or some other unknown figure. She is pointing at the camera, her arm reaching out. I don't know what she is trying to say – who the gesture is for, whether she is notifying the photographer of Libera's presence. Already at this young age, she seems to know that cameras are to be looked at, gazed into. That they are there to capture.

In the photo, Libera smiles at the camera, and though the smile is unpractised, she looks more surprised to be the subject of a photo than her charge Annalisa. Knowing how her life ended, I wonder at the private turmoil behind the smile.

My grandmother told me that Libera worked for Rita's family in Turin and was sent out to Rita once she married. Rita would often have a girl or woman in charge of housekeeping. She would send for them from Italy, and their duties were to care for Annalisa and the home, and prepare meals. Every day Salvatore would send word to Rita notifying her of how many government officials he would be taking home for lunch, and Rita would prepare a menu and give this to the housekeeper. She would instruct all her housekeepers as to how to prepare certain dishes to her liking. She had rules for the women. The prerequisites were: to be able to read and speak Italian well, to have finished *la terza media*, the equivalent to Year 8 in Australia and the UK. My mother says that this was fairly uncommon – at this point schooling for boys and girls hadn't been compulsory for very long. A great number of villagers were illiterate and spoke their regional dialect rather than Italian.

Annalisa and Libera stand on a wide dirt road, behind them is a field of green, then what seems to be a fence on Libera's left perhaps protecting a vegetable garden, then hills in the background. My grandmother isn't what draws me to this photo. What draws me is Libera, as I am drawn to all photos of her. The more context we have for a photo, the more potential for meaning it gains.

I didn't know Libera, but I know her story. My grandmother told me that once everyone had returned to Italy after the war had ended, her family received news that Libera had switched on the gas in her oven in her apartment in Turin and immersed her head in it. Whenever Libera came up in a photo or conversation, my grandmother would always do the same thing. My mother would follow suit. They'd shake their heads, look at the ground, say *poverina. Poor thing.*

When I first found out about Libera, I pressed my grandmother for more information surrounding her suicide – *was she depressed? Did she have any family? But why do you think she did it? Were there signs?* She acted as though it was an isolated, unexplainable incident, implying that Libera was a happy person when she knew her, or happy enough, or perhaps it was that happiness was beside the point. She said, 'How should I know?' and I wonder whether she thought about it after she heard. I always stop at this photo whenever I flip through the photo album, trying to discern some clue or hint of an internal struggle, an innate sadness in Libera.

In *Camera Lucida*, shortly after her death, Roland Barthes is looking at old photos of his mother. He is lamenting the fact that he cannot conjure up a total image of her, and none of her old photos 'speak' to him. The photos of his mother refer to her, but they don't embody her, although some bring back memories of sensation, like a photo of his mother hugging him when he was a child recalls the fabric of her dress and the scent of her perfume.

Then he finds it: the photo that brings her back. It's of his mother and her brother as children. Part of the reason that this photograph of his mother as a child evokes her essence may be because at the end of her life, Barthes cared for her in her illness, reversing the mother–child roles of their relationship.

A little later in the book, Barthes is looking at an 1865 photograph by Alexander Gardner of Lewis Payne in his prison cell. Payne had attempted an assassination on the US Secretary of State W.H. Howard, and was waiting to be hanged. What 'pricks' him about the photo is that he knows what will happen to Payne after the photo is taken. Considering the photograph of his mother, which he dubs the 'Winter Garden Photograph', he applies this same knowledge to her. It's like a rupture in time – the events following the photo both have happened and will happen: 'In front of the photograph of my mother as a child, I tell myself: she is going to die.'

Often the backgrounds of photographs reveal more than their foregrounds, and through the photographer's focus we can see what they are attempting to highlight and conceal. In Spina's *The Marriage of Omar*, the Countess's nephew, Lieutenant Antonino, recalls looking at a book of photographs of the 1911 war before departing Italy for Libya, the oval portraits of fallen soldiers arrayed across its pages like ornaments. A closer look at those photographs revealed piles of murdered rebels lying on the floor, their clothes like rags hanging from their stick-like limbs, as though they were nothing but hunting trophies. Spina is most likely taking liberties here, but the point remains that often photographs have dual messages – that which the photographer intends our eye to catch, and that which is in the background, only discernible if we have context.

Looking at these photos, it becomes clearer that the albums don't provide a whole portrait of their lives, or a complete representation of the places in which they lived. Public and work life receives limited space, is often relegated to the background. There are clues, such as the Fascist flags flapping in the distance, or my grandmother's *piccole italiane* uniform. But in family photographs, public and political life is tangential. The story that an album tells is normally controlled by one member of our family. Just like all stories, it is a construction, excluding some unsavoury moments and family members in favour of others. The stories of our lives, idealised. Tellingly, Salvatore's photos – the one of the hanging, or the rocky grave in the desert – did not make it into the official family albums. These photographs were relegated to his bachelorhood scrapbook or the boxes. They are dateless, placeless, nameless.

Another shadow world, in the sense that it follows us everywhere, our family history. Family histories are inherited legacies that bequeath immortality, belonging and identity. The events of these histories are turned into narratives with climactic points such as migrations, transformations, and struggles overcome. Older generations pass them down to younger generations who store them away. Photo albums don't just furnish these stories, but they survive as their text – my grandmother would turn a page, gaze at a photo, and tell me the story whose recollection the photo had sparked. We ourselves also edit these stories, so that the more unpleasant components of our history are erased and therefore are lost to time.

It is understandable, to want to edit our histories or those of our families because an event produces a feeling of grief or shame. In his 2013 article 'The Memory of Fascism and of the Anti-Fascist Resistance among Italian Youth', the Italian sociologist Alessandro Cavalli writes about the degree of knowledge – or lack of knowledge – that more recent Italian generations have regarding fascism. In order to associate public history with private family memory, we need to have a personal connection to the events of the past, most often passed down by our grandparents, who are the last generation to have experienced fascism. We don't know much about what or how often or how much the older Italian generation says to their grandchildren about fascism, but Cavalli reasons that in general, such discussions have been scant. The kind of experience our grandparents had under fascism is also a major factor. According to Cavalli, the 'silent majority' of the Italian population who were not ardent fascists, but nevertheless accepted the dictatorship quietly, likely have continued to keep quiet. The 'active minority' of ardent fascists, too, have likely kept silent, considering that history rendered them the losers. Those that probably passed down the most memories are those who have something to be proud of – the *partigiani*, anti-fascists who actively fought against the regime. This group too, however, may not have all passed down memories, particularly those that were traumatic. (Of course, there are ardent fascists within the 'active minority' that have passed down their memories and values. The Italian politician Alessandra Mussolini, for example, echoed her grandfather when, referring to North African colonialism, she pronounced in 2006: 'If it hadn't been for my grandfather, they would still be riding camels with turbans on their heads.')

While an individual photograph provides a glimpse into a shadow world, a photo album creates a whole world ancillary to ours. There, on the shelf in my mother's home, is my childhood bound in two thick volumes. There is my brother's, bound in his. There is my mother's childhood in Palermo, my grandmother's in Libya. My father, who only has one photo from his childhood in rural Sicily, a class picture taken in his first year of school, is the only one who does not have an album dedicated to his youth. Perhaps this is why his past has always seemed like a mystery to me, and why my brother and I cling to the few objects he brought over to Australia on the ship when he was eighteen: an aluminium Bialetti Moka pot with which I prepare coffee each morning, a thin gold chain that my brother now wears, that class picture.

Through arranging the photographs that her parents took in Libya, my grandmother attempted to narrate the story of her life. They began with photos of her as a baby – her mother and father posed with her in front of the house, and they followed the course of her life in Libya. With each turn of the page, she grew. I imagine her now, after her parents had both died, inheriting these photographs of her family and reshuffling them into her own albums. With these albums, she was safeguarding her own childhood.

Among her things, we had found a porcelain baby doll with worn cheeks. Her long-lashed glass eyes closed when you laid her down. My grandmother was an only child, and after her parents died there was no one else to remember what she was like as a little girl or baby. The world in which she grew up also no longer existed, and so all that was left of her youth was her own memory and these albums. Perhaps that was why she loved to recount stories from it – so that she could implant those memories into her grandchildren.

We take and keep photos for the same reason that some people keep diaries or memoirists write memoirs: because once we die, or are no longer able to remember, our memories will slip into the ether. Is there any way to hang onto moments though? And what does it matter, if we aren't around anymore? Journaling, personal archiving, and creating art are all, on some level, ways of attempting to cheat death by reaching for immortality – just as littering social media with youthful selfies seems like a way of immortalising our twenty-something bodies.

I'm not sure if Fox Talbot, or any other developer of photographic innovation after him, was truly successful in his original impulse or goal. Photographs may be, in and of themselves, beautiful, but the beauty they hold is not necessarily derived from the subject captured, it is created by the photograph itself. I still don't think that initial beauty, or more accurately, essence, is really subsumed or embodied by the photograph. I am still more unsure of what it is exactly that photographs communicate. How much do they really preserve or tell us?

Flipping through the albums, my gaze bores through the faces in the photos. I look for missing details in the backgrounds. I have looked at these photos countless times, poring over every millimetre, always hoping to find something new – a clue, or a fissure, a tear in the matte surface. I want the people in the photographs to open their mouths and speak to me, I want a gap to open up that I can slip into, to be allowed into the world of the photo. But the inanimate figures just stare back at me, smiling, unseeing. The people are gone. I can't help but think that the photos provide a flimsy, half-rate kind of knowledge, as Sontag would say, 'a knowledge at bargain prices'.

The way I visually furnished the stories of her childhood then is like so: European colonial villas plonked incongruously in a sparse desert setting, the interiors of her and her family's friends' homes at total odds with the world and culture outside. I imagined her home filled with the same Louis XVI furniture that she kept, so at odds with street scenes of buzzing souks. She never spoke about Libyan people, other than as extras in the cast of the cityscape. I am reminded of her descriptions of men sitting cross-legged at their stalls in souks, or smoking hookah in the cafésof the Benghazi's medina, or elegantly eating couscous while seated on jewel-toned cushions, the hush that befell the city during Ramadan. If anything, the more I read about Benghazi, the more the city of my mind is illuminated: beyond the Italian villas in the European quarter is the medina, and then the *mellah*, the Jewish quarter. I can see the glossy green leaves of parasol-shaped acacia trees, feel the arid soil crumbling between my fingers. I can feel the soft, silent breeze of the sea against my cheeks, and smell the honeyed scent of orange blossoms.

Spina's Benghazi is swamp-like and the tempests that occasionally break the clear skies are dramatic and violent, as though Zeus has returned from antiquity to bring wrath upon a world that has forgotten to worship him. The white muslin curtains of the sandcastle-like villas flap in the whistling breeze. Guards keep watch at the gate of the city. From the hills behind Benghazi, the coastal ruins of ancient Roman forts are visible, among which a lone marabout might be taking a nap in the afternoon heat. Outside the city, children find rusted coins from any number of long-gone civilisations.

Tribe and herd

Human figures - a few adults and children judging by the height - and a herd of cattle among palms, Libya, year unknown

The image of Libya as a fertile land of promise for Italian farmers was a cornerstone of colonial propaganda. In a letter home, an

Italian soldier describes the eighteen months he has spent living in the desert in tents, battling eternal thirst and the fifty-degree heat from the ghibli, which blows sand into every crevice. His experience has led him to question the death being caused by the invasion, all for 'some sand, four palms and a few lemons?'

According to a Library of Congress report from 2005, a little over one per cent of Libya's territory is considered arable, 4 per cent is fit for grazing livestock, and the rest is barren desert. Agricultural projects by Italian farmers in Libya not surprisingly bore little fruit. Spadaro writes that this continual lie – which was spread throughout Italy's thirty years of Libyan occupation – was brought up in 1911 in the Italian parliament as being irresponsible. This concern was swiftly rejected. The idea of a nation made up of Italian settlers tending to the land was too enticing.

Such myths of a North African coast rich with a fertile abundance of crops and soil came from Latin and Greek classics, in which Libya was the site of such fantastical places as the Garden of the Hesperides and the River Lethe. This idea persisted, despite the massive costs of all agricultural undertakings in Libya, because it was so useful in promoting imperialism and the formation of a national Italian identity. And in fact, it was successful: there is still a widespread idea in Italy today that Italian colonisation was different from other countries, founded not on violence and oppression, but on the backs of hopeful Italian peasant farmers.

In Spina's works, the Italian characters are seduced by this false image of Libya, and of the patriotic glory of the motherland – even though they actually live there and can see that myth and reality do not match up. In *The Marriage of Omar*, Count Alonzo continues reading Italian travellers' books because they soothe him. He is comforted by the fact that the Libyans in these books are 'savages', noble and peaceful, and they bear no influence on the travellers, nor any agency – they are merely part of the exotic setting.

In an antiquarian bookstore in Trieste, I happened upon a couple of such books. The first was a large green leather-bound tome, on the Italian colonies and Rhodes. The book, published in 1928, was part of a geographical series on the Italian *patria*, or fatherland. Photographs feature desert steppes and sand dunes, a flooded Benghazi street, Berbers sitting among the palm trees of an oasis, the rubble of sandstones, rocky erosions, caravans of cars careening through the desert, desert rock formations eroded by the wind, robed men leading their camels through sandy plains, *wadis* after the rains have rendered them flush with water, banks rimmed with encrusted salt that looks like coral, wellsprings around which oasis towns have been built, roman cisterns, olive tree clusters, lush vegetation.

It not only seems like an educational text for Italians unfamiliar with the nation's new acquisitions, but it also reads like a preparatory guide for those considering a move there. After a survey of the animal life, the text moves on to the 'hygiene conditions'. This section seems to exist for the sole purpose of reassuring frightened and germophobic Italians that Libya is a safe place to settle. The animals of Libya, the text reassures, do not constitute any serious danger. There are no elephants, and very few insects, although there is a possibility of malaria from the mosquitoes, which are the same as those in Sardinia. It warns that flies can carry jungle rot and trachoma, two contagious illnesses which afflict the indigenous population. Outbreaks of the plague, smallpox and cholera make appearances from time to time, but Italians don't need to worry – the hygienic habits of civilised people are enough to avoid such diseases. What *does* seem to be circulating around the cities in particular are tuberculosis, venereal disease, and Maltese fever.

What is most interesting is the last paragraph, in which the scientific tone of the preceding paragraphs is abandoned. While Libya has a hot climate, which brings with it certain diseases that require necessary hygienic precautions, this will impede neither the quality of life for settlers, nor the economic flourishing of the colonies. The British in Egypt and the French in Tunisia are doing great, after all, just as the Ancient Greeks in Cyrene did, and just like the 'flourishing Roman colonies in Tripolitania in a remote but unforgettable and glorious past'.

A history of Libya is included, from ancient to recent times. The pages are populated with images of mostly Roman ruins of temples, farmsteads, arches, cities like Leptis Magna, coins and statues. The text is careful to note that during the period of Magna Graecia, the indigenous populations were separate from the Greek cities, residing in the countryside or in encampments that ringed the Greek cities, much like during the Italian colonisation. There was no racial mixing, the text is not so subtly saying. The glorious past does not belong to the indigenous populations.

According to this book, the times in which the territories of Libya truly flourished – with advances in economy, art and science – were when it was under foreign domination. Cyrenaica was bequeathed to Rome by the last Greek ruler, which left it independent for twenty unhappy years of unrest and anarchy. Rome, so the book is implying, had to sweep in and colonise the country to save it from itself. What followed was a Golden Age in which Libya enjoyed its period of utmost prosperity under a Roman rule that was 'just and peaceful and strong'. Again, the text is careful to note, like the Greeks, the Romans did not mix with the Libyans. The Romans were eventually driven out. The Arabs came and converted the population to Islam, then the country became swarmed with pirates, and finally the Turks began their apparently fruitless rule.

There are photos of freshly sown fields, of the serpentine beginnings of roads. The text lists the various natural resources: while no natural mineral deposits have yet been found, the authors urge readers to be hopeful – they eventually will be. The government is in the process, the book says, of figuring out how to best harvest and use the vast salt lakes. The fishing industry is also in the process of being developed. Forestry in Cyrenaica has been subject to 'reckless destruction' and 'irregular pastures' by the 'barbarians'. The port being constructed in Benghazi will surely bring in trade economy. The reader is assured that a radiotelegraph service keeps Benghazi in communication with Italy, and that there are six wire telegraph offices, twelve telephone offices and ten post offices. In Benghazi, there are numerous schools, European hospitals, banks and a museum. If development has somewhat slowed down, the authors point out that this is due to what they call 'the work of civilisation', a veiled reference, perhaps, to the war with the Sanusi specifically, or, more broadly, the general atrocities being committed by the Italian military.

Unknown man

Man, Libya, year unknown

In another photograph from the boxes, a Libyan man is sitting cross-legged in a rocky valley. He scans the distance away from the camera. Behind him a white stone bridge and wall that corrals a villa. A faint sketch of power lines run over the bridge.

The photograph looks candid, like the man is having a quiet moment of reflection.

I note the man's silence, how Salvatore held the camera, controlled the image. Like all subjects of cameras and colonies, the man in the photograph is rendered mute. There is no name for him scrawled across the back of the photograph, no year dating the photo.

I used to think that photos were a portal to my family's past. I'd look at the albums like they were pieces of a puzzle that I just had to fit together. Now I know that the photos in my family's albums only pose more questions than they do answers. What I realise that I really want from these photos is what I want from my daily life: to know what is happening beyond the frame.

In *Understanding a Photograph*, John Berger writes that photographs need context to tell a story. They need a narrator, someone who can tell us who people are, what was going on, when it happened, why. Photographs by themselves hold no inherent meaning – the meaning is something that we attribute. The dangerous allure of photographs is that they give us a sense of some kind of real, of unmediated proof – but in fact by themselves they offer no explanation, no context, no sense of what is posed or constructed. The human figures trapped in photographs cannot communicate. Now the man in the photograph is a silent figure in a box of photos in a cupboard in Australia. His captured image belonging to a stranger: war haul.

After Mussolini took power in 1922, and swiftly rejected the previous government's policy of working with (or at least, going through the motions of working with) local leaders, the *riconquista* began. By 1928, he had succeeded in northern Fezzan, and in January 1929, Cyrenaica and Tripolitania were joined under a single governor. The new state was christened Libya, with Tripoli as its capital. In the summer of 1929, however, Sanusi resistance erupted in Cyrenaica again, under the leadership of Sidi Umar al-Mukhtar, who would come to be known as the 'Lion of the Desert'.

The Sanusi tribesmen began guerrilla warfare of raids, ambushes and sabotage. In Cyrenaica, Italian colonists were confined to the walled cities and towns, as leaving meant being ambushed. In response, the Italian authorities commenced a genocide. Known rebels were isolated, their family members hanged if found fraternising with them. They sacked the holy oasis of al-Kufrah. In Muhammad Asad's *The Road to Mecca*, a survivor recounts the attack: the Italians encroached on the city with armoured cars, cannons, and aeroplanes that bombed homes, mosques and palm groves. The residents, consisting of a few hundred armed men, women, children and elderly men attempted to defend their homes. The survivor tells Asad that he managed to escape and conceal himself among some palm orchards. He remained there for the entire night, throughout which he 'could hear the screams of women being raped by Italian soldiers and Eritrean *askaris*'. In the morning, Asad encounters an old woman, who tells him that the remaining survivors have been gathered to watch as a copy of the Koran is torn up, before the palm groves of the oasis are lopped and the wells blocked.

In the oasis of Taizerbo, poison gas was inflicted on the peasants and shepherds who lived there. The very means to live were denied to the nomadic tribes: their wells, which were the main source of drinking water in the desert, were blocked with concrete or sand, and countless communities, including women and children, were forced to march to their new residences in concentration camps. St John writes that, as of 2017, Italian colonial archives were still restricted, and so the exact figures of how many people were detained is unavailable. Most estimates put the number at around 110,000, two thirds of Libya's eastern population. Of these, he writes that the number of those that died of from illness, starvation, or maltreatment is thought to be around seventy thousand.

A tall, four-metre-thick barbed wire fence was built along the Egyptian border, running from the port of Bardia to the oasis of Jarabub. The fence was erected to stop the supply of arms being smuggled from Egypt to the Cyrenaican guerrillas. It was in 1930, in the middle of it all, that Knud Holmboe travelled through the desert by car, from Tripoli to Benghazi.

Knud Holmboe was born in Denmark in 1902, the son of a businessman. A career in journalism was his way out of the bourgeois world in which he had grown up, and he published his first article, about reindeer-herders in Lappland, in the Copenhagen newspaper *Dagens Nyheder*, at the age of eighteen. At twenty-two, he first set foot in Africa, to report on the French colonial war against Riff mountaineers in Morocco. This was his first encounter with the actions of Europeans in their far-seeming colonies. An inner crisis followed, leading to a year spent in a French monastery. He emerged with the desire to learn about Islam, making pilgrimages to Turkey, Iraq, and Persia. He then retraced his steps back west, spending time in the Balkans, the Muslim footholds of Europe. Somewhere along the way, he converted to Islam and learned to speak Arabic. He travelled by ship to North Africa, which is where *Desert Encounter* (*Ørkenen Brænder*) finds him, in the lobby of a colonial hotel in Ceuta, Morocco.

The book opens with Holmboe making conversation with an English journalist. Holmboe explains that he is waiting on permission to drive from Ceuta through Spain to Barcelona. From there, he plans on boarding a ship to Egypt or Syria, and then taking a car through to Mecca. The Englishman questions why, considering Holmboe speaks Arabic, he doesn't travel through the Libyan desert on to Egypt. Each of their experiences in Morocco have been guided by the French colonial government, eager to show the fruits of civilisation: chemical works, government buildings, ports and new industry. Going through Libya might give Holmboe the opportunity to observe North Africa and learn about the various cultures without the veil of European civilising propaganda. Thus begins Holmboe's drive across Libya, from Tripoli to Benghazi. At the time of writing (1930) there was no road between the two cities bookending the Sirte Gulf, and the war in Cyrenaica had been going on for almost eighteen years.

In 1930, after the fence had been built along the border between Libya and Egypt, whole tribes were made to march to concentration camps. According to official Italian census records, the population of Cyrenaica, in 1928, was 225,000. In 1932, four years later, it was 142,000. The resulting orphans were sent to Fascist re-education camps, and in 1937, they were shipped out as soldiers for the Fascist Italian campaign in Ethiopia. Human life was not the only target – to denude the tribal populations of their resources, Italian soldiers machine-gunned livestock from aeroplanes, so that, by the Vice-Governor's own estimation, the number of sheep and goats went from 227,000 in 1930 to 67,000 in 1931.

Holmboe's account of the events are not only known as the best record we have of the atrocities committed by the Italians, but they also act as a bridge between two worlds. Holmboe was not a Western explorer in the traditional sense. He was also a Muslim who spoke Arabic, an outsider in his homeland of Denmark where, as he continuously explains to Muslim Libyans, he was the lone follower of his religion. These two characteristics, coupled with his inability to speak Italian, also made him an outsider among the colonising Italians.

Desert Encounter follows Holmboe as he travels the length of Libya with his two travel companions, an American named Tarbox and a Libyan boy named Mohammed. Along the way, their car breaks down numerous times, they go ten days without eating, their beards grow long and their burnouses become ragged, their skin hardens and burns in the sun, they walk kilometres barefoot because their leather shoes disintegrate from wear. Their trip is punctuated by regular crossings with Italian forts and Berber camps.

In the camps of tribes that have surrendered to the Italians, the people are emaciated from starvation, the women wear torn rags as clothes, and the children's stomachs are distended under the pronounced dunes of their ribcages. Holmboe is told by the inhabitants that they are forced to remain in the same place for months by the Italians, long past the time when their sheep have eaten all the grass. Those tribes who have surrendered are not allowed to carry arms or to decide where they may camp. They are not allowed to fraternise with free Berbers and they must pay taxes to the Italian government. The punishments for these infringements are always execution. Along the journey to Benghazi, different Libyan men confide in Holmboe that they believe the Italians have the intention of slowly eradicating them all.

On the borders of Cyrenaican towns, Holmboe visits concentration camps. In one, he estimates there to be fifteen thousand people, who are imprisoned by a barbed-wire fence and guarded by soldiers armed with machine guns. The children show signs of starvation, and are dressed in rags. Burnouses are stitched together from scraps of fabric, and instead of shoes, hides are tied with string. Many of the people seem sick and many have deformed limbs.

Holmboe and his travel companions come across ghost towns, villages whose inhabitants have surrendered or fled. In these villages, the wells have all been filled with sand or concrete. They walk into empty homes caked in dust and thick with the stench of corpses. Graveyards are filled with hastily made graves.

In silent horror, Holmboe witnesses executions in military forts and along roadsides and in the squares of towns. Men are shot or hung one after the other, their bodies piled into the backs of trucks. In the towns and cities, proclamations are pasted on walls announcing death sentences.

A summary of the book reads like a list of atrocities: a man's daughter is abducted and placed in a brothel, a boy's father is executed by shooting, another man's brother is hanged, another's ancestral property is stripped from him because he lacks 'papers'. Another is sentenced to twenty-five years of hard labour in the salt mines (it seems the government came up with a solution as to how to harvest the salt). Entire villages are slaughtered with poison gas which, though it had been used as a weapon for thousands of years, was first used on a mass scale during the First

World War. It was subsequently banned by the Geneva Protocol in 1925.

Another man confides to Holmboe, 'I suppose they intend to exterminate us all.'

'Balilla'

Boys undertaking military training on Fascist Saturday, girl observing
(Annalisa?), year unknown

Another photo of children, this time a group of boys in
formation behind another boy wielding a flag. They are in a
walled courtyard, wearing the Blackshirt children's uniforms of
the *Balilla*, the Fascist youth organisation that compelled boys
to take part in paramilitary training with the aim of moulding
them into the 'fascists of tomorrow'. It was mandatory for all
Italian children aged eight to thirteen to take part in Fascist
Saturdays, where boys (*Balilla*) and girls (*Piccole italiane*) were
required to exercise, be indoctrinated in the tenets of fascism,
and train for the army. Boys were armed with scaled-down
versions of army rifles called *moschetto Balilla*. The *Piccole italiane*
learned the virtues of nurturing the home and family. Boys were
trained to be faithful warriors of fascism. Girls were trained
to birth warriors. Between the ages of fourteen and eighteen,
boys moved on to the *Avanguardisti* and girls to *Giovane italiane*.
Later, a fifth organisation was added, for children even younger,
between the ages of six and eight. They were the *Figli della*

lupa, or 'Children of the She-Wolf'. My grandmother told me that often on Fascist Saturdays, Rita would make her pretend to be sick and leave her at home alone to play. This small rebellion – an apparent effort to shield her daughter from Fascist proselytizing – is the only clue I have to my great-grandmother's inner thoughts.In Benghazi, Holmboe watches a ceremony in which Fascist boys receive their rifles. It is a public celebration, and Italian and Eritrean troops parade through the city. All the boys and almost all the men wear black Fascist shirts. In the main piazza, a marching band plays as the boys with their rifles stand at attention awaiting the arrival of the Vice-Governor on his balcony. From it, he barks a reminder:

> Remember, in whatever you are doing, that you are Italians, Romans, and remember that your forebears were once in this country. You are Romans fighting against barbarians. Be kind to them, but remember that you are their superiors. Remember that you are Romans!

The rebellion in Cyrenaica continued until the capture of the Lion, al-Mukhtar. Twenty thousand Libyans were brought out of their imprisonment to watch as he was hanged in the Suluq POW camp. Shortly afterwards, in the new year of 1932, the governor declared the rebellion over, and the war that Italy had begun in 1911 was officially won. Towards the end of *Desert Encounter*, Holmboe is arrested under suspicion of being a spy. He is thrown into a mosquito-infested prison cell and then transferred to Benghazi, along with other political prisoners, mostly Sanusi rebels from the mountains. His fellow prisoners have been sentenced to either death or decades of hard labour in the desert salt lakes, for crimes such as being in restricted territory. The sentence entails lugging salt under the harsh desert sun, as the wind whips sand in one's crevices, and thirst swells the tongue and cracks the lips. The salt devours the flesh off thighs and calves. Eventually, the Italian authorities are convinced that Holmboe is not a spy, and he is released. He soon realises that the authorities never believed he was a spy – they wanted to keep him from travelling through a tract of warzone, from Derna to the Egyptian border. After a sojourn in Alexandria, Holmboe returned to Denmark, where he quickly wrote *Desert Encounter*. The book was published in 1931, and immediately banned in Italy. Holmboe was murdered near Aqaba, Jordan in October of the same year, still on his way to Mecca. In 2004, his book was translated into Italian for the first time.

In 1934, Italo Balbo became the governor of the single colony of Libya. He was an air marshal, a long-time fascist and an organiser of the March on Rome in 1922. He became governor at an auspicious time: the rebellion had finally been quelled in Libya, and the colony was at 'peace' for the first time in two decades. Now Italy could focus on economic development, infrastructure and tourism. As a bonus, unemployment levels were rising in Italy, due to the Great Depression, which boosted emigration to the colony. Balbo was also fortunate that, at this point in time, Mussolini was keen to throw money into the colonies. He wanted a strong, modernised Libya, which he thought would support his vision of building a Mediterranean empire. The land that had been dispossessed from the Libyan tribes could now be repurposed for Italian farmers, and new developments could provide work to unemployed Italian migrants. The dream was a Fascist 'fourth shore' filled with modern cities, towns, farmlands and vineyards, the Italian flag flapping from every edifice, proof that Mussolini had returned Italy to its former imperial glory.

In the 1930s, Tripolitania and Cyrenaica, together as Libya, were incorporated into metropolitan Italy. It rounded off the peninsula's Ionian, Tyrrhenian and Adriatic coasts, becoming known as the *quarta sponda* (fourth shore). It meant that the Mediterranean was now encircled by Italian territory, so that the sea became a real *mare nostrum*.

Mare nostrum too, was a notion tied to the Roman myth. The phrase is Latin, for 'our sea'. Originally it was used to refer to the Tyrrhenian Sea, after the Romans had colonised Sardinia, Sicily and Corsica. Once the Romans had extended their control to Egypt and the Iberian Peninsula, the entire Mediterranean became *mare nostrum*. Mussolini dreamed of a Mediterranean in which each shore was a part of Italian territory. It meant that the sea was now effectively bound, that a Sicilian looking across the sea could take comfort in the fact that, were they to cross it, they would still be home.

In 1937, Mussolini made his second tour of Libya, this time with the ostensible purpose of inaugurating the *strada littoranea*, the coastal highway running between the Tunisian and Egyptian borders. The building of the road was touted as a massive achievement of infrastructure that would encourage tourism, and a prime example of the deliverance of civilisation to a previously remote Turkish colony. What the Italian publicists promoting the event failed to mention was that it was built on the back of Libyan labour. During this visit, Mussolini received the 'Sword of Islam' in a lavish ceremony in which over two thousand Libyan horsemen were present. It was held on the outskirts of Tripoli, and bestowed to him by the Berber chief Yusef Kerbisc. Photos of the sword reveal it to be a gaudy construction, with a straight blade and friezes in sold gold, adorned with arabesques.

While it may have looked to the Italian public like a precious Islamic artefact, presented to Mussolini by some noble and ancient tribe, it was actually an Italian approximation of such, made to order by a Florentine artisan firm. An official photograph of the event was released, with Mussolini on horseback, wielding the sword high over his head and pointing skyward. What the official photograph was cropped not to show was the attendant holding the horse's bridle, keeping the animal in place.

Fascist Procession

Officials lined up for some kind of Fascist procession, Benghazi, 1940

In this photo, there are men in their official uniforms. It was taken during the 1930s, the 'glory years' of colonial fascism. A man in white robes looks like he is kneeling at the feet of another man, like he is taking the communion wafer. Even if I had asked her about it when I had the opportunity, I don't think my grandmother could have told me what was going on. Perhaps all she knew was what she wrote in the caption: 'Papà is last on the left.' In any case, by the time this photo was taken, she had already been sent to Turin.

The second volume of Spina's Benghazi epic, *Colonial Tales*, takes place in the 1930s. While the first volume of *Confines* spans the first decade of the Italian invasion, *Colonial Tales* is a collection of short stories set during Italian Fascism up until the Second World War. Its cast is mainly made up of Italian officers, bureaucrats, aristocrats, teachers, merchants and settlers in Benghazi.

Prior to *Colonial Tales*, Spina's Benghazi is a bustling merchant port. The inhabitants of Benghazi are not just indigenous

Libyans – they are exiles from Crete, migrants from Misrata and Djerba, Maronites from Syria, West African migrants, and the descendants of Turkish settlers. The curtains of *Colonial Tales* open on a different Benghazi. Now, the main square is lined with ostentatious hotels adorned with marble columns and arches. Bored Italian military officers, bureaucrats and their families dominate the narratives, and the city is rife with gossip and intrigue that distracts them from their idle lives. Days and evenings are spent making conversation in the cafés that line the *corso*, walking along the promenade for the customary evening stroll, lazing around their homes in hiding from the heat, and attending military parades in the main square, or banquets and balls at the Officers' Club.

The stories centre around conversations, in which the characters voice their opinions on the state of the colony, Italian politics of the time, propaganda, and the expansionist strategy. They are self-aware enough to realise that their presence in the colony is for the sake of appearances rather than necessity. An Italian officer, for example, sarcastically notes the irony of illiterate colonist farmers bringing civilisation to African savages. When the characters venture out of the city, it is to make day trips to various archaeological sites, more to pass the time than out of any thirst for knowledge. The trips, which are taken by various officers, dignitaries and bureaucrats and their wives, are often taken with a resident professor or archaeologist. The earth in these short stories is arid and violent. The characters sweat in the heat and suffer through furious sandstorms. Some disappear. Others visit archaeological sites to reassure themselves of their right of inheritance to the country, but their contact with the land invariably leaves them feeling isolated and alien, as though the land itself rejects the Italians.

When Libyans make their way into the narrative, it disturbs the Italian characters. The world that they have dreamed up is at odds with reality, and the presence of Libyans reminds them of this. In 'The Prince of Cleve', a Libyan lieutenant of noble lineage joins a group of Italians (one of which is the Governor) on an archaeological tour of an ancient Greek amphitheatre. Turning to face the group, he thunderously recites lines from the play *Città Morta*, written by Italian writer and forefather of fascism, Gabriele D'Annunzio. The first of these lines: 'Behold me, O citizens of my native country.' The recitation of the lieutenant, named Nemiri, spooks those present. It's the uncanny sensation of finding the unhomely in what should be homely: the ruins, the lines of the Italian play. But when spoken by Nemiri, they are invariably reminded of their otherness in *his* country, the country of which they have crowned themselves citizen rulers.

In Spina's fiction, the landscape around Benghazi is untouched, marked at regular intervals with the remains of ancient coastal cities, the arches of amphitheatres that emerge like majestic staircases into the sea. Hellenic mausoleums lie a few feet from the shoreline, with Doric friezes and the faint carved name of the deceased still visible. There are Christian basilicas, ancient Roman forums. There are palaces carved into rock, Doric columns, atriums, stone triclinia. There are sarcophagi, niches, loggia, Ionic pillars. Professors litter the narratives, and they drone on about ancient history and customs.

The extensive descriptions of ruins, Roman and otherwise, remind the characters of the temporality of power, rather than their inheritance. The landscape is incessant in its recall of past empires. The ancient tombs haunt them as harbingers of the future. They remind the characters that the civilisations that have been there before them have all come to an end. One day, Fascist Italy will also come to an end, and other empires and powers will emerge in its stead.

This inner revelation taunts the characters. Some feel an impending sense of implacable doom, while others are convinced they are the victims of a curse. They are tormented by the past, and the ruins are not just omens of what is to come, but of retribution for the unseen atrocities that built their colony and continue to bubble underneath the surface.

Man and boys in Berber town

Four figures and their shadows, Libya, year unknown

Another photo shows a man walking around the corner of a squat white stone building, against which three boys sit on a stone bench. It must be afternoon; their shadows are so strong that it looks as though there are eight figures at first glance. The man and the boys all wear qamis and caps and they look startled at the presence of the camera, one boy shielding his eyes from the sun.

I ask myself who these images were taken for, why my great-grandfather wanted to archive them. To photograph something is to consume it, claim it, colonise it.

These photos did not make it into the official family narrative, but he wanted these events on record. His private album is constructed like a personal journal. I know that he was not the type to keep a written journal. The story I had always been told was that over their two years apart after first meeting, Salvatore courted Rita by sending her love letters. Recently my mother told me that after they married, Rita was dismayed to learn that the letter-writing was almost entirely ghostwritten by a more eloquent friend of Salvatore's.

I can now place this photo on the map of Libya that I have built in my mind. Harder though, to reckon with Italy's colonial history, my history, my inheritance and how I profited from it.

I can somewhat picture what Benghazi was like. A white city. A turquoise sea. Rolling waves lap at the lip of the long promenade, lined with palm trees. A grainy wind sends hot red Sahara sand into the crevices of the city, settling on windowsills and staircases, in eyes and ears and nostrils, burrowing into the lace of the women's parasols, the jacket pockets of the men. Red clouds swarm through the porticoes of the sparkling European quarter, lined with villas and imposing imperial apartment buildings, through the medina, a labyrinth of square whitewashed homes, small cafés serving coffee and hookah to clients playing draughts, blaring music from gramophones. In the souk, stalls line the narrow winding streets that open onto the market square. Bearded tradesmen sit cross-legged on pillows in their stalls, which they pack up every day and transport their unsold wares back to the country upon camels. The domed ceiling of the synagogue, with its large Star of David, bobs up into the city skyline from the *mellah*.

In the heart of the city is the main square, christened by the Italians as the Piazza del Re, looked over by the parliament building, Palazzo del Littorio, with its Moorish façade of arches topped with mosaics of coloured tile. Corso Italia, the city's main artery, spills into the square like a river. At seven each evening, the city halts and the *corso* hums with the slow-moving flow of amblers. Perhaps my young grandmother and her parents are among them. Her father holds one chubby arm as she insists on walking, while her mother pushes the empty stroller. The earlier wind has died down, and the sea sends its cool breeze through the streets of the city, gently rustling the branches of the palm trees. The chalet, bars, and restaurants that face out to the immense sea are now brimming with people. The luxurious colonial hotels, Albergo Italia, with its palm garden, and Albergo Berenice, with its daily afternoon orchestra, are filled with tourists preparing themselves for their evening dinner. The outdoor tables at the Café Italia are full of patrons sipping prosecco and cocktails, as the tinkling music of the four-piece orchestra wafts into the road. Italians in suits or uniforms and Fascist badges are seated at the tables. An ankle crossed over a leg reveals a spur, a hand thumbs a military decoration on a lapel, another shifts the sword at a hip. Fingers snap as Eritrean batmen zip around tables delivering telegrams and letters.

The silhouette of Mussolini's head is displayed on the walls, and families greet one another with the raised arm of the fascist salute. Perhaps an armoured tank inches its way down a wide street. It stops at the gate of the city, guarded by armed soldiers. Further along from the city is Giuliana Beach, which looks just like an Italian beach. On the sand are orderly rows of colourful wooden beach cabins. On the other side of the city from the beach, close to the city wall is Benghazi's prison. A medieval-looking construction, it is made up of four towers and guarded by sentries with machine guns. On another beach, a row of men accused of rebellion are being shot one by one.

There are pine groves outside Benghazi, through which the ancient road to the port of Apollonia is said to have run. Apollonia was a Greek commercial centre, one of the five cities of the Cyrenaican Pentapolis. An earthquake had caused half the city to slip into the sea. From a boat, the fish-populated ruins of this sunken city could be examined, like the miniature castle in a fish tank. The region had once been rich with rivers, but now only their barren beds were left, like the fossilised imprints of extinct species in stones and seashells.

Further along on the coast is Cyrene, Cyrenaica's namesake. North Africa's first Greek city on Libya's eastern coastline, it was founded in 632 BCE, and was an intellectual and cultural centre of the Greek world. Behind Cyrene, the necropolis in the hills, larger than the city itself, airy black rectangles that are windows into the resting places of the ancient inhabitants. The ancients living in the sixth century AD must have believed in a pleasant afterlife. The tombs are built like cool temples, with staggered views of the sea. Apollo's fountain in Cyrene is populated by statues of robed men with their heads lopped off. The tail-less, pupil-less lion mid-step, his carved mane resembling fish scales. The cool water rushing down the rocks of Apollo's fountain.

Inland from the tombs, in the hills. The wreckage of a bombed village. Another village an abandoned ghost town. Wells spilling over with sand and concrete. New towns built in the middle of the desert, populated by families wondering how to make olives and grapes grow from sand. Land that was stolen from communities which now populate the concentration camps, or else are gone due to starvation or shooting or hanging in the desert, or in some town square, or in Benghazi itself, the *Piazza del Re*, as an Italian crowd looks on. A soldier's fort oversees one such camp, hundreds of people fenced in with barbed wire, their only sustenance tinned food because their animals are emaciated from not being able to graze. Shackled men wade through the gritty salt lakes in the desert, hauling sand. More shackled men labour under the scorching sun, building the *strada littoriana* – the road that symbolises the deliverance of civilisation.

There is another photo, one I won't show. It's of an execution. Holmboe writes that while he was in Libya, there were on average thirty executions a day – adding up to about twelve thousand a year. 'The land swam in blood,' he writes. The photo shows a man hanging from a noose in the desert. All I have left of that moment, from which all the witnesses are surely now deceased, is this photo.

In Spina's novel, *The Young Maronite*, there is a hanging of a main character, Semereth Effendi. A wealthy Turkish merchant, he has migrated to Libya decades before the invasion and eventually joined the Sanusi rebellion. Captured by the Italian military, he is hung publicly in Benghazi's main square. Although the hanging Salvatore photographed took place in the desert and not in public, when I look at the photo now, I superimpose the retelling of the hanging in Spina's writing. It is told in retrospect, by an Italian officer who had a rivalry with Effendi.

In a long, unbroken confession, he recalls that Effendi's face was inscrutable, displaying neither fear nor hatred or resignation. This lends Effendi the dignity that he was denied in the mode of his death. The Italian officer reasons that he died as either a patriot or a warrior: a hero. He is described as standing in the gallows, looking like Moses clutching the ten commandments or 'Jesus on the cross'.

The narration notes that the officer speaks as though he is reliving Effendi's execution, talking as though he can see it on a film, one that he is condemned to continue watching replay, over and over. The officer recalls the sun's blinding heat and the cloud of desert dust that smothered the square. He repeats Effendi's final words: 'We return from whence we came.' In that moment, he says, he felt the urge to fall to his knees. He finds himself changed now, haunted by his participation in the execution – because to be a witness is to participate. In searching for a sense or meaning to Effendi's murder by the Italian Expeditionary Force, he finds none, and this senselessness stretches to Italy's presence in Libya, and the violence wrought upon it, all in the name of civilisation.

I found the hanging photo among the loose photographs in the box. I will never know why Salvatore took it. Sontag suggests that we take photographs when we don't know how to respond to a particular event or an encounter. It transforms mere observation into a productive act, while also distancing us from the event or encounter by placing a camera between us and it.

In recording these moments of atrocity, he became a voyeur – he separated himself from the moment, and absolved himself from intervening. But taking a photograph amounts to complicity, a tacit acceptance of the status quo. He will always be a participant in this death, and now so am I. I own the last and perhaps the only photo that anyone has ever taken of this man.

I always circle back to the question of why he chose not only to record such horrible moments, but also keep them. Looking at these photos shatters the romanticism that colours my perception of my grandmother's childhood home. When he returned to Italy and showed people the photos of Africa, did he also show them the photo of the hanging? If it is true that he risked his life smuggling them back there, the questions that plagues me is: to what end?

Annalisa and boy

Annalisa and young boy, Benghazi, 1937

Two children, both with their fists stuffed in the pockets of double-breasted military coats. On first glance, the boy seems to be beaming up at the girl, but on closer inspection he is giggling at the actions of someone off camera.

They have obviously been told to pose, and one thing I can discern from my grandmother's photos is that even as a child she was accustomed to being in front of the photographer's lens. She smiles at the camera, close-mouthed, with her chin turned down, as though she is sharing a secret with it. She may just be posing, though, and the boy may be an annoyance; he may be smiling at someone making fun of her. Behind them, out of focus, is a building, perhaps one of their homes.

If I could, I would ask my grandmother about the background of the photo. It's the kind of photo that supplants all memory, that you stumble across in an album and recognise as a past self you no longer have any connection to. It reminds me of all the selves I've lost to the fuzzy selection of memory. Now, looking at the photo, I am reminded of how age shrouded my grandmother, and of the world we have lost in losing her.

If she is six here, this photo would have been taken when she lived in Benghazi. In a couple of years, her parents would send her to live with her grandmother in Turin, in order to escape the daily bombardments which sent her household regularly into underground bunkers, and from which she would develop an anxiety disorder.

John Berger writes that 'what is remembered has been saved from nothingness. What is forgotten has been abandoned.' I worry over who among us grandchildren will be tasked with keeping these photo albums, whether we will be the last generation to remember. Now, looking at these photos, I wonder: when is the exact moment that you lose a person?

A couple of years after this photo was taken, Annalisa was sent to a boarding school in the Italian Alps. By 1941, fewer than ten thousand colonists remained in Cyrenaica, the rest having been evacuated. The beginning of the end of Italian Libya was marked by the death of the governor, Italo Balbo, who was hit by friendly fire eighteen days after Italy entered the Second World War.

When the war came to an end, Libya was split up again, between two of the greatest colonial powers: France took control of Fezzan, while Great Britain was given Tripolitania and Cyrenaica. Italy attempted to regain its colonies after the war, but they were blocked by the winning powers and by Libya's own nationalist forces. Instead, in 1951 the UN recognised the independent reign of King Sayyid Idris, the captain of the Sanusi. Despite these changes, many Italian colonisers returned to Libya after the war, and prospered there under the monarchy, particularly after the oil boom. Rita and Salvatore never returned.

My grandmother had always described the Libya of her youth as idyllic, and in my mind growing up it was an exoticised fantasy. Coming upon the photographs, I thought they would tell me something more of the past, but they too were mysteries. Not just that, but the world that the photographs depict no longer exists. When Gaddafi seized power from King Idris in 1960, he demolished all markers of imperial Italy, mostly in Benghazi: palazzi were left to decay or turned into parking lots, monuments fell, roads were torn up. A country is just as much an idea as it is a territory, an idea that is deliberately fashioned, and Gaddafi's nationalist regime sought to define an independent Libya by eradicating the relics of the past. Only its aftereffects remain, echoing in Libya's ongoing political and civil war, in the concrete structures that Gaddafi neglected to destroy, such as Benghazi's *lungomare* and its Italianate architecture, and now in the reversed migratory passage of African refugees to Sicily.

In his 2016 book, *The Return*, Hisham Matar travels to Libya in the wake of Gaddafi's assassination, finally able to return after a lifetime in exile. He writes that every family, including his own, could name members who had been lost during colonisation. This resulted in a tense climate of friction between the various religious, cultural, and ethnic communities in Libya. The Jewish population, one of the oldest in North Africa, left. The settlers who did stay on or returned to the inland agricultural villages had their property confiscated and were deported in 1970, soon after Gaddafi came into power. *The Return* traces Matar's search for his father, abducted and imprisoned under Gaddafi's government as a political dissident over twenty years before, and surveys the events of Gaddafi's coup against King Idris and his following regime.

Matar, returning to Libya for the first time since he was eight years old, finds his homeland on the brink of civil war. Civilian militias roam the country. As Matar walks through Benghazi, past the neoclassical Italianate buildings on the seafront, down the narrow streets and silent squares, past the newer concrete apartment blocks, he notes the posters pasted all over the city. They are of young men who have died in the Libyan revolution, declared on the posters to be martyrs. Some families have hired billboards to memorialise their sons. Matar notes that once these same billboards and streets bore Gaddafi's portrait, and I think about how before that, they bore Mussolini's.

Man, children, palm trees

Man and two children, Libya, year unknown

A Libyan man on a donkey gazes at the camera with a hand on his hip, two children standing beside him, squinting at the camera. The man wears a military coat, while the two children wear qamis. All three wear the tight white caps customary to Libyan traditional dress. Behind them: rock formations, jagged hills of sandstone, a dirt road, debris of rocks and ruins littering the ground, the thin shoots of date palms dwarfing everything in the photo. Other photographs of my great-grandfather's show desert oases, a gentle stream bordered by scrubland and furry palm trees, reaching towards a cloudless sky.

The sirocco is the dry, dusty wind that originates in the Sahara and blows over the sea and through Sicily. Its name derives from the Maghrebi Arabic dialect word *šulūq*, meaning 'noon wind'. It can last hours or days, causing storms in the Mediterranean (*sciroccàta*) and carrying red desert dust that settles in lungs and crevices. Later, when my grandmother was an adult, the red sand of her youth settled over the city of Palermo.

In the albums, there are photos of Libyan families clustered together in the desert, of my grandmother as a toddler and a playmate clutching the hands of a Libyan *zaptié*, of Italian children running on a sports oval wearing fascist uniforms, and of my great-father Salvatore and some friends posing with their arms around one another and smiling on a rocky Libyan shore. Looking at them, I feel further away from this world of my grandmother's youth than I did when I was younger and she would recount stories to me.

The photos served as two opposing forces. They were a window, not just into another time, but another place. And they were also a reminder that this photographic window was an impenetrable barrier, that the world it depicted both no longer existed and had never existed, at least not in the way that the photos seemed to say it did. Or, perhaps not that it no longer existed. Rather, that it still does, echoing through the present.

Rome

I don't know exactly where in Rome they met again, but I like to imagine that it happened in Termini train station. That after a three-year separation, Annalisa got off her train from Turin, her long hair in the braids she favoured when she was young. The train had passed military convoys along the way, a lunar landscape of the paddocks of dead livestock and the bombed-out skeletons of homes, and hollow-eyed wanderers drifting to the nearest city, and perhaps the make-shift tents or shanties of bombed-out families, and it had been stopped and searched at some country station by intimi-dating officers carrying rifles. The train was full of off-duty soldiers and families transporting what was left of their lives in bundles on their laps. Finally, she was leaving Turin, which at this point had been so sacked by bombings that twenty-five thousand homes had been destroyed. When the train pulled into Termini, a well-meaning stranger helped her with her suitcase down the steps leading onto the platform. She felt a few minutes of panic – how would she spot her parents amidst the bustle? Had they made it safely?

I never once saw my grandmother become emotional, but I like to think that if there was any time for an exception, then this was it. It would have been the first time seeing her parents in years, after what would have seemed like an age of hoping and worrying and waiting for news of them, and perhaps hearing about the bombings in Benghazi, and wondering whether they had been trapped, smothered under a pile of broken rubble. For the first time in three years, she heard her parents' voices: she thought she'd forgotten them, but hearing them was like walking over the threshold of one's home.

Perhaps when they met, she would not have recognised them at first, because her father's face had grown more creased and tired, his eyes weary. Maybe her mother's hair had gone from dark to completely grey. Perhaps her once-corpulent figure was now halved, perhaps her father now stooped. And they too would have met with a different daughter than the nine-year-old they had sent to Turin: now in the first flush of adolescence, she would have been taller, her face thinner, caught awkwardly between childhood and adulthood.

I've often wondered why my family chose to seek refuge in Rome. It wasn't a city in which they had any family – there was Turin, though it was being pummelled by bombs, and there was Sicily, where Salvatore's family was. Perhaps a colleague of Salvatore sourced an apartment for the family, who had lost all their belongings, and were reduced to chasing after the meagre compensation of a suitcase gone astray. Perhaps Rita had been offered a teaching job which led them there.

Much of their time in Rome, where they remained for over three years, from 1943 until September of 1946, is shrouded. There were only a couple of stories that my grandmother recalled from her three years in Rome. Initially, she attended school, but at a certain point, maybe because of the Allied bombings, she stopped. She recalled being always alone. Her mother was teaching, and her father, she would say, went out for hours each day. My mother, when we spoke about my grandmother's time in the city, always made it seem like Salvatore's absences were mysterious. How was he spending those hours – was he delivering messages? Was he attending secret meetings in underground taverns? All those concerned are gone now, leaving only the imagination to conjure answers. I decided to visit landmarks that recalled the tenor of those years, read books that narrated them. I wanted to know the shape of their lives, the form of the world in which they existed. At the very least, I might further furnish or inform my own fantasy.

In the archives of the *Ministero degli Affari*, in the archival fund of the *Ministero dell'Africa Italiana*, there are two files, one under the name of my great-grandfather, Salvatore Gueli, and the other my great-grandmother, Margherita Bertone. Rita's file consists of letters from and about her, all circling around the same issue: the compensation of her lost luggage. The luggage was lost on the day that my great-grandparents left Benghazi, five days before Christmas, on 20 December 1941.

This was the day that they were evacuated from Benghazi to Tripoli. In a handwritten letter written to the Prefecture of Benghazi, Rita wrote that:

> The luggage of the undersigned, together with that of the other personnel, was loaded on coach LB 128, and insured with weak ropes due to the lack of more suitable material. On the tract between Agedabia and Agheila, the coach, in order to escape the enemy's aerial machine-gun fire, accelerated, causing the fall of some suitcases that had to be abandoned.

Her suitcase fell off and tumbled into the Libyan desert. She listed the contents as such:

1 wool dress	500.00
1 blue heavy silk dress	400.00
4 matching undergarment sets	300.00
3 nightdresses	220.00
4 wool sweaters	180.00
6 pairs of socks	150.00
1 pair of embroidered slippers	45.00
2 dozen linen handkerchiefs	120.00
2 silk handkerchiefs	95.00
1 fur collar	250.00
1 wool jacket	105.00

The value of these belongings came to a total of 2,365 Italian lire, which is equivalent to around fifteen hundred euro today.

As she continuously wrote letters to different officials to receive her compensation over the years, it rapidly lost value thanks to the devaluation of the lira. When she first wrote, on 15 January 1942, the amount was worth around 1,249 euro. She was in Tripoli with my great-grandfather, and Italy had lost Cyrenaica to the Allies. She wrote again from Rome on 1 October 1943, a few weeks after the German occupation of the city, and a few months after its first aerial bombings. The amount was now worth around eight hundred euro.

Metropoliz

Via Prenestina, 913, is in a part of Rome peopled by the salesmen who work in the car dealerships that line the strip, and the shoppers who make a special trip to the two-storey Decathlon outlet across the road, and the Italian and migrant families who reside in its concrete beehive apartment buildings. It's a dusty street scattered with parasol pines, bingo halls and tyre shops, electronics megastores and shoe outlets, suppliers of auto body parts, safety equipment and construction materials, wholesalers and petrol stations and car dealerships.

The address in question was once a slaughterhouse and sausage factory in the service of Fiorucci, an Italian producer of salami. At a certain point it was abandoned by the company, who moved their factory south, like many other industrial plants in the area. The catalyst for their relocation was the public project that ran in Italy from 1950 to 1984, called the *Cassa del Mezzogiorno*, or Southern Fund. This project encouraged public works and infrastructure to move to the South by providing credit subsidies and tax incentives. Apparently, the administrative line between northern and southern Italy was drawn along via Pontina, about ten or fifteen kilometres south of Tor Sapienza, the area where much of Roman industry had been situated, and so the place became a sort of urban wasteland.

Alighting from the bus, there is some discussion between my boyfriend and I as we attempt to locate our destination. The footpath is non-existent in some places, cracked in others, where tall shoots of grass and weeds poke through. To our right is a factory lot, concrete walls wrapped around a cluster of buildings, nondescript, except for the murals plastering its grey walls.

We walk over to the driveway of the otherwise anonymous fortress. A sign on a metal pole pokes out of the concrete. The sign is small, thin, yellow, and black lettering announces that we have arrived at:

Metropoliz.

We walk through the arched entrance. Standing behind a folding table is an African man, who tells us that a tour of the museum has just started and that we are welcome to join it. We walk up a ramp into the main building and find our tour guide surrounded by a cluster of patrons, both tourists and Romans. He takes us through the museum's maze of rooms.

MAAM, the *Museo dell'Altro e dell'Altrove,* invites artists from across Italy and Europe to make and donate an artwork or installation that is inspired by the premises. Now, there are over five hundred works by artists. The building doesn't hide its past life: the floor is still rough concrete, as are the walls, which are stained in places. Some rooms still contain the old machinery, nobody has cleared the cobwebs, and two fat cats – one ginger, the other black – wind around our legs each time we stop to contemplate an art piece. In one room, a wall is covered by a mural in which large pink swine hang by their feet from a conveyor belt. On the floor, hundreds of painted red shoes trail from one wall to another. An oil landscape hangs above a doorway. In another room, an outline of Italy is filled with pieces of charcoal. A narrow abstract painting is wedged between rusted factory apparatus. A giant, photo-real portrait of a woman's face in BIC pen. A hole hacked into one wall creates a peephole, with rings drilled around it and painted orange and red so that it looks like Saturn. Wire pigs prance across a rafter. Painted paper fans hang from a ceiling conveyor belt. The cream-coloured shells of sea snails grow from a doorway, and a rainbow of yarn animals walk upside down across a bar of fluorescent light, covered with cotton stuffing so that it resembles a cloud. Meat and tomatoes are simmering on a stove somewhere, unseen children laugh and yell to one another.

Metropoliz, the site of MAAM, is a place that could easily be called a shantytown anywhere else. It is home to a community of over two hundred people, a quarter of them children. The guide tells us that the families who occupy the old slaughterhouse are made up of Italians, migrants, and Romani. They came in 2009, and, with nowhere else to go, set up camp, building partition walls and homes on the property. They set up a community kitchen in the middle of the main building, where, for a modest sum, the public can come and have lunch or a coffee.

After the tour, we wander around to where some of the houses are. Some have murals painted on them. A woman hangs out her washing, two neighbours sit on their respective porches, smoking cigarettes and chatting with one another. A young girl clutching a stack of books pushes open the gate to her home, the garden filled with vegetable patches and potted plants, the exterior walls decorated with mosaics of glass. In front of other homes sit brown leather couches, a child's tricycle, a patio umbrella, a shopping cart full of what seems like junk. Further on, a group of boys plays soccer on a small field. A few more dwellings stretch out, and a Romani and an African man have an intense discussion about where the division between their respective properties lies, which ends with the Romani clocking the African man. Neighbours come to intervene. Feeling suddenly like intruders, we turn around and leave, heading for the bus stop.

Hadrian's Villa

On the bus out to Hadrian's Villa, the scenery along the highway seems super-sized. We pass tall, paint-worn palazzi and shopping centres; an Italian Buddhist institute; the 'Big Ben Café', a combination bar, fast food takeaway, *pasticceria*, slot machine lounge and bookmaker's; pizzerias and auto repair shops; a MoneyGram; a sports centre. Beyond the highway, which is a clogged artery of exhaust fumes and billboards and the blinking bulbs of the betting places and the gaudy pizzerias, lie national reserves and ruins and the golf courses of country clubs. We get off at the main street of Tivoli, a run-down resort town. Trucks and cars barrel past, and the street is lined with small sticky snack bars and newsagents. We walk past schools and villas and through supermarket parking lots, until we finally make it down to the arched gates. At a small hut joined to a closed gift shop in the villa parking lot, we buy two tickets and an audio guide.

The villa itself is set in a massive expanse of parklands, about the size of Pompeii, parts of which were once privately owned (the residence of one such owner is still on the property). It is a vast complex of ruins, which were the summer estate of Emperor Hadrian, who had it built as an escape from the city. I assume that normally, there are tonnes of tourists walking through the grounds, but on this occasion, it is just myself, my boyfriend, and a smattering of other couples that we occasionally cross paths with. Our solitude lends everything a spectral quality, as peaceful as it would have been when Hadrian retreated there, sick of the clamour of Rome.

We walk through the grounds, past white stone slabs and columns jutting out of the ground, statues with an arm or head cut off, crocodiles snapping at the air, shards of intricate tile work with weeds budding up around the edges. It begins to rain, fat drops catapulting off our umbrellas like scattershot bullets. Glassy pools form in the ground. Soon the rain stops, the sun emerges, the white statues glow in the warm light.

Information plaques inform us that each jumble of stone was once something definable. The audio guide blathers on, describing the unrecognisable baths, the dining halls, the ballrooms, in vain. We stop at a murky oval pool around which columns and statues of nymphs and muses and aquatic animals and gods and decorative arches are curved. Another couple ahead skips over a chain-link barrier to walk the whole way around it, so we do the same. I try to reconstruct it all in my mind, to complete the sawn-off columns, fill the baths with water, imagine the ancient Romans bathing or feasting in their robes, eyeing Rome in the distance over the rolling green hills.

In the Middle Ages the villa was a quarry, stripped for building materials to build Tivoli. While the villa was only made a UNESCO site in 1999, it has undergone over five hundred years of excavations, back when 'excavation' was akin to grave robbing. The villa was continuously scoured for treasures, such as sculptures and mosaics, which were then scattered throughout Europe, to adorn the homes and private collections of popes, noblemen and royals. Hadrian's Villa became famous, and its bounty of treasures legendary. Families carried out 'private excavations', unearthing and carting statues and fragments off to manors in France, Spain, Austria. These private excavations continued throughout the sixteenth and seventeenth centuries. In the eighteenth century, when Count Fede took ownership of the villa, he combed it for treasures to add to his own collection, which disappeared upon his death. Finally, the Englishmen on their Grand Tour picked through the rubble, uprooting perhaps a bust or a column capital to send home to their estates in Britain. We pass archeaologists studiously brushing away dirt, gardeners keeping grass trimmed. We and the other visitors all crawl over the villa silently, gawking and pointing and gesturing, taking the time to linger and touch. I walk into the atrium of what had been a banquet hall with columns which had once been load bearing jutting up out of the ground. Now supporting nothing, they reach up into the open sky.

It is a truism that in times of present uncertainty we tend to foster nostalgia for an idealised past. The Fascists were like other populist leaders before and after them, in that they weaponised an oversimplified past – whether personal or public – by mythologizing it. The ideal of *romanità* has been around since the Risorgimento, first when Italians needed to be drawn together under the banner of a collective history and a shared identity, and then to justify Italian colonisation. It was fascism, however, that got the most wear out of it. As far as myths go, it's a seductive one. The Roman Empire, after all, had been the last time that the peninsula and its islands were united. Every Italian city boasts Roman ruins, and Rome was, after all, an empire that contained many cultures within it. Besides, who wouldn't want to lay claim to one of the longest lasting civilisations on the planet? Who wouldn't want to align themselves with this ancient greatness, one whose legacy survives to this day?

Aesthetics were fundamental to the diffusion of *romanità*, which was used to prop up the Fascist regime's shallow ideology. Public life and space were seen as a theatre setting that had to be dressed in fascist garb and choreographed in fascist movement. Buildings were adorned with fasces, an Ancient Roman symbol consisting of a bundle of wooden rods and an axe bound together by a strip of leather, which signified power and authority. People were to greet one another with the Roman salute, a gesture that inspired the Nazis. There was also a new calendar; time began not with the birth of Christ, but that of fascism. Rome had to be 'restored'. New roads like the via Imperiale were laid down, the city centre was connected to the sea by the opening of the via del Mare, railroads were built. New suburbs were constructed. It seems that the Rome that needed to be restored wasn't the material city, but the appearance or feel of what it represented. Only the most notable ruins were considered worth conserving, and many were sacrificed for the sake of renewal.

Italian Fascism was, at its core, a lean, theatrical regime. This fact is perhaps best exemplified by Mussolini himself, who styled himself and posed and gave speeches as if he were the omniscient father figure of Italy, the all-powerful emperor who would lead his little country out of its aberrant smallness and into its past greatness. In Elsa Morante's era-defining novel *History*, Mussolini was described as a dreamer, whose fantasy was: 'a histrionic festival, where among banners and triumphs, he, a scheming vassal, would play the part of certain beatified ancient vassals (Caesars, Augustuses, and so on . . .) before a living crowd humbled to the rank of puppets.'

Fascist actions were compared with ancient Roman events to justify the present with a kind of simultaneous temporal continuity. It was as though the thousand years in between the Roman Empire and Fascist Italy hadn't occurred. Mussolini's March on Rome, when compared to Caesar's coup, for example, could be read as a return to form, one which had simply been dormant for a while.

These tactics are still used today. In the UK, the legal scholar Nadine El-Enany writes of a *Daily Star* headline following the Brexit referendum that borrowed from Trump's US presidential campaign slogan: 'Now Let's Make Britain Great Again.' Along with fear of immigration, imperial nostalgia for a time when 'Britannia ruled the waves' was an undercurrent of the campaign to leave the EU. While part of the EU, the UK was one country among many, but as the locus of an empire, it 'was defined by its racial and cultural superiority'. She points to one of Boris Johnson's speeches after the referendum, in which he romanticised British colonialism as an 'astonishing globalism, this wanderlust of aid workers and journalists and traders and diplomats and entrepreneurs,' and suggested that the 'next generation of Brits' would possess the same adventurous spirit as their forebears.

More recently, in 2018, Reuters reported how the government of India's Hindu nationalist Prime Minister Narendra Modi had appointed a group of pasisteen bureaucrats and scholars to prove that today's Indian Hindus directly descend from the multifaith and multicultural country's first inhabitants. They were to use DNA and archaeological evidence to show that Hindus are the 'true' Indians, and that the events described in ancient religious

Hindu texts are fact. This new Hindu-centred version of the nation's history would be added to school curriculums, because, as the spokesman of the RSS, India's Hindu nationalist movement, was quoted as saying, 'to bring about cultural changes we have to rewrite history'. This is aligned with the RSS movement's philosophy of 'Hindutva', which is the belief that India is a nation of and for Hindus.

Then, as now, the past was a wellspring from which inspiration and ideals for the present could be drawn. In reminding the Italian people of the glories of ancient Rome, and packaging it as their exclusive inheritance, Mussolini was prompting Italians to see and define themselves in a particular way. In a speech he delivered in October 1923, he declared that 'we are all Italians and have to be proud to be Italian not only for the glories of the past, very noble glories. But we do not wish to live off their rent as degenerate and parasitic grandchildren, but above all for this new Italy that is rising. . .' Never mind the fact that if an Italian could count Roman ancestors (or ancestors originating from colonised Roman provinces, such as Sicily), they wouldn't be their grandchildren, but their great-times-twenty-grandchildren.

And like the populist leaders of today – like Modi in India, Bolsonaro in Brazil, and Trump in the US – Mussolini tended to cast a mythologised and therefore oversimplified gaze over history. In his collected writings, posthumously published in forty-four-volumes and titled *Opera Omnia*, he justified the millennial gap between the Roman Empire and the present day by suggesting that the country was in a kind of time warp. He wrote that 'for the Italian people all is eternal and contemporary. For us it is as if Caesar was stabbed yesterday. It is something proper to the Italian people, something which no other people have to the same extent.'

EUR

EUR is a suburb that lies to the southwest of the city, almost at the midpoint between the historic centre of Rome and the Tyrrhenian Sea. It is a large suburb, with three of its own stops on the metro. I get off at the last stop, planning to walk the length of it back down to the first. Immediately, when I emerge out of the metro, it becomes obvious that I am no longer in the Rome that the mind's eye normally conjures.

Before me, a man-made lake laps at the ENI tower. The tower, completed in 1962, is commonly known as the *palazzo di vetro*, or glass palace. Although building began in the late fifties, it follows the architectural lines of the rest of the place, with its flat, square façade of glass. The artificial lake that begins at the tower and borders EUR was planned before the war, but not realised until after it. Cutting across the lake and through EUR's neat grid of streets is via Cristoforo Colombo, originally named via Imperiale. It is a wide boulevard rendered imposing by its hundred-metre width. The spine of EUR, it cuts through the length of it, corralled by Rome's historic centre on one end and the sea on the other. Bordering it behind me are more offices housed in grubby, once-white commercial buildings, apartment blocks, car parks and cafés. The suburb is now home to Romans, offices, businesses, the Central State Archives, a museum, and the Fendi headquarters in the famed *colosseo quadrato*, or square coliseum.

EUR is the opposite of what I find so attractive about Rome: tangled, narrow streets, a confused melange of foot and motor traffic, apartments and churches and ruins stacked one on top of the other in a palimpsest of time and life, piazzas swarming with people like flies to a picnic; a city that achieves a kind of grace from its gracelessness. EUR, on the other hand, is dull in its deliberateness. I am uninterested in the straight and sweeping lines of its domed basilica. It looks like an evangelical spaceship rather than a Catholic house of worship, like it should be in Salt

Lake City and not Rome. EUR feels and looks artificial, hollow, like a sanitised imitation of a city.

This is because it was planned. EUR (pronounced *eh-urr*, with a rolled 'r'), stands for *Esposizione Universale di Roma*, or Universal Exhibition of Rome. In some ways, it was Mussolini's EPCOT, a planned city that made manifest the idealised vision of the fascist metropolis. It would be a white urban centre that took its cue from the ancient Roman fora and recreated the grandeur of imperial Rome. The spot chosen for it was an area in the countryside at the midpoint between Rome and Fiumicino airport.

EUR was originally intended as the site for Rome's 1942 expo, a world fair planned to celebrate Fascism's twentieth anniversary. Its original name, E42, reflects this – E for *esposizione* and 42 for 1942. The fair was to be modelled on Paris's expo in 1937 and New York's World's Fair in 1939. The difference, however, was that the structures built for EUR were going to be permanent. The buildings would be made of stone and reinforced concrete. They would also be the site of a new Roman quarter, and a new urban centre of the city in general. It vaulted towards the Mediterranean, the sea that Italy would soon rule. The permanent structures would become museums that feted and unified Italy and its ancient Roman history of civilisation. There would be the *Palazzo della Civiltà Italiana*, housing a museum that flaunted Italian civilisation; there would be museums dedicated to folk art and tradition, science and technology, and both ancient and modern art. These museums would all circle the heart of the suburb: Piazza Imperiale. There would be a museum of Roman civilisation that faced the Piazza della Romanità, and military museums that would trumpet the State's power by housing exhibits dedicated to corporations and autocracy.

Mussolini had planned for foreign visitors to see E42 as a testament to the new Italy he was building, perhaps thinking that one day it would be dug up like the ruins of ancient Rome's Imperial Forums. Of course, the fair never happened. The Italian writer and journalist Corrado Augias writes that although Hitler had assured Mussolini that the war wouldn't break out until after the expo, Germany invaded Poland on 1 September 1939.

I walk down the side of the lake to via Colombo, which cuts straight through the middle of the suburb, and turn right down viale Europa. Across from me are the state archives, preceded by parking, housed up many blackened steps that lead to a squat building. It is of the usual fascist variety: two floors of symmetrical white travertine columns. I turn back and continue down via Cristoforo Colombo. Six lanes of rumbling traffic make it impossible to idle or meander. There are barely any pedestrians and on either side of the road stand imposing white uniform structures, all solid squares and straight lines.

This was the centre of Mussolini's 'new Rome', one characterised by monumental buildings that ran along and radiated out from the main artery of via Imperiale. Drawing from neoclassical and rationalist styles, they are colossal constructions of marble and travertine. E42 was a projection of the future: a beacon foretelling what the rest of Rome was going to look like, a shining example of the 'fascist style' for all future city planners to emulate. During a press conference for the project in January 1937, the General Commissioner of the Entre EUR, Vittorio Cini, stated that the new style announced by and named after the exposition would be the 'definitive style' for 'the year XX of the fascist era'. This new style, E42, would have as its principles 'grandeur' and 'monumentality'. Rome, he added, is everlasting and universal, and so E42 would be built to be everlasting and universal, 'so that in fifty or one hundred years their style will not have aged or, worse, been degraded'.

Competitions were held for the design of the permanent buildings between 1937 and 1938. These were judged by a jury commission, but it soon became evident what, or who – according to one of the winning designers of the Piazza Imperiale, Ludovico Quaroni – was the deciding factor. Entries had to impress *il Duce* in order to be successful. Essentially, one had to figure out what it was that Mussolini was impressed by. What Mussolini favoured was Classical architecture that recalled the Romans, but presented itself as modern. While claiming to direct his gaze towards the future, Mussolini was really hoping to mimic and grab at the grandeur of the past.

This tension between the past and the future was a problem for fascist architecture. Fascism clutched ancient Rome and the reverent desire to return to it in one hand, and the urge to create a modern city on top of the ancient one in the other. In other words, fascism wanted to be entirely new and avant-garde, while also claiming that it was rooted in Italian, by which it meant Roman, history and tradition. The paradox of fascism's looping, palintropic gaze between the past and the future is evident in fascist-sponsored art and architecture, which seemed to toe a line between resurrecting ancient Roman forms and inventing a new and unique fascist style.

I stop in the piazza in the heart of EUR and turn right towards the *Museo della Civiltà* complex, originally built to house E42's Universal Science Exhibition. The museum, in the geometrical style of Italian Rationalism favoured by Mussolini, has two identical white rectangular wings that run parallel to a green square consisting of some shrubs and parasol pines, which opens onto via Colombo. These two buildings house the Pigorini National Museum of Prehistory and Ethnography. Connecting these two wings is a raised colonnade, at which the viale della Civiltà Romana begins.

Interestingly, there is no signage I can see that explains Mussolini's totalitarian aesthetic, nor the fallen regime that conceived it. The museums that are now housed in its buildings sidestep the issue. Inside, the exhibits display palaeontological specimens and traditional folk art from Italy, copies of Roman art, and ethnological artefacts such as Paleolithic Venus statues, masks from Congo and boomerangs. Outside, the totalitarian buildings are nagging echoes of an unrealised future and a troubled past.

A thin median strip of green grass lined with shrubs and trees runs down the middle of the straight road, which stretches out to another white colonnade at the end. I follow the road, dull office blocks on either side. Some of those ugly 1960s Italian palazzi, whose concrete balconies provide a view of the road. At the end, concrete steps lead to another museum complex, again in the same pattern: two identical rectangular structures flanking the cul-de-sac, connected by a white colonnade. This time grubby steps lead to the buildings and the colonnade, and the structures themselves are brown brick. Across the top of the colonnade is written: *MUSEO DELLA CIVILTÀ ROMANA.* More white colonnades lead to each entrance of the brick buildings. Graffiti on one reads in a green scrawl: *CARLOTTA TROIA.* ('Carlotta whore.' Poor Carlotta.) All of it has been left to decay, although I don't know whether this is some side effect of the pandemic or because cleaning up fascist architecture isn't a popular mayoral pledge. Hundreds of cups litter the ground, perhaps left behind by some graduation party. The cloud cover is turning purple, and a wind picks up. The only sounds in these seemingly deserted surrounds are birds chirping and the white plastic cups that occasionally skitter across the concrete ground, blown by the wind. There is paper and rubbish and disposable masks. Birds peck at crumpled wrappers, wedged under the wheels of parked cars. There are broken glass bottles, empty plastic water bottles, crumpled and flattened receipts, faded lottery tickets, empty cigarette packets, a couple of empty tins of dog food, inexplicably.

Now the name 'Museum of Roman Civilisation' is ironic. With the litter, the graffiti and the emptiness, the imperial architecture seems post-apocalyptic, like the opening scene of a vacant London in *28 Days Later.* It seems like the detritus of a fallen empire, and in a way, it is, albeit one that fell in its adolescence. I imagine Mussolini time-travelling and seeing this: his worst nightmare. His empire, made irrelevant. Buildings built for a purpose that they would never fulfil. I imagine whether, if humanity survives that long, future archaeologists will unearth it a thousand years from now and mistake it for the remnants of success. Being in EUR is like glimpsing another possible future, or at least the death of it.

I retrace my steps to via Colombo. This is the heart of EUR, the monumental Piazza Marconi. It's mostly overrun with motor traffic. Mussolini also aligned himself with the Roman emperors by reviving their passion for Egyptian obelisks. In the middle of the piazza, he erected one by the Italian sculptor Arturo Dazzi. This white cylindrical tower features panels of bas-reliefs which illuminate the achievements of Gugliemo Marconi, a hero of the Fascist Party.

Facing the Museo della Civiltà complex, down viale della Civilta del Lavoro, is the stark rectangular building of the Palazzo della Civiltà Italiana, the Palace of the Civilisation of Labour, or, as it is better known, *il colosseo quadrato*, the square coliseum. The square coliseum is, for me, one of the few dazzling examples of fascist architecture. It took five years to build, beginning in 1938 and ending in 1943. A smooth white travertine cube supported by a podium on a small hill, each façade is identical. It looks like a perfect, geometrical beehive. It is six storeys in height, and each storey on every side has nine rounded arches. At the top of the building, on the front, is the famous inscription: '*Un popolo di poeti di artisti di eroi / di santi di pensatori di scienzati / di navigatori di trasmigratori'*. 'A people of poets, of artists, of heroes / of saints, of thinkers, of scientists / of navigators, of transmigrators.' (Of course, these poets and thinkers and scientists and travellers, in Mussolini's vision, were all of the non-existent 'Italian race'). Underneath the ground-floor arches are twenty-eight neoclassical robed statues.

There were plans for more works that never came to fruition, like Palazzo della Luce, a fantastical building that was to be made using only glass, light and water as its materials. I see EUR as a kind of parallel vision of the dark future that Italy almost met. This interpretation is only intensified by its occasional beauty – a fleeting curiosity to see what it would have looked like reminds one that, had it been finished, Italy would still be a dictatorship.

Augias writes that EUR represents a clear departure and almost a rejection of the labyrinthine network of ribbon-like streets dating from the 'Renaissance' or the ancient city. Here, there is nowhere to hide, to deviate, to be deviant. Everything is uniform, individual only to the point of complementing the other parts. The tenets of fascism are made manifest in this urban architecture – rationality, uniformity, monumentalism, rigor, imperialism – with the architectural motifs of the Roman Empire thrown in. In this way, Fascism rejected the idea of the traditional city – as a labyrinthine locus of chaos, of subversion, of secret places and narrow pathways, of confusion, of dirt, of close quarters, yes, but also of convergence, of difference, of movements.

After the Second World War, EUR was still unfinished and ravaged. In the 1950s, the quarter was cleared of rubble and ruins, and the unfinished structures were completed according to their original specifications. A new sports palace was erected. This was to prepare EUR as a site for the 1960 Rome Olympics, but the fact that it was completed after the regime fell does not detract from its ghostly, spectral quality.

As I observe my surroundings, I feel sure that Mussolini intended for these monumental constructions to one day rival the ancient marvels of the Coliseum and the Pantheon. Using architecture to convey political might to both the rest of the world and one's own populace is nothing new. Hitler used his architect, Albert Speer, Napoleon used Haussmann. The Austro-Hungarian Empire promptly constructed buildings that matched its imperial architecture in its newly acquired cities to give its empire a uniform look and remind the dominated populace of their new allegiance. Augias writes that Hitler acknowledged the importance of architecture for his regime in a 1937 interview with the architectural journal *Baubilde*. He stated: 'National Socialism . . . prefers public buildings to private ones. And as the demands the state makes on its citizens grow larger, it must in turn appear that much more powerful in their eyes.'

The Classical throwbacks – the two exedras that are now corporate headquarters for INA and INPS, and the Piazza Marconi, which is supposed to hark back to the Roman fora, are all unappealing to me. Exedra and fora are intended to be meeting places, but nobody is meeting in these places. You might point to, again, the pandemic as the reason behind their desertedness, but I maintain that it is because there is nothing inviting about them. They do what imperial architecture is meant to do – to incite fear, and remind us that the only place one can truly relax is in one's own home. When one lives under a totalitarian government, the fear is warranted. The urban fabric was used to control the populace under fascism, by erecting new buildings, altering old ones, and modifying the topography of cities through the paving of new roads, highways and piazzas, and the construction of new quarters such as this one. New buildings were carved with the dates of the year from the new fascist calendar in Roman numerals, preceded by the letters EF, for *era fascista*. These concrete works acted as material propaganda, tangible achievements that Mussolini could be photographed in front of and point to as fascist progress in the name of Italy.

Now, Rome stretches out to meet EUR, the train line leading to it uninterrupted by residential suburbs. But then, it was plonked down in the middle of open countryside, a forceful expansion of the city bounds. While countryside, the place in which E24 was built, Tre Fontane, wasn't exactly uninhabited. The households based there lived off small plots of land. Their elementary homes were said to have been similar to those huts used in Italy's colonies, and for this reason, they were disparagingly referred to as 'Abyssinian villages'. The people who lived in these huts in Tre Fontane were among the poorest and most desperate. They also reflected badly on fascism, as Italian 'civilisation' could not be seen to have so many people living within it in such an uncivilised manner. Mussolini ordered the inhabitants immediately removed.

It wasn't the first time people would be removed and dumped for being an unsightly blemish on the city. Masses of people were evicted from their homes when rent control ended in 1930, while in 1911, the entirety of the (now-stylish) area of Prati was emptied out. In the fascist 'monumentalising' of Rome, whole residential, working-class quarters were cleared out and pushed into slapped-together blockhouses at the city edges. They were the large swaths of the city that would continue to live in desperation, but they could no longer be seen, making it possible to pretend that they no longer existed.

In the historic centre, Mussolini had cleared out the areas around the Roman Forum and the Piazza Augusto Imperatore, for example. In their place, massive, wide roads, such as the via dei Fori Imperiale, which cuts through and over Imperial fora to connect Piazza Venezia and the Colosseum, were paved. These once-packed zones of the city were razed, and in their stead came strange spaces, spaces of absence perhaps, because what replaced these places where people once lived and interacted was this monumental minimalism, both stark and colossal, so favoured by Rationalist architects and so void of character or warmth. What replaced them was big empty piazzas or big empty roads that were only good for cars, or later, tourists.

The clearing of Tre Fontane for EUR also wasn't the last time a swath of families would be uprooted in the name of development. In 1960, more people were displaced in preparation for the Rome Olympics. This happens in cities all over the world, and seems to be a common consequence of 'cleaning up the city' prior to holding international events, the most obvious example being the Olympic Games. It brings to mind the eviction of two million people from their homes in Beijing in preparation for the 2008 Games, the displacement of those who lived in east London's Clay's Lane housing estate, which was demolished to make way for the 2012 Games, or, more generally, the development and gentrification of historically Aboriginal Redfern, an inner-city Sydney suburb.

EUR was supposed to decentralise the Roman centre and shift it outwards towards the sea, and in this way, it stands as a mirror site, the asymmetrical double of an unrealised parallel present. It even has its own colosseum, this one disciplined, rigid and phallic, in contrast to the feminine curves of the original. Although it was planned and built to become a bustling hub, like so many planned precincts of cities, like Melbourne's Docklands and Sydney's Darling Harbour, it never did.

Via Rasella

Via Rasella is a short street with a slight incline a five-minute walk away from Piazza Barberina. Wedged between via del Traforo and via delle Quattro Fontane, its name is thought to be a corruption of Rosella, the surname of a noble family that owned much of the property in the area. Once, families like the Rosella lived in palazzi side by side with working-class families, in a time in which one might walk through the streets and simultaneously note the brass doorknockers of rich families alongside underwear drying out of their neighbours' windows. Much like most other large cities, the centre of Rome is becoming more and more uniformly upscale, as the working and middle classes are pushed out to the periphery.

After raining for the better part of the day, the sun is beginning to make an appearance. Via Rasella is a narrow street, over which tall buildings loom and block out most of the sunlight. I had read that on via Rasella, there had been an incident between the Nazis and the partisans, and the buildings still bore the bullet holes from this occurrence. We walk down the length of the street, me checking for pockmarks in buildings, pointing to them, asking my boyfriend – is this it, do you think? Via Rasella bears the usual marks of upscale Rome: restored apartment buildings in red and yellow and umber, a boutique hotel, a café/bar or two. We walk the length of the street and turn back to check again.

This time, we find it. I wonder at how I hadn't spotted it. Set back from the street by a small piazza, it is a rust-coloured building, plaster cracking in places, grubby compared to the others, the lone one unrestored. There are no plaques or memorial markers. Now there are hotels, fancy apartment buildings with inner courtyards bearing lush gardens and fountains, restaurants. It is quiet, just a few couples strolling. The stucco façade is speckled with hundreds of small craters that reach up to the roof, some the size of a large fist, others the circumference of a plum, making it so that the building looks diseased. Left as it had been on that day, it is a testament to a time when ordinary Romans lived in the centre of the city and a standing witness to the time when the very streets of Rome were a battleground.

I'm not certain of the exact date when Rita and Salvatore fled Tripoli and sought refuge in Rome, but it is pretty safe to assume that it was sometime in January or February 1943, when the British Eighth Army took the Libyan capital on 23 January 1943. They secured an apartment for themselves and my grandmother on via Eurialo. Many refugees of war would flee to the country's capital that year, with the Allied bombings of the South rendering countless families homeless like my great-grandparents. Others fled downwards from the North, escaping conscription or round-ups. It was also the year that the north would become the 'Republic of Salò', the puppet state set up by the Nazis for Mussolini.

According to my mother, my great-grandfather was unemployed while in Rome, because he refused to sign up as a fascist member of Salò. But the Republic of Salò didn't exist until September 1943, months after they likely arrived in Rome. Did he work initially, only to be fired after the German occupation? Did he refuse to re-sign into the Fascist party when they arrived in Rome? Was he just unable to find work?

I don't know what to think of whatever association he may have had with fascism, but there is no concrete reason to think that moral scruples held him back. It's not like he didn't have experience of working for a government that was committing atrocities – he had received medals for his contribution to building Italian Libya, after all. Why would my mother or I assume that suddenly he had reached a line he could not cross, in joining a party that was still committing atrocities, now against its own citizens? It is easier to think that he didn't sign on, because it aligns with my mother's memories of him, because it allows us to shrug off any weight that his participation or belief in fascism may pass on to us. And what if he did? How to think of him?

What does it mean that there is no way of knowing? Who are these strangers who made us possible?

A black-and-white film. Roman rooftops in the background of the credits as suspenseful orchestral music plays. Soon, jarringly, the cheerful strains of German song drown out the orchestra. We hear the beat of their footsteps while a disclaimer appears on screen, warning the viewer that while the film is based on true events, it is in fact a fiction. Now we are at street level. The singing German soldiers goose-step across the screen. This is Roberto Rossellini's 1946 film *Rome, Open City*.

When the film premiered, it received international praise for its use of documentary techniques, crowned by the critic Georges Sadoul as 'a new realism'. Many scenes were shot on location in the streets of the city and in working-class apartments. The extras were locals and the cast featured amateur actors. The script itself was written a few months after the Germans left and the Allied troops had entered Rome, and the film was completed in January 1945, while northern Italy was still under German occupation. The first public screening of the film was just five months after Italy's liberation, on 25 September 1945.

The film's narrative also lends itself to this idea of capturing real life on film, playing as it does on the well-known memories of wartime. A man, the film's partisan hero, escapes a night-time raid by the Gestapo. At the Gestapo headquarters on via Tasso, moans and cries of torture punctuate the strategizing of the German Commander and the Fascist police chief.

Women raid a bakery. Characters wonder when and if the Americans will arrive, toppled buildings their only calling cards. Partisans take secret meetings with priests to deliver messages or money. The Italian characters move on foot through the city streets, under the watchful eye of the German commander, the snooping mitts of spies, the ever-looming 5 p.m. curfew, the gnawing of hunger, the constant threat of random round-ups, and the streets overrun with soldiers. Fascists walk past the wall of a palazzo, the graffiti reading 'W [Viva] Lenin', and another wall displays the hammer and sickle. As Romans riot for bread, priests eat diets of watery cabbage soup and women drink ersatz coffee, the Germans are shown in via Tasso in rooms carpeted in rich rugs, lit by ornate candelabras, decorated with beautiful paintings. They play the grand piano and cards and drink liquor, read lazily while reclined on leather couches.

A couple prepares to marry but, on their wedding day, a round-up of the men in their apartment building sees Francesco, the groom, arrested. As he is carted off with the other men in the back of a truck, in the film's most iconic scene, his bride, the pregnant widow Pina, is shot in front of both her fiancé and her son. (This scene was filmed on a street in which a similar round-up had taken place the year before, and the scene's extras were residents.) A partisan is betrayed by his girlfriend, then he and the priest helping him are taken to via Tasso, where the former is tortured to death. The latter is shot in a field, with his back to an Italian firing squad. The firing squad purposely misses, shooting at the ground, and the commanding German officer, frustrated, shoots the priest in the head himself.

The plot is based on real events that occurred during the German occupation, which were still very much alive in the minds of Italians. The priest, Don Pietro, was partly inspired by the one who blessed his fellow prisoners during the Ardeatine massacre, Don Pietro Pappagallo. Pina's death, too, was modelled on a real event, the death of Maria Teresa Gullace, a thirty-seven-year-old pregnant mother of five, shot on 2 March 1944 in front of a former military barracks in viale Giulio Cesare. Her husband had been taken there, victim of one of the German round-ups.

Despite its basis in fact, *Rome, Open City*, is far from it. The film provides a window into what Rome looked like, the camera reproducing the streets, the people, and the effects of the war as they were. But, as David Forgacs points out in his book on the film, both the film itself and the perception of the film as documentary-real are part of a collective myth. This collective myth, built around the memorialisation of Rome under the German occupation, began to take root almost as soon as the Germans were retreating from the city.

Take, for example, the other priest that Don Pietro was based on, Don Giuseppe Morosini, a military chaplain who had supplied the partisans with arms and ammunition. He was arrested after being led into a trap by a spy, and was then executed on 3 April by an Italian firing squad. The scene of Don Pietro's shooting is filmed on location, at Forte Bravetta, where Don Morosini was executed.

After Rome was liberated, newspapers commemorated Don Morosini, framing him as a martyr. In these reports, borderline miracles followed him. The Christian Democrat outlet *Il Popolo* wrote in their obituary that he had directed a school for children rendered homeless by the San Lorenzo bombings. It reported that before he was shot, he turned to his executioners, and both blessed and forgave them. Apparently, the shots fired failed to kill him, and the Italian commander had had to shoot him directly in the back of the head to finish the job.

Another commemorative article, published on the first anniversary of his death, added that, no – it wasn't that the shots failed to kill him, it was that the Italian (not German, note) firing squad actually couldn't bring themselves to kill him, and that, on discovering that they were to kill a young priest, the soldiers silently conspired and swapped looks, looks that clearly communicated that each and every officer should aim their guns above the head of Morosini and shoot into the sky.

In addition, the Italian commander did not take the decision to finish Don Morosini off on his own. It was actually a German officer, who was also present, who gave the Italian commander the signal to do so. In the span of one year, history altered and the ultimate blame for the death of Morosini shifted from the Italian Fascists to the German Nazis.

After the war, Italy was faced with the same problem that it had come up against after the Risorgimento and the Second World War. Mussolini had been executed. His body and that of his mistress Claretta Petacci were taken by truck and dumped on the ground in Milan's Piazzale Loreto. A mass gathered. The bodies were spat on, kicked, sprayed with urine, shot at and poked. The crowd jeered. A photo online shows the bodies being strung up from the gantry of a petrol station by their feet like slaughtered pigs. Hundreds of people circle them, trying to get a look.

The country was having an identity crisis. What was Italy and what did it mean to be Italian? The nation, and the people's idea of the nation, was flung into chaos, described by the historian Christopher Duggan as 'an abyss'. Into this abyss were thrown previous definitions of what 'Italy', 'nation' and 'state' meant. Everything that had gone into constructing the country for the previous eighty-odd years had been razed to nothing.

This crisis had probably been a long time coming. The identity of Italy and Italians had been a shaky subject even before Risorgimento. Duggan writes that unification had two goals: to reclaim the peninsula from foreign rulers and to 'make Italians', a famous phrase attributed to the Piedmontese statesman Massimo D'Azeglio following unification. Italians had to shed what were perceived to be vices ingrained from centuries of 'despotism and clerical rule'. They were subservient, for example, and undisciplined; they were indolent and individualistic. To this end of uniting and 'making Italians', the state, prior to fascism, had turned to war, colonisation, the institution of Italian as the national language. But the question was and would remain: what did it mean to be Italian? On what basis could an Italian national identity be formed?

From amidst this rubble, it was unclear what national narratives could be recovered. Fascism had been thrown off like a ratty coat, and everywhere the Allies were welcomed with celebrations. The divide between the North and South had widened, and the three prevailing ideologies of the resistance – communism, socialism, and Catholicism – had all had problems with one another and the concept of Italy itself. The king and Mussolini's replacement as prime minister, Badoglio, had declared a Kingdom of the South, but it was the Allied Military Government who was in actual power. Besides, there wasn't much support for the monarchy anymore. Italy was a country in a prolonged state of collective whiplash.

Rossellini's journey as a filmmaker is an apt analogy for the way in which Italy now had to quickly reinvent itself. The film made Rossellini famous as an anti-fascist director, despite the fact that, during Fascism, he had made three war features funded by the government. Born into a wealthy Roman family in 1906, he began playing around with film as a young man. He was also friends with Mussolini's son, Vittorio, who had given him the opportunity to work on the screenplay of the fascist war film *Luciano Serra, pilota*. Released in 1938, the film won the esteemed Mussolini Cup prize along with Leni Riefenstahl's film *Olympia*. It's also reportedly true that Mussolini approved of the film, whose screenplay was read to him by his son Vittorio as he shaved. Mussolini, in fact, even gave the film its name. Rossellini would later distance himself from it, and though he was credited as screenwriter, he denied association with it. At first, he also denied making the three war features, stating at the Paris opening of his film *Paisà* that *Open City* had been his first feature-length film. Later, when he began to admit to these films, he justified them by either saying that he had essentially been a puppet director, making them under the heavy hand of the fascist government, or that his financial situation had left him no choice: he couldn't find any other work. He would say that he had always been apolitical, and that his father had been a critic of fascism.

At what point does the need to work end and support for a regime begin? Does accepting government funding to make one's work as an artist automatically translate to support of that government's policies? It seems that nobody can agree on how far Rossellini's fascism went. The critics Raymond Borde and André Bouissy accused him of 'selling his soul to the regime' in order to make films. The critic Nino Frank, however, claims that 'there were never any [openly] anti-Fascist Italian filmmakers ... as everybody who wanted to work in Italy was obliged to ... hoist the insignia of the party.' Merely making films approved by the Fascist Party did not equate to belief in its policies – in fact, the Communist Party even advised its followers to 'join the Fascists to work against them from within'.

In any case, according to the film historian Peter Brunette, Rossellini would not have been allowed to make films in the way in which he desired, were he to make another kind of non-political film. Rather than being outwardly fascist, however, Fascist-era films tended to emphasise 'nationalism, patriotism, loyalty, bravery, and, above all, efficiency, especially in terms of Italy's preparedness for war'. These three war films allowed Rossellini to experiment with the neorealist techniques that he was developing. The only other opportunities for filmmaking were costume dramas, literary adaptations and melodramas, all of which were made with the intent of papering over reality rather than unveiling it. Even these seemingly non-political films had a political message: that everything was good under Fascism.

In his BFI book on the film, David Forgacs writes that Rossellini was part of a circle of fascist film lovers and makers and critics that revolved around Vittorio Mussolini, who was the editor of the influential avant-garde film journal *Cinema*, and was known as a producer and screenwriter under a pseudonym. But even Rossellini's relationship to the *Cinema* circle doesn't mean that he was a fascist. The *Cinema* group of filmmakers included Luchino Visconti, Michelangelo Antonioni, Giuseppe De Santis, and Mario Alicata, among others. Alicata, in fact, was a prominent member of the clandestine Italian Communist Party, as were other figures in the circle. Vittorio Mussolini's presence meant that the group was actually able to publish more subversive articles that went either unnoticed or ignored by the censors. (Vittorio Mussolini would later say that he had no idea of the anti-fascist ideologies of the group.)

This is not to suggest that Rossellini was committed to dismantling the dictatorship subversively. Brunette conjectures that for Rossellini, the Fascist government was simply a given. He was sixteen during the March on Rome – to him, fascism wasn't right or wrong, it simply was the system under which he had lived for his entire adult life. This is not to suggest that he did not have a sincere change of heart. Rossellini was about to start shooting a new film in the countryside when the San Lorenzo bombings took place. Shortly after, he abandoned his cast and crew and left the project. He returned to Rome and immersed himself in anti-fascist circles. It was perhaps only during the Nazi-Fascist occupation of Rome that most apolitical Romans, including Rossellini, became politicised.

It was becoming evident that the war was razing the old Italy to the ground, and in its place a new, democratic Italy would bloom. Rossellini had to, as Forgacs puts it, 'relegitimate' himself. This meant making a project that would redeem Italians and provide them with a new national myth on which the democratic Italian identity could be built. It would replace the shame of having endured Mussolini's dictatorship and the atrocities committed in the name of the nation with a sense of national pride. In essence, he was creating history while it was still happening, so that Italians could quickly start feeling Italian.

In *Open City*, the Italian Fascists are passive actors, puppets manoeuvred by the Germans. One scene shows the German commander slipping up and 'forbidding' the Italian police captain to arrest Manfredi before he corrects himself. The Italian Fascists are not the ones in charge – it is the Nazis who are the real evil. It wasn't just the film making this case – Don Morosini went from being executed by a Fascist firing squad on the orders of a Fascist officer, to being executed, begrudgingly, on German orders.

While the Nazis were undoubtedly in control and higher up on the totem pole than the Italians, Italian Fascists were not completely powerless or without autonomy. They had their own torturers and interrogators. However hesitant narratives want to render them, the SS was still assisted by Italians in drawing up lists of Jewish residents to be deported to Auschwitz.

There are so many still-prevalent myths about this period in Italy. One is the idea that Italians were and are not inherently racist, and that the 1938 anti-Semitic Racial Laws were only put in place because of Mussolini's pact with Hitler. But racism was fundamental to fascism and *romanità*. According to Mussolini, the ancient Romans 'were incredible racists', and the Roman

Republic's defining struggle was the question of the Roman race mixing and living among other races. The Racial Laws meant that Italy was finally, after millennia, dealing with 'the racial problem' that had been its predecessor's downfall. These laws barred Jewish children from schools, Jewish people from most forms of employment, and marriages between Jewish Italians and non-Jewish Italians, among other racist discriminations. (There is no evidence or other claim of a connection between 'a racial problem' and ancient Romans, and Mussolini's insistence that there was one was an indication, according to the historian Jan Nelis, that Mussolini was losing his grasp on reality. He had become incapable of separating what was fact from what was myth of his own making.)

Rossellini's Rome is populated by an Italian people united against the Nazis. They listen to *Radio Londra*, read outlawed copies of clandestine newspapers, furtively insult the Germans to their faces, and assist the partisans. The people all hate and fear the Germans. While it is true that there was widespread fear of the Nazis among Romans, civilian solidarity with the partisans, and many non-Jewish Romans attempted to obstruct the arrests of their Jewish neighbours, this wasn't the whole picture. There were also spies among civilian Italians, and people who turned in Roman Jews to the police in exchange for cash rewards.

Open City was made using documentary-filmmaking techniques, and in keeping with that medium it may be based on true events, but it still selects and presents them from a certain point of view. Myths are shaped by real events, parables and fictions, which are woven together in a particular way to form the accepted narrative. Just like family myths, national myths belong to a shared consciousness, and in the act of remembering we strengthen our own sense of belonging

When the film was screened, to an Italian audience that was still reeling from the war, the question in the minds of most Italians was likely: how to move forward? Most people had been left with nothing. At one point in the film, Pina tells the priest Don Pietro that she has sold everything to subsist. 'Life keeps getting harder,' she tells him. 'Who will help us to forget all these sufferances, these anxieties, these fears? Doesn't Christ see us?' These were questions on the minds of Italians, and in a sense, the film was proposing a response.

This national patriotic myth was played out not just in *Rome, Open City*, but in many other neorealist films, literature, memoirs and records of the resistance. Myths arise when they are needed – when we need an explanation for the world around us, or a model for our collective values, or perhaps when we need a common narrative to tie us together. Perhaps we need them to give us the strength to go on. In another scene, Francesco, the publisher of an underground newspaper, comforts Pina. His words of reassurance seem directed towards the audience. He says:

We mustn't be afraid, neither today, nor in the future. Because we are in the right – we are on the right path. We're fighting for something that must come, that can't not come. Maybe the road will be long and hard, but we'll get there – and we'll see a better world. And above all, our children will see it.

What to do with the experience of war after it has been lived, what to do with the memories that settle, the whiplash that occurs? The Rome shown in *Open City* and the heroism of the Italian resistance movement are not in and of themselves myths, but they were used to feed the need for a national narrative that could guide Italians out of the confusion and rubble, and give them not just hope, but trust in the changes that were to come.

In the first half of 1943, he was still in power, but Mussolini's mind, it seemed, was elsewhere. He was preoccupied with a panoply of physical ailments, including stomach pain and insomnia. His distractions from these were Clara Petacci and miniscule administrative details, which he obsessed over. These details included, for example, what opera was best for the Rome season, or his German translation of Alessandro Manzoni's novel,

The Betrothed. He was likened to a somnambulist, unaware of and uninterested in what was going on around him. The Germans, noticing this, made a plan for taking over the peninsula should the Fascist regime collapse.

When the British and American troops landed in Sicily on 10 July 1943, most of the three hundred thousand Italian troops stationed in Sicily fell back, abandoning the fight to the Germans. At the Museum of the Liberation of Rome, posters that were circulated after the Allies took Sicily in June of 1943 are displayed. One red satirical poster reads: 'Kicked out of Sicily, let's kick him out of Italy!' Next to it another poster has a cartoon Hitler dangling off the butt of a rifle over Sicily and southern Italy. Blood drips from his hands. 'Germans out!' it reads. Another bears the headline: AVE CAESAR! In this one Mussolini is a marionette speaking from a balcony, as a giant Hitler manoeuvres him. Yet another pamphlet communicates that Sicily has been the first metropolitan territory in Italy to be liberated and encourages the reader to embrace and support the Allies as the Sicilians have.

My family had expected to finally find refuge from the war in Rome, but misfortune seemed to follow them. On 19 July 1943 at 11:03 in the morning, Rome was finally bombed, contrary to the assumption that it would be spared due to its cultural and religious patrimony. The job was carried out by seven hundred American planes coming from North Africa and the Middle East, which dropped around a thousand tonnes of bombs on San Lorenzo and Littorio, an inner-city quarter and a small airport in the city's north, respectively.

Fascist leaders in Rome conspired to overthrow Mussolini, hoping to negotiate with the Allies. The King, wanting to keep his crown, was forming a similar plan. Two weeks after the Allied landing on Sicily, the Grand Fascist Council met in Rome, where it was decided by vote that the king should execute his military powers and axe Mussolini. Mussolini bitterly commented on his ousting by spitting that 'Italians are not Romans'. He had tried to make and elevate Italians to the heights of their Roman forebears, but they had failed. He was disappointed with the apparent inability of the Italian people to live up to the greatness of their ancestors. Never mind that this link between Italians and Romans was an invention of political rhetoric, one that he himself had dreamed up.

There were celebrations at the news, though they were tempered by the fact that Badoglio, who we might remember as the Governor of Tripolitania and Cyrenaica, had stated that Italy would continue in the war alongside Germany. Notably, there were no real protests anywhere in the country against the sacking of the man who had plastered his face all over Italy for two decades.

Rome was declared an open city on 14 August 1943, a day after it was bombed a second time. 'Open city' is a military term, meaning that no armed forces can operate within a city's jurisdiction, whether for strategic warfare, resources, or the development or transit of war materials or troops. No military government can declare a seat there. (Cairo and Athens were also designated open cities in this sense.) A *Morning Bulletin* article explains the concept to its readers, quoting the Press Association:

> This means that Rome will be unable to make further contributions of any kind to the Italian war effort or of Italy's prosecution of the war. All barracks must be emptied, troops sent away, government offices connected with hostilities must be removed, munition factories, of which there are many in Rome and its environs, must be closed, military aerodromes in the area must be evacuated, and railway stations and railway lines running through the city must not be used for military purposes.

In the weeks after Badoglio took over as prime minister, he and other senior generals secretly underwent negotiations with the Allies outlining Italy's terms of surrender. Although the Allies had taken Sicily, they still weren't ready to invade the mainland. At the announcement of Mussolini's dismissal, and the celebrations by the people in response to it, German troops began assembling at Italy's border, preparing to invade. The Allies would require support from the Italian army, navy and air force, who, Badoglio promised in an armistice on 3 September 1943, would secure all Italian airfields and ports, and would be pledged in service against the Germans. When news of the armistice was revealed to the public on 8 September 1943, first by Eisenhower and then by Badoglio, nobody wanted to take charge, neither Badoglio nor Victor Emmanuel.

The only direction given to the effectively abandoned military was a directive by Badoglio advising the troops to retaliate if they found themselves attacked. None of the ports or airfields were secured. That night, the royal family, members of the government including Badoglio, and the most important members of the Supreme Command, gathered at the Ministry of War for a meeting. The next day, on 9 September, they absconded from Rome and escaped to Brindisi, a southern city under Allied control. There, they declared a Kingdom of the South. The Italian army, the city of Rome, and the rest of the country was effectively abandoned to the Germans.

German troops swiftly swarmed northern and central Italy. Throughout Europe, the Italian army was either massacred by the Nazis or deported to Germany to undertake slave labour. Those who escaped either fled to the south of Italy or returned to their homes, gathered their weapons, and went to join the closest unit of partisan resistance fighters. In Rome, political and civil authority remained officially with the Italian Fascists, but in reality they now answered to and took orders from the Germans. Italy was an 'occupied ally'.

On 12 September, a unit of Nazi paratroops freed Mussolini by landing on Gran Sasso with helicopters. Over the radio, Mussolini declared the North of Italy to be the Italian Social Republic (RSI), with himself as the leader, though he was effectively a puppet manoeuvred by Hitler. It became known as the Republic of Salò, for the small town on the shore of Lake Garda where the RSI had its headquarters.

The term 'open city' had also been used in the Italian wording of the surrender agreement signed with the Germans at Frascati on 10 September 1943, after Italian troops had failed to halt their advance on Rome. The Germans had agreed to occupy only their own embassy, radio station and the telephone exchange and to keep troops outside the city limits. The agreement was broken almost immediately. The next day, on 11 September, Field Marshal Albert Kesselring, the commander of the southern front, proclaimed himself head of southern and central Italy, which was now considered a warzone in its entirety. All Italian soldiers and civilians present in Rome were ordered to surrender their weapons (although very few actually did).

The next day, the first of what would be countless ordinances and manifestos papered the city walls. It included a series of decrees, in both German and Italian, which made clear that Italy was now a warzone, subject to German laws of war. The manifesto prohibited strikes and stipulated that all 'organisers' would be judged by the German War Tribunal, with execution by shooting as punishment. Private correspondence was now forbidden, and telephone conversations would be supervised. The city's military headquarters were occupied by German paratroopers. Another ordinance on 2 October banned listening to any radio broadcast that was not fascist or German. In light of these events, the expression 'open city' took on an ironic tone.

The two open city declarations – the one made on 14 August and the one on 10 September – could only be effectively binding if both the Allies and the Axis recognised and respected them. Neither did. During their occupation, the Germans used Rome as a hub for the military convoys between the North and South of Italy, and the Allies continued to bomb Rome. Rome was bombed several times every month without fail from October 1943 until March 1944, and the bombings didn't stop until June 1944. Most of the damage was done to homes and public services, with the total death count from September 1943 until June 1944 reaching four thousand. There were over nine thousand injured. The attacking of railways and roads meant that the supply lines to the city were cut, making it more difficult to access food and basic necessities, such as medicine or soap. Three hundred thousand people and soldiers were displaced, while a hundred and fifty thousand refugees from the South flooded into the city.

The national liberation movement that was developed against the Nazi-Fascists in September 1943 was the *Comitato di Liberazione Nazionale* (CLN). It was formed by a coalition of six anti-fascist parties, consisting of the Communists, the Action Party, the Socialists, the Christian Democrats, the Labour Democrats and the Liberals. Partisan units conducted armed resistance, operating in both the cities and countryside carrying out guerrilla actions, like public protests, factory strikes, street combat and ambushes.

In the days following my visit to via Rasella, I learn more about the attack in books and museums. It happened on 23 March 1944, involving a regiment of Nazi soldiers and a group of ten partisans from the *Gruppi di Azione Patriottica*, the Patriotic Action Group (GAP). Via Rasella was part of the daily route that the Eleventh Company of the SS Regiment Bozen took on their way from their morning shooting training to the Interior Ministry. Returning from their training at a shooting range at Tor di Quinto, they would turn left off via del Traforo and march up via Rasella to via delle Quattro Fontane. There were 156 men in the company, accompanied by cars armed with machine guns. These men, donning berets that bore the metal skull of the SS, would march down the street each afternoon at two o'clock. They were a noisy group. Their presence was heralded by the loud clacking of their steel-heeled boots across the cobblestones, coupled with their singing. They sang as they marched not out of spontaneity, but on order, to intimidate civilians.

It was 23 March 1944, and the next day the battalion would be going on active duty. Seeing as this regimented movement of theirs was well-known and established, it made them an ideal target for the GAP. The plan was for eighteen kilos of TNT to be concealed in a street-sweeper's rubbish cart. The cart would be placed in the middle of the road, so that as the soldiers surrounded it on their way through, it would explode right in the middle of them. Precisely forty-five seconds after the soldiers passed by, the fuse to the explosives would be lit by the pipe of a partisan medical student named Rosario Bentivegna, disguised as a municipal street-cleaner. His girlfriend Carla Capponi would be waiting for him at the top of the street, ready to throw a raincoat over his shoulders to disguise him. Immediately following the explosion, the plan was for more partisans to burst out and spatter the soldiers with hand grenades.

While the battalion's usual route was always followed to the letter, the partisans were not counting on the fact that 23 March would be an exception. It was a Thursday, the Fascist Party's twenty-fifth anniversary of its founding in 1919. The battalion stayed longer at the firing range that day. The partisans, who had taken their positions, waited and waited. They wandered around, pretending to read newspapers or inspect the posters that papered the buildings, but staying too long in one place would invariably arouse suspicion. Complicating the matter was the fact that they were all armed, with machine guns and hand grenades, no less. If they happened to be searched, the punishment was death on the spot. Over an hour passed. They considered postponing the attack, but the street-sweeper's cart was too heavy to take back to its hiding place, and they couldn't leave it there. After nearly an hour and a half of waiting, the group was about to abandon the operation, when the clacking of the steel heels and the Germanic chorus of the soldiers was heard. This particular afternoon, their song of choice was a merry tune called *Hupf, mein Mädel* (Turn, My Darling). As they turned down the street, their long shadows preceded them. Bentivegna lit the fuse with his pipe and walked to where Capponi awaited him, as discreetly as possible. It was 3:45 p.m. when the TNT exploded.

By all accounts, the explosion was so massive that it was heard throughout Rome, so loud that my grandmother probably heard it on the other side of the city. The foundations of the apartment buildings on and around via Rasella most likely trembled, or perhaps swayed like Mediterranean cypresses in the wind. Pictures would have fallen from walls, crockery slipped and shattered on the floor, vases tipped and spilt flowers and water, jewellery boxes spilled, and a ring, a family heirloom, rolled under a bed and wedged itself into a dusty crack. At 3:45 p.m., most people were probably taking a nap, or doing their ironing, knitting, or reading. Perhaps someone had just made coffee and was raising the steaming espresso cup to their lips right before it spilled all over them and scalded their chin and chest.

The explosion instantly tore apart the bodies of twenty-four soldiers. The partisans flung their grenades at the men left standing and fled. Twenty-six of the SS soldiers were killed and some of the sixty wounded would go on to die. The Nazis, thinking that the attack had come from above, swiftly opened fire on the apartment windows above them, producing the scattering of bullet-holes that now memorialise the incident. Six civilians were killed, four by the German soldiers and two by, mostly likely, the explosion.

In response, the Nazis raided all the apartments in the area, forcibly entering by breaking down doors. Two hundred and fifty civilians were either dragged from their homes, or off the street if they happened to be passing, and lined up at Piazza Barberini. A snapshot on the Fosse Ardeatine website shows a line-up of people backed up against a wall with their hands on their heads. They wear coats on what would have been a chilly spring afternoon. Soldiers point at them with rifles.

Museum of the Liberation of Rome

Via Tasso, 145, the faded peach-yellow building that now houses the Museum of the Liberation of Rome, is about a half-hour's walk away from via Rasella. It's another brief street with a slight incline, less glitzy then via Rasella, in a residential and otherwise nondescript sector of Rome. The address in question is a stout 1930s apartment building, which at the time belonged to Prince Francesco Ruspoli, who had rented it to the German embassy's cultural office in 1939. After the Germans began their occupation of Rome, the SS turned it into a prison, converting the once-residential rooms into cells, interrogation rooms and offices. Next door, via Tasso, 155, identical to its neighbour and connected to it via two adjoining corridors, was used as lodging for military officers, storage and office space.

I can now walk up via Tasso and enter the building freely, but when my grandmother lived in Rome, all the adjacent streets were blocked-off by cavalry and armed men. One could only pass the building on via Tasso from the opposite side of the street in single file, and the building itself was guarded by SS officers armed with machine guns. Nobody could see inside: all windows that weren't bricked up had their blinds permanently shuttered. But I imagine that anyone walking nearby would have strained their ears to hear a tell-tale scream or yelp or gunshot coming from that ominous building.

My grandmother never mentioned the name 'via Tasso', but an ex-prisoner, in the memoir of his incarceration there, writes that it was a street and a building that everyone in Rome, no matter their connection to the Resistance, knew. It occupied territory in the city's collective consciousness, shrouded in sinister silence. There, everybody knew, people were disappeared, subjected to unimaginable tortures and depraved deaths. So much so that it transcended the material realm and became a concept, a metaphor, a name nobody dared to utter, simply referring to it as 'there, at San Giovanni' (the name of the piazza nearby).

I walk up a few steps and turn right through a door that opens onto a small reception area: a wooden desk on one side, where an old man takes my temperature. He directs me to proceed with the audio tour upstairs.

The museum is small, housed on three different floors, along with the reception area on the first floor. The building had been housing for the petit-bourgeoisie, and each floor constituted one identical apartment. I walk into a small entrance, off which open five rooms of varying modest sizes, originally intended as three rooms (two smaller for sleeping, one larger for lounging), a kitchen, and a bathroom.

I imagine that my family's apartment had a similar structure to it. It was bare, with bits of furniture my great-grandfather had managed to scrounge, rotting wooden stools and crates for chairs, a wonky table, mattresses thrown on the floor for beds. Or perhaps the apartment had been taken from another family, one that had escaped to the countryside, and the apartment was filled with their furniture, couches and beds which still smelled like them, brushes in which their hair was still tangled, their pots and pans and their family pictures framed on the walls.

The floor is the same speckled linoleum it was then. The first room is bare. Inside, on a wall, a film reel is being projected. On the reel, clouds of smoke billow out of apartment buildings, in gusts so big that it looks like a nuclear bomb explosion. The smoke then billows out of more urban apartment buildings, the countryside, factories. Over the parasol pines seen through one of the ancient city doors. It wafts out over the city skyline.

The camera pans over piles of knocked-down cinderblocks and rubble. An apartment building halved and sizzling, what were once the top floors spewed onto the ground in front of it, a group of people in front surveying the damage, perhaps scavenging for survivors or the bodies of victims. A body being ushered on a stretcher into a Red Cross tent. Hordes of people walking along tram tracks. A man standing next to derailed and bent tram tracks, a blown-out skeleton of a car.

People walk down streets, passing bombed-out buildings, huge craters in the roads. Entire city blocks reduced to piles of rubble, palazzi with a large bite taken out of them, or with a cross-section cut out, so that one can see all the material inside: the structural beams, the sagging floors and ceilings. Someone's French shutters have blown onto someone else's balcony, and someone else's entire home is made visible by the collapsing of a wall.

Other palazzi look as though they've been flattened by a giant hand. Ancient porticoes are chipped and surrounded by the rubble of other ancient porticoes. Shrines are stacked against the detritus. A never-ending crowd clamours around the Pope.

The city skyline again, now clouds of smoke bloom and disperse, like thick grey fireworks, or the simultaneous eruptions of a row of volcanoes. The camera surveys blown-out glass windows, curtains reduced to rags and dangling feebly out of them, the destruction and damage of historic edifices and structures. An aerial shot, big splotches or growths flowering over the city.

I assume that the splotches and bombed-out buildings and rubble in the film reel is of the San Lorenzo bombing, the first major inner-city bombing of Rome. The objective in San Lorenzo, a residential area, was to hit the freight yard. After the first round of bombs, the second round were ordered to aim for the clouds of dust, smoke and fire that had arisen. These clouds, however, grew and grew, resulting in bomb clusters being dropped five-hundred metres away from their target.

It recalls a scene in Elsa Morante's novel *History*, in which the protagonist and her young son are out running errands when the San Lorenzo raid occurs, and return home to find that a bomb has been dropped through their apartment. In the book, the sky seems to hum, before releasing thunder. The buildings around them begin to crumple, and the ground see-saws.

In the aftermath, Ida and her son walk past a dead horse, the lopped limbs of destroyed statues and glass shards littering the ground. A crowd forms, names are screamed, some people are covered in blood. She returns to her apartment building to find that in place of her home there are now only piles of dust. Morante writes that:

> Below, some howling or mute forms roamed among the refuse. No moan rose; beneath, they must all be dead. But some of those forms, driven by an idiot mechanism, were rummaging or scratching with their fingernails at those piles, searching for someone or something to save.

The film reel continues: living rooms whose bookshelves have collapsed onto the floor, dining tables broken to bits, empty hospital beds blanketed in ceiling, walls strewn with bullet holes, streets smothered with bits of what were once homes. The pews of a church reduced to tinder.

Queen Margherita, in a hat, polka dot dress, and gloves, surveys the damage, flocked by her entourage. She murmurs condolences, clutches anonymous hands reaching out from amidst the crowd. In the end, the whole quarter was cratered. Four thousand bombs were dropped on the districts of San Lorenzo, Prenestino, Tiburtino and Tuscolano. Three thousand people were killed and eleven thousand were injured. Ten thousand homes were demolished and forty thousand people found themselves suddenly homeless. These bombings were the first of fifty-one that would fall on Rome.

Although Annalisa and her parents didn't live in San Lorenzo, they were a walkable distance from it. Annalisa and Rita would have been at their schools, while Salvatore may have been out, perhaps waiting in line somewhere to exchange ration cards for a meagre portion of bread. The school buildings shook and the footpath tremored. Sounds like thunder claps. I wonder what steps Rita took to calm her class down, whether she let her students go home to check on their parents. I like to think that all three dashed back home once the dust had cleared, drawing three separate lines that wound through the narrow city streets and converged on their apartment, rushing past all the other

Romans hurrying home, and that when they got there, all at the same time, they embraced one another.

Exhibits cover the walls, showing Rome as it was during the years of the war, up until Liberation. The rooms are similar to how they were kept then: bare, shabby, with thin barred openings above the doorways, around which the paint peels. These lead on to the small entrance room and were the only source of fresh air, which, as an ex-prisoner wrote, entered in small gusts whenever the door to the apartment was opened. To be able to perceive such a slight change of air must mean that the air in the cells was thick with human stench – the kind of rancidness that makes one's eyes sting. The kind of air that feels as though it's too dense to fully take into one's lungs.

In a room that was once a kitchen, judging by the range hood still attached to a wall on one side and a marble sink on the other and the pale blue wall tiles, a thin, still-half-bricked-up window lets in a sliver of light and looks on to what seems like a school building outside.

Behind a glass case, the museum has placed the scraps of clothing recovered from the body of Colonel Montezemolo in the Ardeatine Caves. A rectangle of a white cotton shirt. The pocket from his jacket. One scrap is embroidered with his initials – perhaps his handkerchief.

Another, larger room is still papered in the lush wallpaper that covered it before the Nazis took the building. This one is again plastered with photos and newspaper cuttings. In a glass case mounted on the wall, the blood-stained shirt, white and crumpled, of Professor Gioacchino Gesmundo, again from the Ardeatine Caves. A collection of items under glass, found on the body of the partisan opera singer Nicola Ugo Stame: a pitch pipe, an ivory crucifix, a mother of pearl Madonnina, and an ebony mouthpiece. There is a pocket watch with the glass smashed, recovered from the body of Otello di Peppe.

Sometimes the interrogation had been so intense that the prisoner in question would return to the cell unrecognisable, their face tenderised. Missing teeth or fingernails. Other times they were brought back unconscious, transported by four officers and covered in a blanket. The officers would lay the prisoner down in the room and unveil them to the others, in a sort of 'macabre exhibition'. I imagine how the walls would have been greasy from their skin oils, how their clothing would have been constantly damp with sweat and their heads itchy with dandruff and dirt.

Another room, Cell No. 2 on the second floor, is windowless and small as a tomb. Once a bathroom, this room was used for solitary confinement. Arrigo Paladini, a historian who would go on to become the director of the Liberation Museum, was kept here for a month, from his arrest on 4 May 1944, until Rome's liberation on 4 June. He was arrested, tortured, and sentenced to death for taking part in partisan activities. Then, it was a black, airless room, where the scratched-out scrawls of previous prisoners could be felt under his fingertips. On his escorted trips to the toilet, he had the opportunity to see other prisoners – some could not hold themselves upright and had to use the wall to help themselves along, others were skeletal, their faces partly a 'cadaverous' white, partly 'swollen and black' from beatings. There was no bed, and Paladini slept huddled on the bare floor.

Now glass covers the walls to preserve the writings scratched onto them: prayers, messages of encouragement, drawings, song lyrics, accusations, warnings, last wishes, calendars. There is a rough drawing of a crucifix. A message of encouragement to future prisoners reads:

Love Italy more than you love yourself, more than the realm of your beloved, more than life itself and more than your dear ones, beyond limits, and with unshakable faith in its destiny. Only then death will find you in peace, without regrets as the martyrs gone before you.

An accusation naming a spy perhaps: *IT WAS ROMANI*. A warning to be wary of an agent, 'Coniglio'. *Chi cade per la patria vivrà in eterno* (those who die for the homeland live for eternity) and *VIVA L'ITALIA*. Final farewell messages to lovers, quotations from Dante and Petrarch. Messages in Greek, Latin, and English.

The exhibits reproduce newspaper headlines, front pages and clippings, ordinances, pamphlets and snapshots, telegrams from those years. They convey one of the principal concerns of the period: hunger. There are newspaper clippings of bread strikes and protests. Behind another display case is a cardboard ration card that looks like a bingo card with its grid of numbers. There are photos of thick queues of people lined up outside a bakery, which the caption tells me had people lining up for hours.

Food rations allocated to individual adults added up to barely a thousand daily calories. People who had money to spare spent it on the black market, where prices for ordinary things ballooned. In the spring of 1943, for example, the price of eggs on the black market went for fifteen times the recommended price. Like in most other European cities, cats had by now disappeared from their usual haunts: the ruins and the streets. A leaflet from Communist Women for Bread and Peace, dated March 1944, informs us that the bread ration was reduced to a meagre fifty grams a day per citizen. The bread in question was black with mould, mixed with sawdust. There were protests from Roman women outside bakeries, many of whom were shot.

The flurry of communiques, posters, and ordinances would have plastered the city walls and set the tone for those nine months of occupation in Rome. In sparse bureaucratic language, they impose new rules, regulations, and orders. A communiqué reads, in both Italian and German:

On 22 October 1943, Italian civilians who were part of a communist gang shot at German troops. They were taken prisoner after a quick skirmish. The military tribunal has condemned ten members of this gang to death for attacking members of the German armed forces at gunpoint. The sentence was carried out.

The Chief Commander of the German Troops.

Ordinances inform citizens of new curfews and restrictions, enforced by the death penalty. The people of Rome must keep 'calm and disciplined'. They are forbidden to drive personal vehicles or ride bikes.

Clandestine pamphlets call men, women and students to contribute to the Resistance and assist the Allies. They provide assurance that the Allies are coming to liberate Italy and instructions on how to resist the Germans while they wait. When civilians come across Allied forces, they must cooperate and obey orders, while ignoring the orders of the Germans. Railway workers should stop trains from carrying German troops or provisions, road workers should do what they can to stop German trucks from continuing on their route. Young people should not show up when they are conscripted to military duty. To circumvent any anti-American sentiment, pamphlets assure Romans that they continue to be bombed because the Germans won't respect Rome's status as an open city.

Interestingly, the image of a new Italy is already being drawn in the many pamphlets. Hope seemed to arise from the growing rubble, hope for a new utopian order. A pamphlet from the Action Party, dated 1 May 1944, is addressed to Italian 'workers, peasants, technical craftsmen, intellectuals, all workers!' It describes the current Italy as one mired in carnage and grief. However, from this 'blood work', a new Italy will rise, a . . .

> . . . free Italy . . . the Italy of democracy and work . . . Don't give up, Italian workers . . . This last May of war finds us all united and ready, the dawn of our liberation radiates from it.
> Long live the Italian workers!
> Down with Nazism and Fascism!
> Down with the reaction!
> Down with the monarchy!
> Rome, May 1, 1944.
> Action Party

There is a strange tension in the rooms of the Museum of Liberation, which now houses offices and conference rooms as well as exhibits. The rooms memorialise the atrocities committed against Roman Jews, the massacres of Forte Bravetta, Fosse Ardeatine, and via Rasella. As faithful as the museum is to these past events and atrocities, the structure of the museum and the banal office space seems to sanitise, if not the events, then the physical space in which they happened. In a building that was once cloaked in fear and obfuscation, guarded by cavalry and armed guards, the nerve centre for the Nazi surveillance of Rome, one can now walk in freely, the ticket price an optional donation.

The display cases preserve objects from the past, such as the four-pointed nails used by the partisans to puncture the tyres of Nazi-Fascist vehicles and the muddied handkerchiefs procured from the pockets of the dead in the Ardeatine Caves, but they are under a physical barrier of glass. We can't feel the rust on the nails or smell the dirt from the caves. The glass reminds us – or at least makes us feel that – these events are history. Likewise, when the museum was established, only parts of the bricked-up windows were removed, in order to leave some impression of the rooms' prior darkness.

It makes sense, however, to repurpose via Tasso in this way, dedicating it to the memory of the partisans who were tortured and slaughtered in these very rooms. After an event like a dictatorship, the question arises of what to do with its material constructions and the memories they house. These buildings in which atrocities happened become, in a sense, timeless spaces, voids, in which no future events can happen. The space itself becomes haunted, in the sense that it cannot (and should not) let the past go. It's not as though they could revert via Tasso back to its original residential use, after all. Now, it teaches us how to remember, provides a blueprint of how to consider the past.

The Australian Consulate

The Australian Consulate is housed in a large, white, slightly Moorish villa in Rome's upscale, residential Nomentano, a quiet quarter of villas and public parks and neat piazzas. The villa in question is set back from the road and heavily gated. In the garden are palms and parasol pines. I have always tended to think that embassies and consulates are sorts of havens to the citizens they represent, so far away from home, but the Australian Consulate in Rome seems to not conform to this idea. To enter, one must have an appointment and state one's name and appointment number at the buzzer, where a disembodied Italian voice will decide whether or not to open the automatic gate. I already know I am not getting in, but I try anyway, explaining that I only need to drop off a document, and am summarily turned away.

I return to my rented apartment. I send emails explaining my situation, and I receive a response saying that if I want to renew my passport then I need an in-person appointment, and if I want an in-person appointment, then I will need to come back to Rome (or Milan, as it is suggested to me, the heart of COVID in Italy) in no less than three months. I am addressed as 'Mr. Gacioppo' or, after I have corrected the faceless email composer, I am not addressed at all. I am informed that due to a 2015 law, all overseas passport applications must be lodged in person, and the policy at the Australian consulates is that all in-person contact must be by appointment only, and that, again, the closest opening for an appointment is three months away. I curse the person penning the missives. I harbour suspicions that because of my surname, whoever is writing to me (who I have not informed of my dual citizenship) believes that I am an Italian who has recently acquired Australian citizenship, and not Australian-born.

I am incredibly indignant for someone who didn't bother to read the instructions. I still don't have a valid Australian passport.

I suppose if I didn't have an Italian passport already, I would feel more panicked, rather than simply frustrated. Obtaining my Italian passport was easier and quicker than renewing my Australian one: I stopped by the Italian Consulate in Sydney during their opening hours, a man behind a desk went through some files until he found mine, I gave him my passport photo and paid a modest fee, and I picked up my passport a few days later. It's strange to think that if I didn't have my Italian passport, in Italy I would be considered a migrant, or at the very least an expat. It's not so easy for Italians born in Italy to non-Italian parents, or for Italians who migrated to Italy when they were young, and grew up there, unlike me.

Earlier that year, I was attending a Black Lives Matter rally in Trieste's seaside Piazza Unità. There were about a hundred of us in the piazza, a decent turnout for such a conservative city. The crowd was mostly made up of young Afro-Italians and their white and Asian friends, and a few families and older people. People held up meticulously crafted signs, with messages in glitter pen and marker and paint. They read:

BLACK LIVES MATTER
MIGRANT LIVES MATTER

True to Italy's historical discomfort with the capitalist system, some targeted global capitalism, the economic system which does not just breed, but relies on structural inequality. The signs recognised the inextricable ties between capitalism, wealth inequality and racism. Two young Afro-Italian guys each held a sign:

IT AIN'T A RIOT,
IT'S A REVOLUTION

And:

YOU CAN'T HAVE CAPITALISM
WITHOUT RACISM

At the bottom of each sign was the web address for (what I learn) is an Italian Marxist group. The signs and the speeches that evening were indicative of what was happening in the rest of Italy. After the initial shock of witnessing the broadcast of George Floyd's murder by a policeman, it seemed that many white people in other countries, like Italy and Australia, had initially reassured themselves that violent racism and police brutality were American problems. Migrant Italians encouraged Italy to turn its gaze inward, as did Indigenous Australians in Australia. Racist violence and discrimination happen in our country too, the newspaper articles and the rallies were saying. We too endure under a system which works actively against us.

After a troop of dancers had performed a dance to the beat of drums, a Moroccan-Italian woman in her twenties took the microphone and addressed the crowd. Most of the discussions that evening had centred around the issue of citizenship, particularly of Italians born in Italy to migrant parents. She described the process of attaining citizenship in the country in which she was born, for which she was only eligible at the age of eighteen, the paperwork and the visits to the *Questura* (police headquarters). She stated that, walking out of the *Questura* clutching her hard-won citizenship papers in her hands, she had expected to feel exuberant, but instead she thought to herself *'siamo piu carta che carne'*: we are made more of paper than flesh.

It was through a turn of luck and good timing that I found myself in possession of two passports, two citizenships, and I was preoccupied by how something so seemingly fundamental could be granted so arbitrarily. I decided to get in touch with the movement *Italiani Senza Cittadinanza* (Italians Without Citizenship). After exchanging many messages on Facebook, I was put in touch with a journalist named Paula BaudetVivanco. We were supposed to meet while I was in Rome, but on the day we had scheduled, a classmate of her daughter tested positive for the virus. All the students and their families were required to sequester themselves for two weeks. We arranged to chat over Zoom instead.

Paula is in her forties, with short brown hair that frames her face. A bright red scarf is slung around her neck. She came to Italy at the age of seven. Her parents were political dissidents under the dictatorship of Augusto Pinochet Ugarte. They took her and her eleven-year-old brother with them as they fled from Chile to Italy. The family was already under scrutiny – her uncles had been political activists during the presidency of Salvador Allende. In Italy, she learned Italian attending school, with the help of her classmates and teachers.

Paula tells me that her parents did not ask for political asylum, which would have made for an easier process, but moved as economic migrants. This meant that not only was her youth spent facing the difficulty of growing accustomed to a new country, it was also spent on shaky ground, as her parents continually renewed their *permesso di soggiorno* (residence permit), 'at the mercy of institutions' and ever-changing laws. This difficulty, she tells me, was mitigated by her love of Italian school, her friends, her teachers, and a discovery of a love of Italian literature.

For the first fifteen years, Paula's presence in Italy was legitimised by her parents' residence permit. She was in her early twenties and working as a journalist when, at the turn of the new millennium, she was officially denied Italian citizenship.

In 1951, a few years after the adoption of the Universal Declaration of Human Rights, Hannah Arendt's first English-language book, *The Origins of Totalitarianism,* was published. In one of its central chapters, Arendt meditated on her scepticism of the notion of human rights from her experience of having been a stateless refugee. We tend to assume that human rights are and should be granted to us by way of our humanity. In Arendt's words, 'the right to have rights, or the right of every individual to belong to humanity, should be guaranteed by humanity itself'. But Arendt points out that our rights are conferred to us through our citizenship rather than our humanity. It's only as a citizen that we can enjoy the right to an education, to work, to healthcare, to vote, to life. Without citizenship, these are not rights, they are privileges.

If one's rights as a human depend on one's citizenship status, then depriving one of citizenship must therefore dehumanise them. To be deprived of citizenship is to be shunned from the world. Arendt writes that a stateless person may have more freedom of movement than an incarcerated criminal, and they may possess more freedom of speech while interned in a democratic country than a dictatorship, but the fact remains that they remain rightless. They have no right to exist. If they have a residence, it is thanks to the charity of their host country and not to their right to have it. They may be entitled to their opinion, but without the power to vote, it doesn't matter.

Our citizenship isn't just our passport into humanity, it dictates our class within humanity. Different states give different rights to their citizens. Under Chile's dictatorship, for example, Paula's parents were given neither the right to vote, nor freedom of expression. There are currently 250 million migrants living away from their homelands worldwide. Wanting to migrate, however, in order to attain a citizenship that may perhaps grant us better rights than those we have, or to escape poverty, are not considered grounds to request asylum.

Paula was denied citizenship because, at the time, she could not declare an adequate income. The fact that she had grown up in Italy did not factor into the application. What was needed was to prove that she had had a continuous and satisfactory income for three years prior to applying for citizenship and would continue to maintain that income during the two years it would take for her application to be processed. I haven't met many, or any, twenty-year-olds who could fulfil this requirement, and it seems a particularly unrealistic one in a country in which there is an employment crisis for young people. Paula tells me that the pandemic has added another layer of difficulty for young people attempting to maintain an income so that they can apply or have their citizenship applications accepted. Finally, Paula was granted citizenship at thirty-three. There is an irony in escaping a dictatorship to live in a European democracy in which one will not be allowed to vote until in one's thirties.

With others who have faced similar experiences, she founded the *Rete G2* in 2005, the network for children of migrants, or second-generation Italians. The conceptual goal of *Rete* was to feel seen by the Italian government; the material goal was to manifest change in what they saw as 'unjust laws'. In service of this, the group campaigned directly to ministers in both the House and the Senate. They went to the President of the Chamber of Deputies to explain to him that the current Italian law did not reflect the demographics of Italian society. It did not acknowledge the children of migrants, particularly those who were not born in Italy. There was no specific channel for them to claim residence or citizenship in Italy. They could have lived in Italy since they were six months old and still be treated like a recent migrant, once they came of age.

The *Rete* found support and recognition through Italian Catholic charities, such as *Caritas* and *Sant' Egidio* and *Arci*, and through the Italian unions, such as CGL. They took part in a campaign called '*L'italia sono anch'io*' (I am Italy too). The *Rete* campaigned for a direct and tailored path to citizenship to be offered to those who had migrated to Italy as children and a quicker pathway for children who had been born in Italy to migrant parents. The campaign was fundamental in leading to the approval in the House of a text that recognised their principles. It was pushed to a vote to reform the law in the Chamber in 2015. And then everything stopped. The reform remained blocked in the Senate, she says, until the new generation of Italians without citizenship came of age.

In the autumn of 2016, this new generation started a new movement, *Italiani Senza Cittadinanza*, of which she is a founder. The movement, she tells me, was born from the desire of young Italians not just to be recognised by their own country but to have the same rights as their peers. This group of young Italians without citizenship numbers at around a million to 1.5 million, many of whom are still in school. They spend their school years learning about the Italian Constitution and the rights of Italian citizens through their curriculum, and when they come of age they realise that they are excluded from these rights. Capitalising on her journalist credentials and contacts, Paula acts as the media liaison for this movement.

One of their campaigns was called *Cartoline Cittadine* or 'citizen postcards'. It involved publishing photographs of the movements' members as children in Italy, which made the front page of one of Italy's major national newspapers, *La Repubblica*. Later, I google '*cartoline cittadine*'. The 'postcards' feature photos of children alone or in class photos wearing the smocks that Italian children wear to school. Alongside the photo is a brief biography. I find Paula, wearing the navy smock with a white Peter Pan collar emblematic of Italian schooling, her hair in a short bob pushed back by a headband. She is posed in front of a waxy green bush. The text next to her portrait reads that it was taken on her first day of school in Rome.

Another card shows a class picture of a little girl named Marwa in a green dress, smiling and surrounded by her classmates. She writes that she had to wait twenty-three years until she could celebrate her Italian citizenship. Until that day, she often felt a strange sensation. It was a generalised anxiety in which every day was a test that continued to be postponed. It was a sensation that 'alienates you and renders you different from your classmates', one that won't end until 'you officially belong to your country, Italy'. Other 'postcard citizens' still don't have Italian citizenship. Younes is a twenty-two-year-old university student from Naples who still can't vote, despite being passionate about Italian politics. Nor can Chouaib, a twenty-two-year-old from Treviso who arrived in Italy as a baby. The cards serve to put a face to over a million young Italians without citizenship. Each card notes the school that the individual attended. None of the cards that I see online note a country of origin, probably deliberately. It doesn't matter where we came from, the cards seem to say. We are here now, we were raised by Italy, and here is the proof.

The movement also staged flash mobs in various cities. I search for these on Instagram and come up with the *#fantasmiperlegge* (Ghosts by Law) campaign. A group of 'ghosts' in a piazza wearing white sheets with eye holes cut out, like a Halloween costume. Someone holds up a poster that cites Article 3 of the Italian Constitution:

All citizens have equal social dignity and are equal before the law, without distinction of sex, race, language, religion, political opinion, personal and social conditions.

It is the duty of the Republic to remove those obstacles of an economic or social nature which constrain the freedom and equality of citizens, thereby impeding the full development of the human person and the effective participation of all workers in the political, economic and social organisation of the country.

The problem is that while the writers foresaw a need to protect citizens from discrimination, they perhaps did not foresee future migration patterns. The Italian Constitution and its rights only provide for citizens, meaning that non-citizens in Italy tend to be 'invisible' in the eyes of the law. One could interpret this fact, that the absence of citizenship impinges on equality, as creating an imperative or duty for 'the Republic to remove these obstacles' to equality.

It's not just being 'invisible' or outside the scope of rights that being an Italian citizen bestows, it's also the inability to vote. Paula tells me that at every election – whether it be local, national, or European – Italians without citizenship are unable to participate in votes which concern and affect them. The text to reform the law concerning Italians without citizenship arrived in the Senate chamber in June 2017. However, instead of voting to either pass or reject the reform, it was postponed and then it was ignored, perhaps because the next year, 2018, was an election year.

The following year, 2018, Matteo Salvini became Deputy Prime Minister and Minister of the Interior, positions which he held for just over a year, until he was thrown out of office. In that brief time, he managed to enforce a counter-reform of the citizenship law, extending the wait for a response to citizenship applications from two to four years. This is along with the income test, the requirement that one must provide proof of all changes in residence, ten years of unbroken residence in Italy, not including the four years during the application process, and the collection of all the required documents, such as rental contracts, letters from bank managers, work contracts, proof of university enrolment, and certified translations of documents from the country of origin. The application takes months to process. If it is unsuccessful, then the applicant must start again from the beginning.

Living with this uncertainty – that being able to continue living in one's country translates to the continual successful renewal of a mountain of paperwork – results in a life filled with anxiety. Travel outside of Italy is complicated, for example, because it must be reported. The misplacement or loss of the *permesso di soggiorno* means that someone might not be able to access their doctor. It means a childhood of accompanying one's parents to the *Questura* to collect and renew their papers, waiting in line for hours, and then an adulthood of doing the same. This, Paula says, 'is something that marks you deeply. The longer this thing lasts, the more it marks you . . . in the way you see things, in the way you see yourself and in the way you relate with your country'. Possessing citizenship of a home country gives one a past, but lack of citizenship in the new country negates the future. All of one's focus is on the next day, the next month, the next year. How can someone put down roots if they have no idea where they'll be in a year?

The two main systems for acquiring citizenship are *jus sanguinis* (right of blood) and *jus soli* (right of soil). Most of the world's nations follow *jus sanguinis* laws, through which citizenship is not guaranteed by birth but by blood. If a person's parents are citizens of a nation, then that person acquires the right to their parents' citizenships, regardless of where they are born. By this means, citizenship is a blood right, an inheritance. If each parent has a different citizenship, then this can result in a child with dual citizenship. This means that, for countries that follow *jus sanguinis* laws, then a child born in Australia, who perhaps has never been to Italy nor speaks Italian, but has one Italian grandparent, has the right to Italian citizenship (and therefore, the right to vote), while a child born in Italy to migrant parents has to wait until they are eighteen to apply for it. Or someone like Paula, who grew up in Italy but was not born there, has to wait or may never be given the right to vote. (Since I turned eighteen, the Italian government has sent ballots to my parents' home in Australia, while a person born in Italy, once they turn eighteen, must apply for this right.) In fact, under Italy's *jus sanguinis* laws, anyone born outside of Italy with an Italian ancestor dating back to the Risorgimento can claim Italian citizenship.

The very concept of *jus sanguinis* is racist. It draws on what Arendt refers to as 'race-thinking', the idea that people can be grouped by certain natural or biological traits, rather than by being part of the same community. This 'race-thinking' became and becomes racism when it is developed to propose that certain groups of people not only share natural traits but that they also deserve 'natural privileges'. Both *jus sanguinis* and racism assume, in other words, that there is something unique and special to bloodlines.

Jus sanguinis is a fairly modern invention. During the Roman Empire, for example, Emperor Caracalla promulgated the *Constitutio Antoniniana* (the Antonine Constitution), which made all free men of the Empire, from Britain to North Africa, full Roman citizens and gave all women of the Empire the same rights as Roman women. Citizenship was granted regardless of culture, faith or ethnicity. In its original incarnation, it was about duty and rights: one's relationship to the state, and not to one's cultural group – which were understood as separate things.

Just thirty-five countries recognise *jus soli* or birthright citizenship, and they are mostly in North, Central and South America. In the United States, birthright citizenship was introduced in 1865 with the Fourteenth Amendment to the Constitution, three years after the Thirteenth formally abolished slavery. The Fourteenth Amendment guaranteed Black Americans (and anyone else born on US soil) citizenship by virtue of having been born there.

Birthright citizenship wasn't always so rare. For example, the UK abolished *jus soli* in 1981 with the British Nationality Act. After the passing of this act, Commonwealth citizens were no longer recognised as British subjects and babies born in Britain were not guaranteed citizenship by way of being born in the UK. To be guaranteed citizenship, a baby must be born with one parent who is either a British citizen or settled in the UK. France also restricted *jus soli* citizenship in 1993 with the 'Pasqua Law'. Both these actions were criticised as directly discriminating against 'Black immigration', most often from formerly colonised countries. It also institutionalised an idea of national identity winnowed down to kinship. The timing of these amendments to citizenship laws are perhaps a response to the world becoming more accessible and open.

In the last few years, the terms *ius soli temperato* and *ius culturae* have been proposed as reforms in Italian discourse on how to rethink citizenship in such a way that is appropriate for the changing demographics of Italy. The former is similar to *jus soli*, with the proviso that one parent of the child born in Italy has been resident in the country for at least five years at their time of birth. The latter, *ius culturae*, would instead render children who migrated to Italy with their parents before the age of twelve and who have undergone at least five years of Italian schooling automatically eligible for citizenship.

Paula bristles when I mention *ius culturae* and *ius soli temperato*. According to Paula, Italy already has *ius soli temperato*, whereby those born in Italy to non-citizen parents can apply for citizenship between their eighteenth and nineteenth birthdays, a process which was made easier by the 2013 law *Decreto del Fare*, but which still needs improvement. Conversely, she does not like the wording of the term *ius culturae*. First of all, Italians who were born elsewhere are already a part of Italian culture, with or without citizenship. Secondly, the idea that 'we must prove how Italian we are to have citizenship' is insulting. I see what she means. What is Italian culture, in any case? Does it mean knowing how to properly boil pasta? Does it mean speaking perfect Italian? There are plenty of Italians who don't eat pasta or even speak perfect Italian, who will never have to prove their Italianness.

There are also plenty of dual citizens abroad, those who have an Italian grandfather or great-grandmother, who don't speak a work of Italian, but whose citizenship is unquestioned. Paula tells me that 'we are already part of this territory because we have grown up here, we don't have to prove anything, nor do our companions'. It is their contention that the very fact that they live their lives in Italy should allow them the same rights as their peers.

They are still searching for a fitting term. She says that they have started discussing using the term *ius respiro*. The Italian word *respiro* means breath. The proposed *ius respiro* refers to both the idea that 'we have not been able to breathe for a long time' and the 2020 protests of the Black Lives Matter movement, catalysed by the words of George Floyd as he was being murdered by a police officer. She says that 'in a completely different context, we too have felt breathless for years in Italy, and so we have started using it provocatively. So that others realise that we are not given the opportunity to breathe like our peers.'

I notice that the movement tends to draw from the Black American civil rights movement. During our conversation, Paula also mentions the short film that the movement made along with the Afro-Italian association Arising Africans, titled *Io Sono Rosa Parks* (I am Rosa Parks). The film, she tells me, connects the efforts of and discriminations experienced by the million Italians without citizenship to the catalysing effect of Rosa Parks, when she refused to give up her seat to a white man. The film is narrated by twelve Italians of diverse origins, among them Ghanaian, Albanian, Ecuadorian, and Nigerian. *Io Sono Rosa Parks* uses Rosa Parks and the civil rights movement as a metaphor for the million Italians without rights due to their lack of citizenship, and the bus as a metaphor for Italy: i.e., they refuse to get off the 'Italian bus'. I am uncomfortable with the metaphor, as it makes use of a history that is so unique to the Black American experience. But of course, I can never reach a full understanding of the experiences of either Paula or other Italians without citizenship.

Racism is entwined with Italian history and culture. Consider: the racism from northern Italy towards southern Italy since the Risorgimento, the racism inherent in Italian colonialism, the preoccupation with the concept of race that had taken hold in Italy and across Europe at large, and Italian Fascism's racism towards people from the Balkans in Istria and Friuli-Venezia-Giulia, which was a crucial component of irredentism, the movement that sought to 'reclaim' the Italian-speaking territories that were occupied by the Austro-Hungarian Empire; and of course, the 1938 Racial Laws. The idea of racial purity and difference, in other words, is one that has dogged Italy since its formation.

I tell Paula about my experience listening to the Afro-Italian woman at the Black Lives Matter rally, and repeat what she had said: *siamo più carta che carne*. I ask her what citizenship means to her, given that it is so fundamental to securing one's human rights, and yet based on such seemingly arbitrary and bureaucratic factors. She tells me that *carta*, paper, is a constant in the lives of Italy's migrants or non-citizens. In a room of her home, she still has a fat packet of all the documents that she had to carry around with her when she was a *straniera*. (*Straniera* in Italian is used to mean foreigner, but its most literal translation is 'stranger'. When she was a 'stranger' in her country.) In the packet are all the documents, the birth certificates and rental contracts and *permessi di soggiorno* she has had since she was a child. This 'mountain of paperwork, of bureaucracy' was something that she carried on her shoulders to prove that, not only was she allowed to stay, but that she 'existed'. Bureaucracy, especially in Italy, is often used as a weapon or an obstacle to accessing one's rights, and I wonder whether it is some unshakable fear that her citizenship could be taken away from her again that moves her to keep the documents.

Paula tells me that far-right Lega Nord mayors often impose small bureaucratic obstacles in the way of migrant parents to make their daily lives more difficult. This was the case in a small town called Lodi in the Lombardy region in 2017, when a Lega Nord mayor was elected to local office. Prior to her election, families deemed economically eligible received discounted rates for school bus and canteen services. Eligibility was determined by the Equivalent Economic Situation Indicator (ISEE), an index that determines a family's wealth. The new mayor, however, introduced a resolution which dictated that parents born outside the EU would be required to submit additional documentation to prove their lack of holdings in their country of origin – even though almost all the children affected were born in Italy.

'We are paper above all,' she tells me, 'they made us this way.' Life without citizenship is a constant battle for one's rights, an endless collection of documents, of waiting in line, of uncertainty, of being invisible, of never standing on stable ground, never being able to fully settle. Paula becomes emotional. She says that citizenship for her is peace of mind, the ability to feel at home.

Bar San Calisto

In the late afternoons, my boyfriend and I would spend a couple of hours at the Bar San Calisto, one of the few watering holes left in Trastevere where Romans from all over the city converge inside and around the small circular wooden tables in front. Here, a beer is still one euro fifty, an espresso eighty cents. A huddle of students wearing army and torn denim jackets roll cigarettes, their table littered with white espresso cups. Two chic women masked by sunglasses talk in hush tones over wine. A few workmen still in their uniforms take over a couple of tables and drink beer. A couple of *punkabbestia* chat over beers, their dog docile at their feet. *Punkabbestia* are a subculture in Italy which branches off from the anarcho-punk movement. They can usually be spotted by their torn denim, leather and metal clothing, profuse tattoos on their hands and necks, and their distinctive hairstyles, such as mohawks or shaved heads. They also, as a rule, are always accompanied by a dog (the term, *punkabbestia*, is a portmanteau of 'punk' and '*bestia*', or beast: 'punk with a beast').

Bar San Calisto may be the last vestige of a pre-Airbnb Trastevere, one of the few establishments that still caters to those who live in the city, and not primarily to tourists. It is a Roman institution, which has been in business for more than half a century. Its 1960s wood-panelled décor and yellow masonry lends the feeling of stepping back into a classic Rome of the *La Dolce Vita* era. The interiors are even featured in one of the dreamy sequences of Sorrentino's *The Great Beauty*.

There are men in suits loosening their ties after work. A homeless man places his espresso atop one of the bins outside and stirs sugar into it. A group of old men in caps and woollen pants and collared shirts, who come there every day, have dragged a table from the bar and set it on the other side of the piazza, in front of the San Calisto church. They periodically walk across the piazza to the bar and order coffees and drinks, which they then cart back to their table, continuing to smoke their cigarettes and play cards. A young couple sits in the corner of the terrace, watching and whispering.

It has certainly been written about before, but it seems essential to note that Italians (central and southern Italians in particular) comport themselves with a certain theatricality that adds a romance or charm to their movements and the way they move through daily life, the way they coin and utter sentences and communicate with one another and the world at large. The setting for this theatre of life is the piazza, where the mundane events of daily existence seem to glimmer, making one feel one is living in a film, whether it be a comedy or a tragedy.

Part of the reason for this grace of movement must be down to the structures of Italian cities themselves. The very shape of the street and the piazza and the buildings seems to provoke life. Bernard Rudofsky, an American architect, was enamoured of the Italian city structure, in which piazzas and streets provide social and architectural cohesion within the city space. If, for Rudofsky, the American city was a desert, the Italian city was an oasis in comparison. While in the former, the street's primary function is that of the highway and parking lot, in the latter the street is the pulse of the city, the point of convergence, of meeting, buying, socialising and debating. The piazza has historically been the core of every Italian town and city.

Known as the city's *salotto a cielo aperto* (open-air living room), it speaks to the special relationship Italians have with urban space. In Italy, the private space of the home simply extends into the public, and there is little division between the two. Recently I was talking to an old housemate about this – about how she feels freer and more at home in the streets of the city than cooped up in her apartment. This is not an uncommon sentiment amongst urban Italians, who are accustomed to living in the smaller spaces of apartment buildings, rather than the typical Australian or American house with a garden. The piazza has historically been a space for commerce, socialising and relaxation, where all age groups and classes can be found to merge. It comes most alive in the summer, when it and the streets are swamped with people, and live music can be heard around every corner, the air carrying the light, fizzy scent of impromptu festivities.

Sitting at Bar San Calisto invariably makes me nostalgic. I long to visit Rome during its post-war years, when writers such as Natalia Ginzburg and Elsa Morante and her husband Alberto Moravia flocked to the city, back when living in the middle of the city meant living cheaply. Morante and Moravia, known anti-fascists, had fled Rome during the German occupation and hidden in exile in a small town halfway between Naples and Rome. After the war they returned, to an apartment near Piazza del Popolo, on via dell'Oca. Piazza del Popolo literally means 'The People's Piazza'. It's a massive cobblestone square, centred around an Egyptian obelisk. My boyfriend and I had gone there a few days earlier. It was, as it always is, full of people: university students and families and skaters and tourists. The sun was setting, and the sky was a dusty rose. We had sat at one of the white-tableclothed tables at the historic Bar Canova, whose terrace spills onto the piazza. I watched as an older woman with a white bob and a fur hanging over her shoulders led her young granddaughter by the hand to a table and treated her to hot chocolate. It was, evidently, a rite of passage, although I imagined that when the grandmother was younger, a simple drink at Bar Canova was not an outrageous ten euro. Next to us sat a table of German students on holiday, who were about to begin on their dinners of pizza. (In Italy, the only people who eat at six in the evening, which is what time it was, are tourists and children.) I thought about how so many of the historic cafés in Italian and French cities where writers and artists whiled away their days no longer serve the people who actually live in those cities, how what they serve has become nostalgia at exorbitant prices.

Morante would remain alone in the apartment off Piazza del Popolo after their marriage ended, almost until her death. They kept Siamese cats and filled the house with cream-coloured couches and covered the walls in paintings. Due to the success of their literary careers, it was the first time in Morante's life that she'd had disposable income. Morante's eventual translator, the American William Weaver, who lived close by and translated both their works, remembers that they never cooked; they either held dinner parties catered by a cook, or else went out to eat at a trattoria.

These Roman years were filled with writers and art critics and musicians, who had returned to Rome after the dust settled from the war. The city was rebuilding itself, was filled with the kind of hope that results from being reduced to ashes. The city, like Italy, had been released from the myths and expectations of fascism, and before it the Risorgimento, and out of the nothing that was left came the work of creating new myths, of constructing a new city and country and identity.

In post-war Rome, there was hardly any traffic, making the city entirely walkable, and tourists were still too afraid to set foot there. Weaver recalls going on long walks with various famous writers, including Moravia, meetings in tea rooms and bars, and dinner parties, countless and loud. Morante bored easily. Sometimes, at parties, she would come upon a series of journals or books and spend the entire evening reading studiously, ignoring what was happening around her. Other times she would engage the room in guessing games of her own invention – a morbid kind of *Would you rather?* which involved choosing between two people which to push off a 'high tower.'

In the last months of the occupation, life in Rome got harder. There were more bombings, and food rations were further reduced, while the price of what little food was available skyrocketed. My grandmother, whose body should have been broadening with the bloom of adolescence, instead seemed to be shrinking, her clothes hanging loose on what would later prove to be a naturally ample frame. She would later recall returning home from school to an empty apartment. She would return so hungry, she said, that she would make herself *focaccine*: a spoonful of flour mixed with some water and fried in a pan without oil. *They tasted so good*, she'd recall.

Morante's third and most famous novel, *History: A Novel*, is a brick of a book, which spans several years in the life of Ida

Ramundo, from 1941 until 1947. Its English title does not reflect the wordplay of the original: *La storia*. In Italian, *storia* has a double meaning: both 'history' and 'story', so the title of the book can be read simultaneously as *The Story* and *The History*. It's unfortunate that there is no real way to convey this wordplay in English, because this double meaning is reflected in the novel's grand sweep of historical events seen through the distinct ways in which they reverberate in the private lives of the characters, like the concentric rings that ripple out after a pebble is dropped in a body of water.

History follows the protagonist Ida throughout the war as she strives to survive and protect her sickly young son, Useppe. It's a harrowing novel of hunger and waiting. The small family is bombed out of their home, they move to a refugee squat on the outskirts of the city, they move back into the city, they struggle to find enough to eat, they wait for the war to be over, they meet others who have been bombed out of their homes or cities and are struggling to eat and are waiting for the war to be over. They are haunted by their hunger and the death that surrounds them and afflicts those they love.

In the 1944 of *History*, Rome has filled up with homeless people and refugees, who camp on church steps and below the Vatican. In the public parks, emaciated sheep and cows graze, transferred from the bombed-out farmlands. The bombings outside the city continue, causing apartment windows to tremble and polluted black dust clouds to wash over the city. The Reich occupies the lavish hotels and plans the following day's massacres over extravagant banquet dinners. Villas and office buildings have been turned into torture chambers. Their windows are boarded up and the notes of dance music can be heard playing from gramophones.

Streets and roads are periodically blocked off, while public transport, workplaces, and public spaces are invaded by the Nazi-Fascists, who randomly round up all the able-bodied men between the ages of sixteen and sixty in an apartment building or quarter, and cart them off in trucks or police wagons for slave labour in the Reich or military duty in the north. The paths of the trucks through the urban streets are trailed by women screaming for their sons or husbands or brothers. All the Jews in Rome's Ghetto have been rounded up and carted on cattle trucks to their murders in concentration camps. The city starves. People eat cats and canaries. Ida spends her days searching for food for Useppe, subsisting herself on boiled vegetable peels, tree leaves, flies and ants, grass torn from the cracks of the ruins. Ida, while a passive, timid character, spends the entire book surviving, a feat.

On the night of 4 June 1944, the Allies finally enter the city. Morante describes the event like so:

> Suddenly, a great clamour was raised in the streets, as if it were New Year's Eve. Windows and doors were flung open, flags were unfurled. There were no more Germans in the city. From above and below, shouts were heard: Hurray for peace!! Long live America!

My grandmother had a memory, oft told, of the day that Rome was liberated by the Allies. It was always the same. Cheers resounded from every window, and people poured into the streets, rejoicing. Below her apartment, there was a soap-maker, who everyone in the quarter referred to as *il saponaro del Duce*, the soap-maker of *il Duce*. According to her, everyone in the neighbourhood had shunned him for producing Mussolini's soap, but on the day of Liberation, a pale procession of people came streaming out of the soap factory, their eyes blinded by the sunlight they had gone so long without.

It turned out that the soap-maker had been hiding Jews in his factory. I don't know how much truth there is to this – I have tried to verify accounts of this soap-maker, but have turned up nothing, and so I am cautious of how much stock to give to the tale. But it is a story that I want to believe. Perhaps because of how neatly it fits into the genre of parable – the lesson here being, not to judge others on face value. Or perhaps it is because it fits with the idea of a Rome united against the Nazi-Fascists, one in which citizens help one another, one in which some people were saved, and in which the ending closes on such a lovely scene, of people streaming out onto a sun-soaked street and feeling the warmth of freedom and first summer light on their faces.

While *Open City*, despite its harrowing events, seems built on hope, Morante's *History*, published almost thirty years after the war and into Italian democracy, is void of it. For Morante, the promise of the war's end did not bear fruit, and the post-war years for Ida and the rest of the characters are somehow even darker than their precursors, plagued as they are by trauma. They are haunted by all they've been through, by the violence inflicted on them by the whims of governments and warmongers, and there is no way out.

My grandmother's own descriptions of her life in Rome were minimal, and she would often repeat the same scant specifics over and over. One detail that she would mention was that the Allies bombed every day at midday, and so they spent hours sheltered in the Vatican. Even this, though, seems as though it may be myth – the home addresses listed on my great-grandmother's archival documents are located on the other side of the city to the Vatican. Surely they hid somewhere else? This is the problem with family stories that turn into family myths, particularly stories about traumatic periods. They rely on memory that is a product of that trauma, memory that is fragmented and obscure. She didn't talk about Rome because it hurt her, so much so that her mind had tried to wipe it out.

Unlike my own family story, which had a happy enough ending or at the very least a continuation, *History* is one of those stories where almost everybody dies, during and after the war. They die in traffic accidents, they die of cancer, they die of alcoholism, they die shot by Nazis, they die from frostbite on the Russian front, they die of seizures, they die of drug overdoses, they die under mysterious circumstances, their bodies recovered on beaches. A newborn kitten, painstakingly carried and brought into the world, is casually abandoned by its mother. It dies too.

All the deaths are senseless, all occur after years of strenuous survival, all are the result of grand events out of their control. Ida and everyone she encounters are powerless in the face of the decisions of the anonymous men who wage wars, order massacres and bombings, and pass laws that disenfranchise, discriminate or degrade ordinary people. It seems that Morante herself, disillusioned by the unfolding of history's events, wanted to do away with the myths that had built up around Italy and the war, to poke holes in them and show that they did not return on their promises.

Casa dell'Architettura

The building which is now the Casa dell'Architettura near Termini in the Esquilino quarter was once the Roman Aquarium, and was constructed from 1885 to 1887 by the architect Ettore Bernich. It is circular in structure, with columns and pilasters and aquatic motifs. In the garden there is a pond with a bridge and Roman ruins. This is a fact of living in Italy, but especially Rome: the ancient Romans insert themselves constantly into the everyday, by way of an arch jutting out of a block of 1920s flats, or taking up space in the middle of a bar's outdoor terrace. No longer the aquarium, the building was threatened by demolition for much of the twentieth century, until it became the seat of the Municipality of Rome and the Order of Architects of Rome.

Now there is an outdoor bar in the building's lush, gated garden, its small round tables arranged under and around leafy cedars and yews. I am sitting at one such table, under an enormous tree, awaiting Giorgio de Finis. A light breeze rustles the leaves above me and it seems as though I have found an urban oasis. Around the corner, in front of Termini station, is Piazza dei Cinquecento, where I have just come from.

Main train stations tend to be the places where tourists and the normally hidden parts of the city converge. An acquaintance of mine works at the Kiko Cosmetics in Termini where, she says, her main clients are rich Russian tourists and sex workers. Because of the pandemic, the Russians have yet to return, but the sex workers are just beginning to, and they are favouring eye makeup over lipstick, which would, after all, be covered by a mask. The streets around train stations tend to be the workplace of such workers, but also of money exchangers and lenders, hotels, hostels, street hawkers, cheap bars and internet shops. Termini in Rome is a truly democratic space – everyone in Italy catches the train to travel domestically, no matter their class status, and going through Termini is the only way to get out of the city. Perhaps in the wealthier suburbs, one is shielded from the components of their city they would rather forget, but in Termini one has no option.

Igiaba Scego, in her book *Roma Negata*, writes about Piazza dei Cinquecento. It is always full of traffic – of stressed-out travellers half-running as they drag their suitcases to the station, of young people sharing cigarettes as they wait for buses, of businessmen and women lined up at the bars, knocking back an espresso before their train leaves, of homeless families huddled together in the shade, of people hanging out on benches or meeting up with one another. It's also a hub for Rome's migrant community, and Scego writes of Somali women dressed in brightly coloured *garbesar*, the Peruvians enjoying meals of fried chicken and *sibice*, and the Nigerian mothers accompanying their daughters to one of the nearby African salons. Scego pronounces the piazza as 'Babylonian . . . the piazza of the Somalis, the Eritreans, the Ethiopians, and also all the other migrants'.

Under the portico across from the piazza is where all the halal places are: the kebab shops, the halal Indian, Broast chicken, the halal pizzeria. There is a Huaweiju Chinese and a Hong Kong diner and SEOUL restaurant serving Korean. There are souvenir shops and a MoneyGram, a Capital Luggage Deposit and a combination print/souvenir/fax/phone shop. There is a *sala slot*, which translates roughly to 'slot machine lounge', and a few pop-up street stalls of clothing that smells of polyester, plastic packaging and the back of a truck. Men, young and old, cluster around the plastic outdoor tables, down espresso and drag on cigarettes.

It all recalls what ancient Rome would have been like: a point of convergence in the centre of a diverse empire, one to which people from all corners of the known world would have flocked to make their fortunes, a mix of temples dedicated to different religions, various cuisines, a mess of commerce and merchants.

Giorgio de Finis arrives, late. He is thinnish, shortish, fiftyish, with greying hair and a greying moustache. He is the director of MAAM, the museum that operates out of Metropoliz.

In 2009, the abandoned slaughterhouse, which consists of an area of about twenty thousand square metres, was occupied by a movement which fights for the right to housing, called *Blocchi Precari Metropolitani*. When, in Italian, someone says that a building is *occupato* or 'occupied', they mean what we more often call squatting – although without the negative connotations generally attached to the term in English. This may perhaps be because the occupiers often turn these buildings into *centri sociali*, or social centres. The act of occupying a building is considered a political one, taking a disused space and reclaiming it for the community.

A tradition in many Italian cities, *centri sociali* often operate as little self-governed communities, like Christiania in Copenhagen on a micro-scale. Despite the efforts of local governments to shut them down (they often take up valuable space that enterprising developers are eager to exploit), there were three remaining in Bologna when I lived there. One close to where I lived, in an old military barracks in the heart of the city, was called *Labas*. It held weekly organic markets with the produce of local farmers, ran a free afternoon day care for local families, and staged concerts and swing nights at the weekends. They organised fundraisers for migrants and those in need. The inhabitants were students, workers, pensioners, refugees and migrants.

Labas and the other *centri sociali* in Bologna were and are under constant threat of being kicked out by said city councils and developers, and so it is common practice for famous street artists, such as the Italian artist Blu, to cover their exteriors and interiors in murals, thereby endowing them with artistic significance and protecting them in the eyes of the law (Article 9 of the Fundamental Principles in the Italian Constitution: The Italian Republic 'safeguards natural landscape and the historical and artistic heritage of the Nation'). This works up until a point. After a few failed attempts in which people from all over the city rallied to physically protect the building, the residents of *Labas* were violently evicted in August of 2017, when the city emptied out as it does every summer.

The slaughterhouse on via Prenestina was bought by a construction and civil engineering multinational called WeBuild in late 2003. The price paid was 6.85 million euros, with the intention of turning it into a massive block of flats, flats that would total fifty thousand square metres. Another beehive. Permission to build wasn't granted by the city council until ten years later, in 2013. In the meantime, in early 2009, the still-disused slaughterhouse was occupied by BPM to provide housing for around seventy families. They christened it Metropoliz. De Finis clarifies that *Blocchi Precari Metropolitani* isn't just fighting for the right to a council flat, however. Their fight is more philosophical. They are fighting for the right to their city, for a city that serves the people and not financial interests.

He makes sure to tell me that Metropoliz is made up of families from both Italian and migrant backgrounds. They are from Italy, Morocco, Tunisia, Peru, Ecuador, Eritrea, Sudan, Ukraine, Poland. It's not just people coming from outside, he says: 'poverty concerns all of us'. It is also the first Italian housing occupation to include a significant number of Romani families. He tells me this is significant, since Romani tend to live in their own communities and don't generally deal in politics or political movements. The Romani families who live in Metropoliz left their camps not just to come and live there, but to build a self-governing community in which all decisions are shared. It is by its nature political, in the sense that the continued existence of Metropoliz, like all *centri sociali*, is a perpetual political battle.

De Finis stumbled across Metropoliz later that same 2009, when undertaking a walk organised by Stalker, an urban art collective that engages with liminal and marginalised city spaces. The walk consisted of a series of wanderings along the Grande Raccordo Anulare, the ring-shaped road that orbits Rome. In a sense, the road defines the limits of the city, and during these wanderings, they wove in and out of junkyards, outlet villages, farmland, shopping centres, and built-up residential areas of 'American-style villas', and then Romani families camped out 'amongst the cane thickets'.

This prolonged wandering went on for a few months, and in that time, he came across Metropoliz, which had just been occupied. On the roof, there were people acting as lookouts. This is usual in the early days of an occupation. The police, if they catch wind of a recent one, will arrive almost immediately and easily kick everyone out. However, the more time that passes and the more roots an occupation puts down, the more complicated it becomes for the occupiers to be evicted. He describes the first time he entered the factory as like going back in time, like 'entering the Egyptian pyramids after a thousand years'. The factory itself had not been used in decades, and it was still filled with heavy machinery, upon which dust had accumulated so thick and compacted that it was like sedimentary rock. There was also the fact of the building's prior life. It had functioned back when meat was slaughtered, processed and cured in the same vicinity, and so the pigs 'came in alive and the sausages came out, so it was also a rather gruesome place, with a history of blood and death'.

Two years later, he proposed with his colleague Fabrizio Boni a project called *Space Metropoliz*. De Finis had experience making documentaries about different pockets of the contemporary city, like the Romani camps on the city outskirts. But this time he wanted to make a film that wasn't a 'sad story' that 'nobody wants to hear'. *Space Metropoliz* was to be a 'lunar-themed art film'. The film would follow the Metropoliz community as they prepared for a trip to the moon. It would be filmed at Metropoliz, and so artists, astronauts, astrophysicists and philosophers were called on to aid in turning the slaughterhouse into a set filled with lunar-themed art installations. Murals were painted and sculptures were carved, and, on the roof, a telescope was constructed.

The idea behind the plot or concept of *Space Metropoliz* is that there is no longer any space on earth for migrants, artists and the poor, and so we may as well leave and start over, *carte blanche*, on the moon. The act of occupation is more or less a constant battle with authority, a perpetual fight for a community's continued existence. Both going to the moon and making the film together with the Metropoliz community had the goal of creating a space in which the nagging of hunger and uncertainty of having a roof over one's head, the pressing necessities of survival, were absent. When a life narrows down to need, when one's own existence becomes a question and not an assumption, that need dehumanises that human life, both personally and in the eyes of others. War narrows people down. They become cannon fodder, pawns, victims and refugees. And so does being forgotten by the system in which one lives. The film imagined a fantastical world in which, as de Finis said to me 'everybody eats'.

After a year of making the film, the community asked de Finis to remain. And so came MAAM. The concept was to invite artists from all over Italy to come to Metropoliz and create a piece inspired by the space, which would then be donated to it. The museum still regularly hosts artists who donate their work, which means that its collection is ever-growing. In this way, two elements – that of the celebrated art world and that of a world which nobody wanted to see – would be united, and thus evitalise a forgotten space in the city's underbelly. The creation of the museum also served another, perhaps more pressing purpose – to protect Metropoliz.

One of the main strategies used by police to forcibly evacuate an occupation is to destroy the very walls of the building occupied, so as to render it uninhabitable. Covering these walls in valuable art that speaks to and depends on the physical space of Metropoliz means that the artworks cannot simply be carted away and shown in another museum. They became barricades, much like the street art that adorns the walls of other *centri sociali*. De Finis tells me that this works, because while 'people are no longer respected, art will be for a while longer – you don't throw away five or six hundred works of art as lightly as you throw two hundred people, seventy of them children, on the street'.

He tells me that people now come to Metropoliz from all over Rome, and I recall the assorted group that had gathered for the tour. There were about fifteen of us – a smart-looking older couple, a few art students, a family of tourists, a young teen couple, a woman and her father. It became a place not only for people to see art but also to be confronted with a reality that is being shunted to the outskirts of our cities: that of the housing crisis driven by rising rents and the dislocation of council housing. And perhaps visitors also see that those who are affected by the crisis are not defined by their need. In the course of its history, MAAM became one of the top three museums of contemporary art in Rome, along with the MACRO and the MAXXI. It was listed on official city websites. De Finis was later offered the position of director of the MACRO, a position which he held for two years, and in this way, he tells me, MAAM was further protected.

Now that their community and homes were more secure, they set about fixing it up – patching up the roofs and ceilings of the houses, removing asbestos from balconies. And then, in 2018, in response to litigation from WeBuild, the civil court awarded compensation of 28 million euro to the construction company. The compensation was more than four times what WeBuild had originally paid. It was to be paid by the State, for failing to evacuate the premises. Metropoliz was just one of twenty-three properties subject to seizure decrees, along with another two for which evacuations were already in process. In Rome, eighty-two buildings are under occupation, housing eleven thousand people. It was found that, by failing to carry out forced evictions, the Interior Ministry had infringed upon 'the right of ownership and the right of business'. The State did not intend on paying the money, and so evacuations were scheduled for all the twenty-three occupied properties, to be carried out gradually, at a rate of four a year.

The judge justified the ruling by stating that 'the unauthorized occupation does not harm only the interests of the owner, but also the citizens' general interest in an orderly and peaceful coexistence and it assumes an unequivocal subversive value'. The fact that these occupations persisted revealed a failure on the part of the police to maintain 'public order' and protect private interests.

In rapid succession, de Finis lost his position as director of the MACRO in December 2019, and Metropoliz was scheduled to be evacuated in February 2020. Simultaneously, the same administration that removed de Finis as director of the MACRO and scheduled the evacuation of Metropoliz funded another of his projects, called *Museo delle Periferie* (Museum of the Peripheries). This project consists of an international museum and research centre that will consider the 'phenomenon of the suburb' within the urban context. It will host residencies and research projects, a library, a permanent collection and exhibitions, publications and 'encounters'. It will, in essence, study and valorise subversive museums and projects such as MAAM.

The paradox lies in the fact that, with one hand, the city council wants to wave away subversive occupations like Metropoliz and its inhabitants, and with the other, it wants to foster arts bodies like MAAM. It's a paradox that plays out in most every city, for example, the funding of some street murals and the painting over of unsanctioned ones. The problem, as de Finis tells me, is that MAAM cannot exist without Metropoliz. The fact that it is inhabited defines MAAM. Its walls would not be painted if it were not inhabited, and its very value lies in the fact of its inhabitation.

It's a bit like what happened in Bologna in early 2016, when the city council lifted pieces of the city's famed street art and placed them in a museum exhibition that cost the visitor over ten euro to see. My flatmate at the time, himself a street artist, spent a few days assisting Blu to cover his remaining murals in grey paint. Blu is a Bolognese street artist so internationally renowned that one of his murals had up until that point protected a *centro sociale* outside the city's medieval walls. The idea behind removing the works, and thereby erasing the value that they had added to buildings, and to the city itself, was to protest what the artists saw as a perversion of the meaning of street art. Street art, they contended, depended on the very context of the street, and its value lay in its subversive and egalitarian aim of offering art to the masses. It's an old story. We want the lucrative fruits of subversion, but not the challenge it presents to, as the judge on the Metropoliz case put it, the 'public order'.

Metropoliz was still functioning as of October 2020, when I visited it. This may have been due to a public petition put forward by the Metropoliz community. It could also have been a happy side effect of the global pandemic. But things generally take their time in Italy, which is, in cases like these, a blessing.

De Finis, the director of MAAM, tends to talk in long stream-of-consciousness monologues, making many references to things I don't know about. There are times when I get stuck on a point he has made, and return to the conversation – or lecture, perhaps – then realise we're on a new topic, thankful that I am recording everything. He tells me that his interest in urban phenomena came about in his past life as an anthropologist in Mumbai. He describes Mumbai as 'a city of eleven million people living in slums'. On returning to Rome, he discovered that in Italy, too, people live in slums, and that our world's cities were going in the direction of Mumbai, rather than vice versa. That is, the quality of life in our cities will get worse, rather than better. This is because, according to de Finis, we live in a world where the rich are only getting richer and the poor poorer, where our cities are crowded with people who don't have enough money to eat. This is not solely an Italian problem. A poll in 2020 revealed that 2.4 million children in the UK were living in homes which were 'food insecure'. Later that year, UNICEF stepped in and provided aid to a developed country for the first time. Twenty-five thousand pounds were donated to provide children with breakfast. This is a problem of cities the world over, who serve the economy and property developers and not the people who live in them.

De Finis is representative of an ultra-left wing in Italy that has, in the last decade, done away with politics, in the sense that they no longer believe in the institutions under which we live. They see the world order as the enemy, they see us living in a world in which cities are banks and their inhabitants live 'like parasites' in buildings which are no longer homes but the gold bars in bank basements. According to them, we are no longer human, but algorithms that drive slot machines played by finance guys in suits.

It's a cynical way to be, and sometimes makes a lot of sense to me. I go for a night walk a few nights later, noting the identical green tents and mattresses and bodies blanketed in newspaper that line via della Conciliazione, the road that leads to sumptuous St Peter's.

These tiny tent cities pop up periodically around the city, in the porticoes of banks or under shade-bearing ruins, but most especially throughout Vatican City each night, where they are much less likely to be ousted from their spots. Later that night we return to our rented apartment, a cavernous space fit for a large family, with gleaming state-of-the-art kitchen appliances that have never been used, a few cracked plates and a scratched frying pan and other odds and ends in the otherwise empty cupboards, the oak bookshelf meagrely stocked with a few cheap second-hand paperbacks, the walk-in wardrobe furnished with a total of five hangers.

Seeing all this homelessness and desperate living circumstances, people being forced to choose between occupying an old slaughterhouse or camping on the street draws parallels between Rome during and after the Second World War, and Rome now. Then, too, finding shelter was a problem, then, too, there were families and individuals left with nothing but a tent on the streets of Vatican City, or populating abandoned factories.

Later that night, off a little side street a stone's throw away from Piazza Navona, my boyfriend and I attend a dinner party with diplomats from Italy, Spain, Pakistan and Peru, on the rooftop terrace of a rented Airbnb. It is a small and cosy apartment, the terrace almost as big as the interior. From it, we watch over Rome, see cupolas popping up out of the red mess of buildings stacked on top of one another, other haphazard terraces, windows, chimneys.

All the dinner party guests apart from my boyfriend and I have moved to Rome in the last few months, and they laugh about the difficulty of finding an adequate apartment in the historic centre, where it has become easier to find an Airbnb than it is a place to live. No one really lives in Rome, or the centre of it, they say. There are only thirty thousand inhabitants in the historic centre (a figure which may be an exaggeration, I don't know), and the lodgings have now all turned into Airbnbs, or they are inhabited by Rome's rich upper crust. Gone are the days when via Rasella was attacked, when the working class lived side by side with the well-to-do.

It is a dark, starless night, and I look out at the view, the urban canopy of cupolas and sloping terracotta rooftops. I peer into other people's terraces, try to discern which are inhabited and which have been empty for months. The tenant of the Airbnb explains that the owner is livid that they are having to rent out their investment to him for a third of the price that they would be making any other year, and I try to calculate all the disused lodgings, the kitchen benches and gleaming sinks and crisp bed sheets and bookcases empty but for a few now-dusty guides to Rome and paperbacks picked up from a second-hand shop.

Rita wrote another letter in Rome after the war, on 5 March 1945. This one was addressed to the Ministry of Italian Africa in Rome, since the Prefecture of Benghazi no longer existed. It occurs to me that over the years, she had sent almost the same letter to offices and headquarters and administrations that continually ceased to exist. I note that the list of items changes slightly, one black silk dress becomes three, the price of a dozen linen handkerchiefs shifts from 120 lire to 180, a black midseason wool coat is added. The claimed compensatory value jumps from 2,365 lire to 2,775. Perhaps she looked in the wardrobe one chilly autumn day for the coat and discovered that it too had been lost; or maybe she was reminiscing about a night out dancing in Benghazi and realised that the dress she was wearing in her memory was missing. Maybe she was desperate for an extra hundred lire.

In 1945 Rome was full of refugees, newly homeless families, returned soldiers and what was left of the traumatised Roman Jewish survivors and the men who had been sent to slave labour camps in Germany. Some still awaited the return of their sons or husbands, lost in POW camps or in Siberia. They had, the year before, moved from one apartment to another around the corner. The value of those 2,775 lire, which she had spent years seeking and still sought, was now down to around 208 euro.

At first, I thought it was humorous, this stubborn sense of principle, but then I thought about how desperate they must have been, about what that money could have bought. I realised that rather than transporting secret messages, Salvatore was probably just scavenging for food. According to Rita's letters, they stayed in Rome until at least 1946. Then Salvatore was offered a job in Palermo, capital of a Sicily that was being rebuilt, a new beginning.

Palermo

Palermo.

The Conca d'Oro. Engraving taken from the 'La topografia di Palermo e de suoi contorni' (Palermo and its surroundings) by Domenico Scinà, 1818

In the ragged curve of the gulf that plunges halfway down the page, there is a small, neat square: the city. But the city is not the point here. The point is the sea that takes up half the page, the speckled patchwork of agriculture that takes up the other half. Surrounding this monumental amphitheatre are scribbly protrusions created by the cartographer's shading, marking out the jutting peaks of the mountains, like folds of flesh that pin the basin. To the top left of the page, probably the most evocative part of the map: the craggy hulk of Mount Pellegrino, its peak marked by a thick squiggle.

The map is a more easily digestible substitute for terrain. It offers the clearer perspective brought by distance. It doesn't matter whether we select a map that contains a small space, like the blueprint of an apartment, or a colossal space, like an atlas of the globe. The edges of the paper impose limits, comfortable borders for our line of sight. The apartment is as significant in its blueprint as the globe is in its atlas. On paper, they are equals. From our omniscient perch overlooking the lines, curves and shading denoting landmarks and landscapes, we project our own hopes for the future and reminiscences of the past onto what is mapped before us. Perhaps we look at the blueprint of an apartment and picture our coming lives there, plan where to place furniture and where to make improvements. Perhaps we look at the atlas and reflect on past trips, mark out the places we would like to go.

When I was a child, Palermo existed for me as a kind of shadow home, or perhaps a shadow past. There was no discernible map to it, no solid structure that I could conjure. But its obscure form hovered there behind the veil of the photographs and the stories and the crackling international phone calls to my mother, on the other side of my grandmother's and aunts' and cousins' arrivals and departures, the loot of jewellery gifted to me for my baptism by faceless figures: an illusory world that existed beyond my everyday surroundings, felt rather than known.

I went there three times as a child, one of which I was too young at the time to now recall. My memories of this Palermo are fragmentary, shifting, and above all, trivial. Certain images come into focus as others fade out. It seems as though I spent those visits being shuttled from one cool apartment to another, rubbing the sore spots on my cheeks from where they had been kissed and pinched. Between the apartments were streets overrun with feral cats. They mewed between rubbish skips and crouched under cars. We sat in the over-stuffed sitting rooms of ancient women, the walls of which were thickened by glass-fronted cabinets displaying porcelain animal figurines and framed pictures of children and weddings and communions and ancestors. Before each visit, we'd stop at a cake shop for *pasticceria mignon*, the Italian art of the miniature pastry: *sfince,* fried pastries laden with sugared ricotta and dotted with candied fruit; finger-sized eclairs; miniature *cassate*, sponge and ricotta cakes encased in marzipan; *bignè*, choux pastry loaded with cream or custard and studded with wild strawberries; *babà al rum*, a boozy sponge cake doused in liquor and sometimes cut in half and lined with whipped cream.

These little cakes would be slotted into a shallow pink box and tied with ribbon to be offered at the meeting. Once there, fresh espresso would be poured into small cups, and plates would be laden with glistening marzipan fruit, petite *cannoli* and fragrant almond biscuits. Outside the window, down below, the din of traffic roared sea-like, drowning out the whistle of the actual, nearby sea. Inside, the clinking of teaspoons on saucers, and reminiscences.

Don't forget us, our visits insisted. We still exist.

These trips were not for touring. We did not visit any monuments or museums. Our itinerary was my mother's old life, perhaps an effort on her part to build a bridge between that past life and her current one on the opposite side of the globe. Historical landmarks were gesticulated at in passing. I recall my parents pointing out the pink *Palazzina Cinese* each time we drove past it in the car. We never stopped there though, never walked through the massive parkland that surrounds the chinoiserie-style 'Chinese' palace. My mother and grandmother, who referred to the palace as *la Favorita*, after the parkland, had told me a story of how the king had the palace built for his favourite mistress, hence the name. I can't find an official version of this story anywhere. I can't even find an unofficial corroboration. Instead, what I find is that it was simply one of the many residences of the Bourbons, who had the walls decorated in meaningless symbols that were supposed to represent an unintelligble 'Asian' script.

Perhaps we didn't even set foot in the historic centre. I barely remember going to the beach, though we must have. The few snatches of street scenes I recall reveal that the city seemed to be filled with men cut in half. They would crouch in cardboard boxes on every street corner, bleating 'please, I have no legs'. I would beg my parents to stop and give them some change as they dragged me away, wondering who had taken those men's legs. This was 1990 and 1994 and 2001, years between which Palermo drastically changed, but I took no notice.

Page 2 of the online pdf of Adriana Chirco's book Antiche Strade e Piazze di Palermo. No date.

An inversion of the usual colour scheme, this white on a black background. Its axis is a thin crucifix. A white shape, intersected and slashed into white squares and shapeless shapes, a geometric pattern without pattern. All the irregular asymmetrical mess of the interior human body, real lungs in a chest. There I am, making my way along one of the thin black lines of the bottom left quarter of the quartered old city.

It was early afternoon in August. In Italy, the hours following lunch are a void, a brief abyss that opens up each day. We all know these hours. When I worked as a receptionist at a modelling agency in Sydney, it was the time in which barely anyone called. For some unknown reason, everybody whispered. The hours until the end of the workday seemed as though they would go on into eternity, and I would slump over my computer, my hand resting in my chin, struggling to keep my eyes open.

It's that time in which life seems endless. Inertia clouds the faculties. It's both too late and too early. In Anglo-Saxon countries, we struggle through these hours, as if fumbling our way out of a blackened room. In the Mediterranean, these hours are succumbed to. It is a time in which it is understood that no plans are made. Streets are silent, blinds are drawn, shop shutters shut. Perhaps somewhere far off, a dog barks. It is a time in which the sun is too hot, and bellies are too full, and languor seeps into limbs, sending most everybody into their homes, themselves.

It was 2019 or 2020 and I was dragging myself through one of Palermo's historic quarters, la Kalsa. Officially its name is Mandamento Tribunali, 'district of courts', but this is something I've only ever seen on a map. The name that everyone calls it comes from its old Arabic name, *al-Khalesa*, 'the chosen'. The use of this name suggests a kind of fidelity to those who originated it, Arabs who constructed it out of the limestone that lies beneath the city. Back then, it was a fortified citadel where, in the mid-900s, the emirs had their courts on the banks of the Kemonia

River. Now, it is a labyrinthine medina of three and four-storey apartment buildings and ancient palazzi.

I believe I was on la Kalsa's edge, a block away from the old port, walking there along one of the quarter's few long, straight streets, among low, amber-coloured buildings. Parked cars lined the narrow street. Abandoned pamphlets and balled-up receipts lay in the gutters and rubbish-filled plastic supermarket shopping bags slouched beside front doors. Beside deconsecrated churches, fig and frangipani trees stretched their limbs on triangles of green.

I recall how my feet, along with the rest of my body, were slick with sweat, and my sandals slapped back on the fat sun-baked cobblestones each time I took a step. But the street I think I was on is paved with asphalt. Either this is a spliced-in detail of another memory, or I was on a different street. I do know that I was with a couple of Australian friends, and we were wandering around the mute streets after lunch at a Palermitan street food truck by the water. Above us, the green tufts of leafy ferns and basil plants sprouted from wrought iron balconies.

Many of the palazzi in la Kalsa have been restored in the past few years, many others are empty inside, their windows resembling the cranial features of jack-o'-lanterns. These are still boarded-up, their facades spackled and tagged with spray paint. Around the restored parts of la Kalsa, the large cobblestones are swept clean each day, and on their edges, in front of the doors of the three-storey dwellings, are tall potted plants. There are cafés and fruit vendors. In other parts, perhaps a street over, the smooth limestone of the palazzi turns rough and mottled, skips brim with plastic bags of household waste, and corralled around them are cardboard boxes and mattresses and used furniture.

Another trip, years before, to the lone black square amid the map's jigsaw of white shapes. This is Piazza Magione, a sparsely grassed piazza with play equipment for children. The ancient facades bore murals of the Madonna. Then, the nightlife in la Kalsa was rougher. Less of the quarter had been restored. The piazza was lined with sticky bars whose plastic tables took up its entirety, seating at least a hundred people.

Drink carts sold cheap gin and tonics of questionable quality, and a caravan served traditional street meats: *stigghiòla*, the emptied-out intestines of lambs or calves, roped onto sticks; *quarume*, veal tripe; *musso*, veal offal; and *frittola*, which my aunt calls 'la mano misteriosa' or 'the mystery hand', because the vendor reaches into a vat of nondescript leftover animal interiors fried in lard and delivers you a 'surprise' wrapped in waxed paper.

In the heat of that more recent early afternoon, a car approached on the street perpendicular to the one we were walking down. On the corner was a vacant dirt lot. At its centre rose a small pyramid of household waste: bulging plastic bags, soiled nappies, empty plastic detergent and Coca Cola bottles, broken furniture and old toys. The scent of the stewing rubbish mixed with the salt of the sea air. The car came to a quiet halt. Behind the wheel was an elderly man. In the passenger seat was his wife. When he emerged from the car, I could see that the man was well dressed, in defiance of the heat. He wore a white button-down shirt and a tweed jacket and wool pants. From the backseat, the man pulled out a few full plastic bags, which he tossed onto the pile. He got back into the car and he and his wife drove off.

Rubbish is a dirty secret in Palermo. For some reason, Palermitans have an aversion to depositing their waste in designated locations. In vacant lots, shrines to the Madonna are erected to prevent people from using them as dumps. I once saw a businessman emerging from one of the city's most expensive *pasticcerie,* balling up his receipt in one hand and furtively flinging it onto the street.

When Goethe was travelling through Sicily in the late eighteenth century, his German temperament was shocked by the filth that covered the streets of Palermo. In a shop on the main road, probably via della Libertà, he observed the way in which the shopkeepers dutifully swept the refuse on the pavement in front of their shops into the street's centre. He observed that periodic gusts of wind blew this rubbish back up onto the pavements, through the open front doors of the shops, covering the windows. When he asked the shopkeeper why something couldn't be done about the city's filth, the shopkeeper joked that the rubbish served a purpose, although public opinion couldn't settle on what. While some people believed that it was to hide the poor state of the roads, which were proof of the embezzlement of public funds, he believed that the nobility preferred the streets dirty because it provided 'a soft, elastic surface for their carriages'.

In his book on Palermo, the Palermitan writer Robert Alajmo mentions the late photographer Enzo Sellerio, who, when asked by a journalist how he could stand to live in a city smothered in rubbish, sardonically responded that he didn't live in the city, he lived in his home.

Perhaps this local habit of trashing public spaces and retreating to one's gleaming home comes from a sense of owning only the space within one's four walls, as what lay beyond was for so long the domain of foreign rulers. The historian Moses Finley writes that, apart from a few brief moments of independence in the Middle Ages, Sicily was always under foreign domination. For most of the last few thousand years, Sicilians were exploited through taxation, rent of their own land, and looting. This was a condition that did not improve or change all that much when Italy was unified. The exploiters merely changed, from the Bourbons to the northern Italians. The police, the government, the municipality, in the minds of many Palermitans, are neither their compatriots nor their representatives. They are still in the employ of the Savoy and the Bourbons, they are the French, Arabs, Romans, Phoenicians.

Or maybe it's something inherited from Arab Islamic urban planning. While Western attitudes to the city focused on facades – on front yards and public parks and wide, pristine avenues – the Arabs traditionally disregarded the street, or public space, in favour of interior courtyards and gardens. What was behind the façade was more important than the façade itself.

Or perhaps it is precisely a feeling of ownership that drives the filth out into the street: a way of reclaiming the city from invaders or driving them away, both colonial and tourist. Like a child who breaks the head off their doll so that their sister can't play with it.

Later, on my aunt's balcony, she jokes that it is because without the muck to obscure it, Palermo would be too beautiful, and perfection is only allowed in Paradise. I watch as an old woman peels off from the flow of traffic below and parks next to a car that is already double-parked. She takes her handbag from the front seat and totters into the bakery. The owner of the middle car emerges from the supermarket and commences honking his horn, the customary signal to alert this old woman to his presence. It is unclear whether the woman has received his message. He honks for a while, and the sound of the horn simply joins the street symphony, like the rhythmic beat of a drum.

I look back at the map of the historic centre, the city's ancient core. The sterile black lines don't show the filth, the man-made blight, there is no trace of decay and rubble in the white shapes. They are neutral. The city itself, stripped of its surroundings, is presented here out of context. Markers of imperfection are absent, and perhaps because of this, the representation is lifeless.

'Town Plan of Palermo', 1943 road map used by American military and navy departments

A typical road map, the kind my parents once used, of the city. There is the port, to the right of the map, the urban area clustered around it and denoted by grey geometric shapes. The buildings radiate out, become less dense, leaving space for agricultural land, faint lines and waves and dots. This map shows the intricacy of terrain, but not the humanity that subsists upon it. On the map are ten red circles, some small, some larger. The circles indicate bombing targets. The targets include barracks, the harbour and Ucciardone prison close by, the railway station, the hospitals and historical monuments. They will bomb the mental asylum and a juvenile boys' detention centre. The Quattro Canti will be bombed, the Teatro Massimo, as will il Cassaro, the main street of the city, on which a famous church will be destroyed, two other ancient churches, and Porta Felice.

The map represents a spatial abstraction that circumvents our human incapacity to fully grasp the concrete world. It imposes an order that is absent from the living things it represents. The order derives from not just reducing space to a graspable scale, but flattening it, removing its body, removing our bodies' experiences of it. Within the map, the facts of space – the mountains, the sea, the wind, the humans that live in the dwellings suggested by the geometric shapes, who work the land surrounding it – become theoretical. It makes it difficult to fathom the destruction that a simple red circle on a map will wreak.

In his book detailing the Allied invasion of Sicily, Rick Atkinson describes General Lucian Truscott surveying the skyline of the Conca d'Oro from a hillside before taking the city with his troops. The city, a hazy sea of warm terracotta that tumbles down to the actual sea, has already endured months of Allied bombing. Atkinson draws on the descriptions in officers' diaries to illustrate the state of the city the troops marched through. One officer recorded endless streets of 'crumbled houses' and 'whole blocks of shapeless rubble. Parlour, bedroom and bath exposed . . . by the fantastic projectile that strips away the façade and leaves intact the hat on the bureau, the mirror on the wall, the carafe on the night table'. The bombing had been indiscriminate. Over sixty churches had been hit, as was the National Library, where books lay torn open. La Cala, the old port, was so full of rubble that it was no longer recognisable. Its seabed was later discovered to be blanketed by debris from exploded and sunken ships and landmines.

This map marks a turning point for the city. It exists on a strange temporal plane – it is both a representation of what is going to happen, and what has already happened. A satellite photograph shows what the map put into action. Suddenly, the buildings and the land become real. At the port, the smoke mushrooming from just-dropped bombs resembles cotton wool. Photographs of the city streets depict melted roofless churches, wrecked roads, apartment buildings perfectly halved, a mountain of rubble in a collapsed cathedral, the ancient city doors and people's homes reduced to wreckage.

After the war, an independence movement had been gaining ground in Sicily following the birth of the Italian Republic. In an effort to curb the call for independence from the mainland, the island was made an autonomous region a few months before my grandmother's arrival from Rome. A not uncommon belief was that all of Sicily's troubles stemmed from unification, and it had been suggested that rendering it autonomous was a way of assuaging this sentiment. It was also thought that the greater degree of autonomy granted by the island's new status would industrialise it. The *Cassa per il Mezzogiorno* also funnelled national funds into Sicily, which, according to the historian Moses Finley, acted as a kind of 'reparations' for the North's decades of mistreatment, abuse and exploitation of the South.

Instead of industrialising, Palermo became a 'metropolis of bureaucracy'. It was a capital again, and now it had its own ninety-deputy legislative assembly, along with a cabinet of regional ministers. Thousands of new jobs were created. At the same time as my great-grandfather Salvatore was offered a job in Rome, he was also offered one of the thousands of new jobs that had recently been created in Palermo's civil service sector. He wanted to return to the island of his youth, and my great-grandmother Rita preferred to stay on the mainland. They left it to my grandmother to decide the fate of their lives, and she chose Palermo.

In 1946, my grandmother arrived into the aftermath. The historic centre was still covered in rubble and dilapidated homes and caved-in churches. The bombing of dwellings had forced much of the city's poorer population to flee to cramped lodgings and shacks and even caves. Not a lot had changed by the time my grandmother moved there, and not a lot changed in the years after. Maybe she had now become accustomed to seeing cities riddled with the aftershock of war.

I was recently told by my mother that, initially, the family rented a couple of rooms with use of kitchen and bathroom from a woman who lived in and owned the Villino Conigliaro on Piazza Leoni, right at the top of this map, almost outside of it. By *villino*, I mean a detached home with a garden. Searching for it online, I find a website for a boutique holiday apartment complex. I learn that it was a Liberty (Italian art nouveau) villa, partially destroyed during the Allied bombing. In its place, a new building was erected in the guts of the old. Until 2017, the courtyard remained in a state of abandon until it and the horse stalls and servants' quarters were all converted in 2017 by the owners of the bed and breakfast.

Of the two rooms that they had rented, one served as the bedroom of my great-grandparents, and the other served as both the sitting room and bedroom of my grandmother. At that time in Palermo, 5 p.m. until 7:30 p.m. were what my mother calls 'le ore delle visite.' One had to be prepared for visitors from five onwards, with tea, coffee and cakes or biscuits. Visiting hours ended around seven thirty, and my grandmother would study in the midst of ladies' chatter and the smell of coffee brewing. I like to imagine her at a desk by the window, looking out at the centuries-old olive tree and palm tree that are still there in the courtyard. Searching on Google Maps, I see a wide, white-gated building, obscured by the tree-lined street. The villa is two storeys, the second lined with French shutters that open onto small balconies. In the centre of the roof is a large eagle, perhaps a family crest.

Behind the backdrop of my grandmother's new life, political dealings had been and were still converging, building to a point that would forever change the very shape of the city she now lived in. Conveniently, after Sicily was made an autonomous region, the makeup of deputies selected for the legislative assembly was less than 10 per cent separatist, and by 1951, the independence party was almost entirely eradicated. There was a new problem, however. The first regional elections revealed a communist and socialist majority in Sicily. In response to the threat that the Left would take the regional assembly and carry out reforms, both the Right and centrists rallied around the Christian Democracy party.

The Christian Democrats asserted their dominance with, it is fairly safe to say, assistance from the Sicilian mafia, Cosa Nostra, which had experienced a resurgence with help from the American troops. The oft-told story is that when the Americans swept through Sicily, many members of Cosa Nostra, which Fascism had effectively stifled (the party didn't want another power controlling the territory), were released from prison. The occupying military had installed mafia bosses in mayoral seats and other governing roles in towns all over the island. Consequently, in the late forties, there occurred 'a campaign of terror', consisting of the murders of numerous trade union leaders, spreading the message that unions were not welcome.

'Oh, I didn't know that,' my mother said on the phone one day. 'Where did you hear that?'

'*You*,' I replied, in accusation.

She had just told me that my great-grandfather was never offered a job in Rome, that my grandmother was never given a choice of which city to move to.

'I don't know what you're talking about,' she said.

I wondered if she was gaslighting me, or perhaps she had forgotten, or perhaps it was that I'd recently acquired his documents from the State, which contained no Roman job offer and she was backtracking, or perhaps I was crazy and I'd somehow imagined all those times the story was told to me. Later, just as I'd accepted that the story was my own confabulation, a cousin of my grandmother told me the story, unprompted. I remember once, when I caught my mother out in a lie, or perhaps a changed opinion, she explained that it was a cultural difference. Italians often made statements, she said, and later vehemently refuted said statements when they were repeated back to them. It seemed as though almost all her idiosyncrasies could be explained away by 'cultural differences'.

Where had I originally heard the story? Maybe it was my grandmother who told me. I recall liking this story because it explained my grandmother's decisive confidence, showed how her parents had given her the reins to decide on their futures. My existence did not stem from chance; it stemmed, at least in part, from a choice my grandmother had made.

My family history, like any story, has been infused with myths and dogmas and lessons, to form a narrative constructed from other stories from different sources: snatches of dialogue overheard between my mother and aunt in Mondello late at night, or recollections that the siblings shared when together over meals. These are not stories that simply exist in some repository that my mother and her siblings draw from when the storytelling mood takes them. With each narration, the story is created and re-created, modified and altered.

My aunt guesses that they surely arrived in Palermo via train, but I like to imagine that they took the train to Naples and caught a ship there, arriving like so many migrants and conquerors before them. Over the centuries, the city and the fertile valley in which it stood had earned the moniker of the *Conca d'Oro*: the Golden Shell. The mountains cradled the city, which, after the Allied bombings, was a cluster of rubble at the port, great hunks of roof and walls tumbling into the sea. Behind and around it, however, the valley was still green. This was before it was petrified in cement, a lush green land rich with the sweet smells of sun-coloured citrus trees and fat vine leaves bejewelled with clusters of ruby grapes and the bleating of tart-smelling goats clambering down the mountains that embrace the basin.

All their belongings were clasped in their suitcases. What did they carry? Everything they owned, the paltry sum of items that hadn't been lost. Still a child at fifteen, Annalisa wore her hair in braids. Looking out from the stern of the ship to the edge of her father's approaching island, she must have felt something. Perhaps hope, or relief, or fear, or perhaps she was by now too tired to feel anything.

Now, what was once green is grey, what one sees upon nearing Palermo's port at sunset is a clatter of buildings all stacked together, some cupolas, some rooftop terraces. As one pulls closer one sees the lights of the homes that dot the mountains, one hears the nagging of car horns. But, at that hour, fists of pink clouds punch the sky as they did both eighty and four thousand years ago, and the mountains still cut the same silhouette. Stepping off the vessel, one arrives in the port, lined with trawlers and massive ships coming from Naples and cruise ships. The boxy white ticketing offices of different naval transport companies line the port. It smells of salt and exhaust fumes.

Ancient map of Palermo by Matteo Florimi, a Sienese editor and publisher born around 1540 to a family of chalcographers, 1580

A pre-crucifix Palermo, before the Spanish had laid down via Maqueda. The urban cluster is ringed by medieval walls. The intricate network of filigree streets is cut through by the spine of il Cassaro, which stretches from the mountains to the sea. Lining il Cassaro are palaces and cathedrals, along with Palazzo Reale and Castello a mare. The old port curves into the city, and the beginnings of the new port, to its left, are already visible. Outside the city walls, surrounding the city, is a pastel quilt of farmland. The port is filled with sailboats and warships.

When looking at a map, it is impossible to feel the hot lashes of the sirocco against one's face, which is like being slapped with a hairbrush. It is so hot that the dust in the air dazzles. The white buildings and wide footpaths glow so blindingly that I have to shield my eyes. The outlines of the palm trees lining the centre of the boulevard shimmer like a desert mirage. My whole body slumps downward, my limbs lead weights, and I drag myself into a bar to keep from crumpling into the shadow of an alley.

The first time I experienced the sirocco, I was at my aunt's old house above Palermo, reading on the *terrazzo*, which is what in Italian refers to a large balcony, big enough for a potted garden, tables, chairs, and a clothesline. From this position, it is possible to look out over the city and to the mountains on the other side. My aunt was hanging clothes up to dry in the sun. She looked out towards the valley below and said, 'The sirocco is coming soon.' I asked whether it had been forecast in the news, and she replied, 'No. But you can feel it in the air.' One of my cousin's daughters was fidgeting, rushing on and off the terrace. The other daughter had taken to her bed. That morning she couldn't be coaxed to drink her milk – she just buried her face in her arms. The Sicilian writer Leonardo Sciascia observed that 'before it can be felt in the air the sirocco has already taken possession of our minds, our knees'. This hot wind whistles through the

Sahara and over the sea stretch separating Africa from the island. Its arrival is heralded by an aura, like a migraine. The blood boils, the brain swells, when you close your eyes you see fireworks. You want to stuff your body in a drawer.

I read somewhere that during the Renaissance, when Palermo's aristocracy got into the habit of building lavish villas, they would outfit these residences with 'sirocco rooms', where the family would retreat for hours when the red wind blew. These rooms were windowless subterranean caverns dug close to wellsprings. Their walls were limestone, and this combination, of limestone, underground air and water, produced a cooling effect.

Winds in general have a marked effect on our lives. Wind guides or hinders ships, it uproots trees if it is strong enough, it affects our moods, it facilitates the migrations of plant life by carrying seeds from one location to another.

The sirocco is a reminder of the desert south of the sea, of the proximity of Africa, of the fact that this stretch of sea is narrow enough, or perhaps that the wind is strong enough, for its red sand and dust to be carried across. It's an invisible message to the island that it is not as isolated as it feels, and it brings whispers from far-off lands, reminding us that this wind that whips our faces or triggers our headaches has done the same to unknown strangers.

At the bar, I order an espresso and stir in a packet of sugar, an addition I only make when I need to pick my body back up in the heat. I continue down via della Libertà to the north of the city, past the Politeama theatre, to my mother's old apartment.

When I look at the map, I try to locate myself within it, situate what would become my mother's street, determine the route by which my grandmother entered the city. But I find it impossible to do so. This old map is a composition, in that it makes the city seem composed, but the Palermo I know has nothing ordered about it. How to square the careful lines delineating roads and separating fields with the actuality of standing on a busy street in the city as cars rush past?

A map of Palermo does not show the daily complications of traversing it. It does not show the wildness of the traffic pumping through the roads. I have become accustomed to half closing my eyes when crossing the road, refusing to jump at the motorists who only stop when they are about to run one over, and who otherwise swerve around my moving body, and who sometimes, at a zebra crossing, will proceed to honk their horns at me. I ask myself whether this happens to everyone, or if my foreignness is something that can be read on my body.

While the lines that represent roads on a map are motionless, the traffic, for better or worse, is a vital element of this city. The map does not pierce one's skin like the vicious summer sun, does not emit the car fumes mingling with the thick smoke that billows from the rudimentary street grills, and the smells of fried food and sea air and petrol wafting from the ships in the port. In other words, the map does not reproduce the all-encompassing *feel* of being in the space. It doesn't conjure up the fish stall that takes up the entire walkway and some of the road, the glittering sardines and translucent prawns and spiky sea urchins halved to expose their orange, star-shaped innards, and the gaping heads of swordfish glistening on beds of ice.

It erases the watermelon man, whose stall consists of four walls of massive red- and yellow-fleshed watermelons, creating a room, in which, my uncle tells me when we drive past, he sleeps on a cot in the summer. One can't hear the buzzing of the farmers driving their Piaggio *Ape*, three-wheeled pick-up trucks, down the mountains and into the city. One can't stop and watch as they select a street corner and double park someone in. One can't observe how from there they sell their harvests from the truck beds: blood oranges and dappled lemons and bundles of milky lettuce.

1945 post-war plan for the reconstruction of Palermo following the Allied bombings

Left of centre is the old city centre, that familiar quartered square, patterned like a stained-glass mosaic. Around it are growths, some grids to the south of the city, mostly to the north and north-west, by the port. Surrounding these hard, exacting lines of construction are the soft lines and white space of pastoral land.

Even though the city depicted in this plan never came to be, this map makes it seem like it may as well have. In a sense, it tricks the viewer. It takes the facts of the existent city and shapes them into something recognisable enough that it seems true. Things are judged by their forms. A newspaper article is a product of reportage, the characters in a novel are fictional, and a map, even a plan for an as-yet unrealised place in map form, alludes to a real place. This is why fantasy books so often include maps of their world: to make it more real for the reader and allow them to orient themselves within that world.

More and more, I have realised in my writing and research and interrogation of things that I always took to be immutable facts, that the waters of memory are murky, embedded with a few muddy and rusted relics, whose original forms are lost and open to many forms of interpretation. Unlike the map, the story mutates and changes shape with time, and there are as many versions of it as there are tellers and tellings. It is commonly accepted as fact that memory is not a recording that our minds have made, which we can then replay at will. Rather, it is a reconstructive process of the mind, one which combines the imagination with the first or second-hand memories of others.

We take the stories that we have heard and remake them in our minds and tell them again, and each time they change. The kernel of fact at the centre of the story is like the grain of sand that settles in the oyster, that is folded under layer upon layer of tissue and becomes a pearl: something else entirely from its origin, something that no longer exists.

While I was writing this book, my grandmother's condition worsened, and my mother could no longer care for her at home. My grandmother was put into an aged care facility, and a few weeks later, fifteen minutes after my mother and my uncle had left after visiting her, she passed away. It seemed an impossible outcome. In the last few years, as she had survived hospital stays resulting from infections, had survived after stopping her medications, and after weeks of refusing food, we had taken to calling her Lazarus. We thought she'd live forever.

I watched the funeral in Australia on a livestream at four in the morning in Trieste, from a camera positioned in the ceiling. I could see the coffin, the priest, the backs of my family's heads sparsely seated in the front rows. I could see from the way that my mother and brother's heads hung and their hands brought tissues to their faces that they had started crying.

A week or so later, my uncle gathered all her children and grandchildren – from Brisbane and Wollongbar and Palermo and Trieste – over video chat. He read from a letter she had written us all a decade before, in preparation for her eventual death. He'd made a little speech about her before reading, mentioned a story we'd all been told hundreds of times. It had been her dream to be a professional fencer, and she'd been offered a place to train in Milan, but her father wouldn't let her go. She would have made it to the Olympics, he said, something that she had said and repeated and that her children had repeated and that her grandchildren then repeated, so that it became one of our family's scriptures, one of our matriarch's lost futures.

Instead, she attended the University of Palermo, where she got degrees in law and political science. It had been her dream to be a lawyer, he said, but when she found herself a single mother of three at twenty-nine, she had to let that dream go too. Gradually an image had formed around her, one which she had promoted, of a woman whose potential had been cut short by the circumstances of her life. After his speech he read her letter, which was more effusive than her usual jocular stoicism, but was true to her judicious and precise nature. She had indicated which piece of jewellery went to which grandchild, had written private, loving last words, had named all her children and grandchildren without singling out the favourites. She requested that we go to Mass once in a while and light a candle in her honour.

I found recently, in a drawer in my study, a few vintage postcards I had picked up at a market in Seville a year ago. One showed two women dressed in white, sitting on an oriental rug under a horseshoe arch covered in Moorish tiles. The second is a detailed black-and-white panoramic drawing of Seville's cathedral. The third is a colour drawing, a blue sky over green hedges and palm trees, a view of the garden of Seville's Alcazar. All the postcards are stamped and addressed and written on. One is addressed to my parents, another to my cousin, the last to my grandmother. It all came back to me: I had written the postcards in Seville, had bought stamps, but hadn't been able to find a post box before leaving. The postcards had stayed in my backpack, and were shoved into a drawer on returning, I'm sure along with a mental note to send them from Trieste.

I evidently never sent them, a fact I only stumbled upon after it was too late. By that point my grandmother was gone, and I realised I had lost my last opportunity to send her one final postcard. It had seemed trivial at the time of shoving the postcards in the drawer, but now it felt incredibly lonely, to read the message I had left for her, knowing I would never address anything to her again. She had never received it, had never known I intended to send it, and suddenly it all seemed connected: my absence meant I had missed the last year of her life and I couldn't even get it together enough to send her a postcard. Now that postcard reminds me of one of the many times I might have expressed love, but failed to.

The map described above was a plan for a once-future city, dreamed up by some urbam planner. It can still be detected in the current city, particularly in its northward expansion, where my great-grandparents and grandmother and later mother settled. And yet, like life, the city did not stay true to the plan, and now this map is a map of a non-existent city, just as our imagined futures are derailed by time. It is a kind of broken promise for a future that never came to fruition.

Our own lost futures are like this map: they go on existing alongside what actually happens, unlived shadow lives that unfold alongside and inform our actual lives. They are so fundamental that I know more about my grandmother's potential futures than her actual past. When I think back to my past selves, I clearly recall my expectations of what I or my life would become. Life, of course, rarely turns out how we expect it to, but those past, never-fulfilled desires are still essential to who I am now.

Topographic Map of Ancient Palermo, 1827. By Salvatore Morso, born in Palermo in 1766. Despite his family's modest means, he would go on to become a professor of Arabic

The city in its beginnings. A simple map, like a child's primary-colour drawing: a coloured close-up of a settlement on a small, green peninsula. In the middle, a cluster of buildings line the only road, running the length of the cape. Outlining this cluster is a red wall. The wall is dotted with sentinels. Two blue bodies of water push into the green of the land like bunny ears. On their banks, a few docked ships. Scattered on the surrounding land are dwellings, stretches of wall, green fields.

Regarding Palermo, my family stories, passed down to me by my mother and grandmother, were almost all I had to go on. I did know the stereotypes of Sicily – the mafia, the crude backwardness, the obscene piety, the desperate poverty, the entrenched corruption. These stories felt like they came from a different world to the stories of my family. I was in the Public Gardens of Trieste a while ago, sitting on a bench while watching the son of a friend play in the playground, when a well-dressed older woman with grey hair swept back in a bun came and sat next to me. She had her grandchild with her in a pram. The baby's older sister was out playing on the equipment. The woman began talking to me about her youth, how innocent she was at twenty, still a virgin. She pulled her granddaughter from the pram and stood her on her lap. Eyeing her smiling face, she said, 'It's all different these days. This one will probably be doing it by the time she's twelve.' The woman asks where I'm from. I explain my birth in Australia, my Sicilian parents. 'Oh!' she says. Yes, she could hear the South in my accent. She went to Sicily last year. She was so surprised by how modern it was. Running water, up-to-date technology, all the modern conveniences. 'I had expected all the women to be dressed in black with scarves covering their hair. Perhaps it's still like that away from the coast.'

Growing up, my parents preferred American films, and most of the Italian books in our home were translations of English classics. I took things that my family said for unquestionable fact. I didn't know, for example, I looked it up, that the national Trenitalia train network ran all over Sicily. I had been told by my family who lived in Palermo, for years, that such a network did not exist. 'It might as well not exist,' they said when I told them I was, in fact, taking the train. 'It's slow and it breaks down all the time. Whatever you do, take the bus.' I took the train, all over the island.

One of the last times I visited, Palermo was hit by a massive flash flood. The torrents seemed to take specific paths through the city, preferring certain roads over others. We watched videos of people atop their cars, or wading waist-deep in water with their phones and handbags held above their heads. I suggested to my cousin, who was complaining that the flash flooding was due to the mayor apparently refusing to clean out the underground sewage system, that water tended to flood where old rivers once or still were underneath the city. She laughed and assured me that there were no rivers in Palermo. I understood there weren't currently any rivers in Palermo. But perhaps there had been? 'No,' she firmly told me. 'No, no, no. Trust me.'

The peninsula on the map described above is known as the Phoenician foot, though it looks more to me like a tongue in an open mouth. The map itself is a representation of what the beginnings of Palermo are supposed to have looked like. This 'foot' is named for some of the first settlers of what would become the Sicilian capital, which is thought to have originally been a village of Sicanians, one of the first indigenous tribes of Sicily.

The basin which embraces Palermo was once rich with rivers. Two of these rivers, the Kemonia and the Papireto, mirrored one another, creating a peninsula where the city centre would one day sit. The Kemonia sprang from where the lush parkland of Villa d'Orleans is today and flowed seaward from there, through Ballarò and la Kalsa, and the Papireto from the northwest, and across il Capo and Conceria. La Cala, the ancient port which arcs into the city, was once a natural inlet at which the twin rivers converged and flowed together into the bay. When the Phoenicians arrived, Palermo literally was 'all port'. What remains of the rivers still meets there.

The Phoenicians were seafarers who navigated the Mediterranean, founding trading posts as they went. They are thought to have established Carthage, on the Tunisian coast, and the Carthaginians in turn turned the trading posts into colonies. The Phoenicians sailed into the green and blue valley and dropped anchor on the banks of its rivers, scratching out the beginnings of a city and calling it *Zis*.

Then came the Romans, the Arabs and the Normans. The Arab historian and geographer Al-Idrisi wrote in 1139 of a Norman Palermo in which 'the rivers traverse all of the capital of Sicily, where there are also inexhaustible sources of water. Palermo abounds in fruit trees . . . and inside the walls there is a triumph of orchards, magnificent villas and many slow-moving streams, brought down from the mountains in canals.' The two rivers nourished the soil and crops flourished; the scent of citrus pervaded the basin, which was filled with the lush green growths of trees and crops. It was easy to sow and food was in abundance. The city itself was surrounded by what has been described as a 'vast orchard'. From the East, the Arab rulers imported bitter orange, lemon trees, mulberries and sugarcane. They grew papyrus in the swamplands. The melodic trickling of running water – that of the rivers and reservoirs and lily ponds and canals and fountains – could be heard all the time.

The Kemonia was torrential and wild, regularly flooding and wreaking destruction, while the Papireto was the more temperate of the two. It was said that the Papireto was a tributary of the Nile, connected through an underground canal, and underneath the foundations of the city, originating all the way from Africa, there was a mummified crocodile. The Kemonia, which now runs underneath the city, was also christened by the Arabs as the *Fiume del Maltempo*, or the 'River of Bad Weather'.

Despite the Kemonia's tendency to overflow, the changing rulers of Palermo built along the banks of the two rivers. One invasion after another, as slums were crammed on their shores, the rivers narrowed. The Papireto thickened, coming to be used as an open sewer. What once fed the city became a dumping ground for its waste. The basin became humid and malaria festered in the stagnant water. What was left of it was eventually interred by the Spanish in the late sixteenth century, like the corpses in the catacombs. A muddy subterranean canal is all that remains.

If a city can be read like a book, then Palermo's underground rivers are the subtext, a subtext many of its inhabitants unwittingly navigate as they walk its streets. But the subtext and the accepted narrative do not always correspond. In order to hew to the narrative on the occasions in which they do not, we might see things that aren't there. We might ignore some facts in preference of others. But who writes the narrative, or better, who sets its conditions?

Historically, Palermo has been no stranger to floods. The earliest recorded flood was in 1557, when the valley was hit by a prolonged tempest. Water welled four metres high at the city walls. A few years earlier, a dam wall had been built, so as to protect the city from this exact event. The Kemonia, by now underground, raged. The floodgates broke. A tidal wave of water and debris and mud stripped from the surrounding mountains rushed at the city. The city walls, two metres thick, were torn open. The wave flowed onto the path cut by the Kemonia, killing two thousand Palermitans and destroying five hundred homes that had been built over the underground riverbed. The flood plunged the city in its currents before gushing into La Cala and out to the sea.

The last major flood occurred over another tempestuous winter in 1931, when floods hit the city centre during a storm. While rain poured incessantly, the subterranean rivers, which had been thought dry, swelled and found one another. They again reclaimed their ancient paths. The city was plunged in water. Via Roma became a two-metre-tall lagoon, and in other parts of Palermo the water reached six metres in height. Gusts of the tramontana wind whipped the city, knocking down walls. Photos online show people walking along floating bridges made of wooden planks. Underneath them runs a venerable river, bordered by buildings whose entrances have been swallowed up.

In another, the shadowy figures of two priests wade through a flooded road, palm trees sticking out of the water at odd angles and onlookers stand out on their balconies surveying the situation. The front page of *La Domenica del Corriere* shows an image of two men helping a woman climb out of a canoe and onto a balcony that is now just above water level. Another depicts what looks to be via Roma, cars stopped in the water and carts overturned. Ten men huddle together on the back of a horse-drawn cart. In another, an entire wall has been knocked down into the earth, revealing the foundations of the city.

Over the years, the Kemonia was diverted to the Oreto river to the south. A 2009 article on *Live Sicilia*, however, reports a city flood. The Kemonia had reclaimed its ancient bed, rising up on via Porta di Castro. The article reports that while the river is underground, a few minutes of rain is enough to reincarnate its ancient iteration. The journalist writes that the inhabitants of the area are ignorant about the history of the river, and uninterested in it. They insist, he writes, on blaming the mayor, who according to them refuses to clean the underground sewers.

Underneath the article, two commenters condemn their fellow Palermitans for lacking knowledge of their city, while two more accuse the journalist of being a liar. They point to the fact that water also flowed into streets under which the Kemonia doesn't run, or they deny that it still runs underneath the streets. According to one commenter, this theory could only make sense if a crack had ruptured in the pavement, allowing the water to surge. One advises: 'Try to keep the manholes and the sewers in perfect condition instead of stealing money and making excuses!!!', while the other adds: 'The fact is that the mayor should take more care of our city which needs a lot of help!!! In addition to removing the garbage from the bins, the city should be made cleaner, with more road maintenance, and among the many things our bike lanes are ILLEGAL!'

Morso drew his map in 1827, long after the rivers had been interred. His map is an imagining by the future cartographer of a past city, a ghost or corpse buried underneath the cobblestones he paces, just as much an abstraction or a fantasy to him as it is to me, although he and I, too, knew and know very different iterations of the same city. The map he draws features approximations of dwellings in miniature, the unbridled Kemonia reduced to a swath of blue, the old walls a cinnamon-coloured outline. There is no life in the map itself, no captains guiding the ships from the sea into the ports, no farmers tending to their flocks, no people walking the streets. The map is the setting for a story, and it is up to the viewer to populate it, to drive the narrative forward.

Recently I was walking through the Ballarò market. The steam billowing from frying meats and *panelle*, squares of parsley-dusted chickpea flour, merged with the scent wafting from the freshly baked bread in the *panetterie*, the pungent smell of fresh fish, and the metallic sweetness of animal parts: meaty cow tongues, ropes of intestines lustrous like mother-of-pearl, and folds of spongey Easter-yellow lungs. Whole pink octopus, just pulled out of boiling water, were sat on plates. The vendors at the market, originally thought to be a souk, were Sicilian, Tunisian, Pakistani, Afghani. 'Ballarò' is said to derive from 'Bahlara', the name of a nearby village inhabited by Arab merchants.

I had walked past the dried fruit and yellow peaches and figs ready to burst from their flesh. Piles of red, orange and yellow spices, boxes of green pistachios and almonds fat as thumbprints. Thick bricks of cheese, from white to bright yellow, and bouquets of basil and oregano and parsley. There were vats of black and green olives, and ropes of paper-skinned garlic bulbs. Among the stalls were the outdoor plastic tables of restaurants, and I sat down at one. The waiter served me cold wine from a jug. I ate boiled octopus and potato doused with lemon and olive oil and parsley; *sarde a Beccafico,* cleaned sardines enfolded around a mixture of breadcrumbs, raisins, pine nuts, garlic and parsley; and *caponata*, a sweet-and-sour marriage of fried eggplant, olives, tomato sauce, capers and celery.

It seemed impossible that the ground underneath me was once navigable by ship.

Old city map from 1778

This map is again centred around the X axis of the city. The city centre here is a parched riverbed or striated muscle tissue. Via Maqueda runs outside the city walls to the left, creating one axis of a new, smaller cross parallel to the larger one, called Addizione Regalmici, designed by the Sicilian engineer, Nicolò Palma. The new continuation of Maqueda is the beginning of what will become via della Libertà. Below, unconnected to the former construction, by the water, is a fishing village, Borgo Vecchio.

Once a week, over Zoom, I give conversational English lessons to the cousin of a friend. My student also happens to be an architecture professor at the University of Palermo. After a month of regular lessons, she tells me she can't take it anymore: she doesn't want to order a meal in a restaurant or declare what colour a dog is. We decide that she'll start giving me lessons on Palermo's architectural history in English.

During our first lesson, for which she has prepared a slideshow, she shows me the progression of Palermo through ancient to modern maps. As she speaks, she runs through the maps: Palermo as a green tongue in the middle of two rivers dotted with little ships, Palermo before the Spanish had laid down via Maqueda, Palermo during its first expansion. Here the rivers frame the city walls; here, in 1665, they are just thin ribbons, putrid sewers. Looking at a medieval map, she points my attention to the walls around La Cala port. Here, facing the sea, they were thicker, hollowed out and filled with soil so that, should pirates and invaders approach and fire cannons, the earthen walls would absorb the hits. In another map, a quilt of squares and rectangles surrounds the city, a neat paper representation of a far more rampant reality: plumes of wheat swaying in the sea breeze, wine-dark grapes bursting on leafy vines, oranges and lemons ready to be plucked from branches, almond trees blooming pink with flowers and the branches of fig trees sagging under the weight of luscious fruit.

I have been told that when I am asked about the book I am writing, I visibly wince. I find it difficult to explain, even to myself, what it is I am looking for in these cities, but most especially Palermo. It is the only city in which I have my own memories, my own romantic version of the past. It is the only city I can walk through and note that the buildings are squatter than I had remembered, the promenade shorter, the piazza smaller. Was my memory mistaken, I ask myself, or did it change in my absence?

After my first adult trip to Palermo, I returned almost every summer. I had initially thought that my subsequent visits would intensify my memories, but they only served to rewrite and replace them. Now, instead of comparing everything to childhood recollection, I compare the current city to the one I was in the summer before. When I walk through the streets, the memories of the last couple of years rush back to me, rather than recollections from my childhood or the stories I was told about the past.

I find my own memories, however, to be more dependable than the stories I have been told. Like fairy tales, these stories change with every telling, and my relatives disagree over the different versions.

I only realised this recently, that my mother has systematically shifted facts in our family history to serve whatever purpose is at hand. For example, she had always told me that my grandmother had a degree in opera from the conservatory of music in Palermo. I had believed this, until a few years ago when my grandmother corrected her – she had actually dropped out, because an instructor, in her opinion, did not recognise her talent. Recently, my mother remarked: all the women in our family suffer from stage fright. You, me, your grandmother – that was why she dropped out of the conservatory. (Was my memory of my grandmother's explanation another confabulation?)

My mother also once recalled how, as a child, her father would pick her up from school in the afternoon in his chauffeured car, laden with sweets. But, my aunt said, this only happened once.

Perhaps this is why I find myself so drawn to maps of Palermo. Like a narrative structure, every mapping is a retelling of the city, and in every retelling details change, whether they are superficial or fundamental. As my student flicks through the various maps and versions of Palermo throughout time, the city morphs and transforms. But while the city may change, this map will not. This version of the city is resistant to time. No matter how many times I turn away and come back to it, the lines will never deviate, never blend or shift.

Master Plan of Palermo in 1885, designed by the Sicilian engineer Felice Giarrusso.

The original city centred in black, the proposal for the new city clustered around it in red: to the south, the west and the north. The original shape of the city is no longer distinguishable. The fishing village, Borgo Vecchio, has now been subsumed by the city. While the white lines delineating roads in the quarters of the old city are curved and flowing and narrow like rivulets, the new roads in the new red quarters are all straight, thick grids. These red sections are the proposed additions to the city, dividing it into sixteen sections with streets styled on the Haussmann model. My student pronounces this first transformation to be, in her opinion, 'the first sack of Palermo'.

By the time my grandmother arrived in 1946, Palermo had for the most part morphed into the planned city described above, with the addition of the destruction wrought by bombings. It still took up the centre of the Conca d'Oro, surrounded by green farmland and orchards that clambered up the foothills. It still glimmered under the sun and smelled of the sea and citrus. There, to the north of the old city, the new city stretched out. Palermo's horizontal axis, via Maqueda, which ran past the Teatro Massimo to become via Ruggero Settimo, had been extended into via della Libertà. In 1891, a national exhibition opened in Palermo, which lasted for two years. The exhibition was set up in the new city, in a quadrangle formed by via Dante, via Principe di Villafranca, via della Libertà, and the street on which my mother would eventually grow up, via la Farina. The pavilions built for the exhibition were designed by the famed Palermitan Liberty architect, Ernesto Basile. The pavilions showcased art, Sicilian ethnography, agriculture and industry. After the National Exhibition, a further northern addition to the city was made.

By the time my grandmother arrived, via della Libertà was an avenue lined with Liberty or Eclectic (a collage-type style that drew from many schools such as Medieval, Baroque and

Classical) villas and small palaces and castles and gardens and palm trees. All of these had been erected between 1905 and 1934. The villas that lined via della Libertà and its surrounding streets and which were otherwise strewn throughout the city and its outskirts might be described as whimsical or quirky. They featured frescos and murals, sinuous staircases, turrets and terraces, stained glass decorations and floral masonry patterns. They had protruding pitched roofs that recalled northern European roofs and circular windows. Some had Moorish horseshoe arches and symmetry and central courtyards, which had been brought to the city thousands of years before by Arab architects. Some mimicked medieval castles, with towers and gothic windows. Some had light-filled, gazebo-like towers rising from their roofs, and others English-style conservatories, where Palermo's rich drank tea surrounded by winter gardens.

Despite the rubble, the old city was still filled with the pink domes of Arab-Norman buildings and garish Rococo churches and the secret garden courtyards of convents. Beneath and beyond the destruction in the old city, there was a wealth of fruit orchards and noble palaces, set in a verdant valley in which fennel, chicory, asparagus and cabbage grew wild.

My student flips over to another slide: the 1945 plan for the post-war reconstruction of the city. In this map, the city continues to expand to the north, the urban area three times what it was originally. And yet, it is still surrounded by green, there is still seemingly a method to its rebuilding and expansion. Looking at this map, one glimpses a city that never was, but might have been. Like all plans for the future, the planned map exudes hope.

Perhaps my grandmother and her parents saw themselves in their surroundings: they, like the city, would rise from these ashes.

Master plan for Palermo, 1956-1962

A black and white map of what Palermo would become. Via della Libertà extends northward. The sea laps at the ancient centre and the expansion around it morphs and grows, edging out towards the mountain ranges, north past la Favorita parkland and towards Mondello Beach and Sferracavallo Beach, it crawls up the mountain towards Monreale, and down south, closing the gap between the city and Romagnolo Beach. The quilt denoting farmland is gone. A road ringing the city emerges. There is no longer any shape to the city, no longer any definition or order. Like a weed, its grey growths creep up the mountain sides.

My aunt often remarks that the twenty-minute drive from the city to her old home in Monreale, a town that overlooks the city from the mountains, used to be like driving to an altogether separate place. At a certain point, the city stopped, and gave way to the pastures and orchards of farmers. Now, the city meets the town, merging to form one body.

It is only when we look at a series of maps that claim to represent the same space that we notice the constant shifting of natural boundaries and margins. Concrete spreads over grassland, rivers dry up, marshlands become beaches, forests flatten. Terrain is like a body in the constant flux of ageing, a map like a snapshot or portrait that captures a single moment in time. And like a snapshot or portrait, the map inspires mourning for the loss of the past landscape it depicts.

Now most of those villas that had welcomed my grandmother's arrival along and around Libertà are gone. My student shows me photos of old villas alongside what replaced them. Villa Cusenza, a three-story Gothic and Classical confection of arched balconies and windows topped by an airy turret and decorated with Liberty-style flower motifs, became a nine-storey apartment building. Villa Deliella, designed by Ernesto Basile in 1905, a two-storey structure with a conservatory and an open-air tower, was famously demolished in 1959 the night before it was granted cultural heritage status. It became and is still a parking lot. Palazzo Barresi, a building with six-storeys of balconied windows, was knocked down to become a glass cube of offices.

The cityscape filled up with concrete high-rises, boring plaster buildings with boxy balconies, or faded billboards, or parking lots. The cement labyrinth now takes up the entire basin, so what was once green is now grey.

The evolution of the city as tracked in these maps and photographs is known as *il Sacco di Palermo*, which refers to the systematic concretization of the Conca d'Oro. It began in 1958, when Salvo Lima became mayor of Palermo. He would remain in this position for four years, before going on to become Sicily's most powerful politician. Vito Ciancimino was the city's rough-mouthed commissioner for public works, who later became mayor himself. The former's father was a mafioso, and he followed in his father's footsteps. The latter was a barber's son. Both had been early in joining the conservative Christian Democrat (DC) party as the Second World War was ending. It was a smart choice, since from the end of the war in 1945 until 1992, when the *Tangentopoli* corruption scandal brought the party and the entire Italian government down, the DC was never out of power.

This was both despite and because of the popularity of the Italian Communist Party. The DC had the support of the Vatican, which was terrified at the prospect of the atheism that attends communism. The DC also had the unwavering support of the United States. According to a 1976 *New York Times* article, the CIA covertly financed the Christian Democrats to the tune of three million USD per year from the end of the Second World War up until 1967. In 1972, Richard Nixon approved CIA funnelling funding of ten million USD. Another *New York Times* article from the same day, January 6, reports that the CIA had made secret cash payments of six million USD 'to individual anti-Communist political leaders in Italy since Dec. 8 in an effort to prevent further Communist Party gains in national elections there'. A high-level US government official described the action as 'support[ing] our friends'. The 'support' wasn't only financial.

A decades-long campaign of 'psychological warfare' was carried out, involving propaganda and influencing the DC through the extension and withdrawal of aid to discriminate against, silence, smear, and exclude members of left-wing parties or unions.

DC support did not only come from the Vatican or the United States. Votes in the South, which was a DC stronghold, were delivered by, as Peter Robb puts it, '*friends*' in Sicily, although these 'friends' were not the same 'friends' that the US official had been referring to. ('People didn't talk about the mafia in Sicily,' Robb writes, 'but they talked a lot about friends'). It later became clear that these 'friends' and the DC had a symbiotic relationship.

In the years preceding Lima's tenure as mayor, land reform had broken up many of the feudal estates. Agriculture was declining and peasants flocked to the Sicilian capital, which was now devastated by the war. Building boomed. Parks were paved over. Alexander Stille describes it as the transformation of 'one of the most beautiful cities in Europe into a thick, unsightly forest of cement condominia'.

The prior owners, or descendants of the owners of the old villas still live on and around via della Libertà. For the most part, they gave up these villas without a fight. A family friend, who lives in a penthouse with a wraparound terrace on a street adjacent to Libertà, also owns two floors of apartments in another building on the same road. The apartments were promised and given by the city council in the sixties, in exchange for the family villa. I have been told that the municipality approached the owners of homes and gave them two options: either to sell or to have their property seized.

The demolishing and building stretched out into the decades. The area of construction grows on the map like mould, creeping out of the initial northern expansion of the city and down south to the industrial area. The gurgles of cement mixers and cranes and falling walls were the soundscape of my mother's youth, when the air was made hazy by the dust dispersed by constant demolition.

New neighbourhoods on the city's outskirts were built to accommodate the growing population. But these new areas, intended for the city's poor and middle class, were more cheaply built than those around Libertà. They were crowded and bunched up close to one another, and each mimicked the one before it. It's an eerie sensation, walking or driving past these areas, the intimate interiors of lives shaped by a greed and disdain that I cannot accept, cannot make sense of.

These buildings in the new neighbourhoods were constructed with watered-down cement. Now, the spackled boxes look diseased, as plaster regularly peels off like a scab. The poor construction doesn't discriminate between rich and poor. My aunt once lived in a building that had been showing signs of wear for a while. One day, a fillet of thick plaster dropped from a balcony bottom, wrecking a car below. The bottoms of the balconies reveal their rusted skeletons. Under many balconies, sheets of green tarp are fixed, so as to prevent more errant damage.

It was later found that, over Lima and Ciancimino's four-year tenure, 4,200 building permits were granted by the city. Over three thousand of these permits had been granted to just five people, who were fronts for mafia-owned construction companies. Cosa Nostra controlled construction, property development and real estate. Italy became the world's biggest per capita consumer of cement. Buildings and bridges and roads that led nowhere and ended abruptly were continuously planned out, over-funded, half finished, and abandoned.

Ciancimino was arrested in 1984 and Lima was killed one morning in March 1992. While leaving his villa in Mondello with friends, two youths on the back of a motorcycle overtook Lima's car and began firing shots. The car jerked to a halt, Lima and his two companions clambered out. While the other two shielded themselves behind a dustbin, Lima was shot dead while attempting to run. His friends, spared by the assassins, left the scene. The country's prime minister at the time, Giulio Andreotti, whose own mafia connections would not only be the subject of future films, but also be put on trial, attended the funeral.

Now they are memorialised in the altered city skyline and the subsequent maps of contemporary Palermo. No longer the Conca d'Oro, it is now often referred to bitterly by Palermitans as the *Conca di Cemento*. I recall the first time hearing this new phrase, in the backseat of the car of some old family friends, as we wound up Mount Pellegrino. As I gazed out at the blue sea lapping at the grey sea of the city, the latter hemmed in by the stark mountains, I still found myself awed by the brutal, violent beauty of it all. I like to think that, though the cities we arrived in were vastly different, the mountains both my grandmother and I saw on our arrivals were the same.

A rendering of a past Palermo by Francesco Scoto, 1665

A map that looks like the page of a storybook, illustrating a storybook city. A cluster of buildings with triangle roofs straight out of a child's imagination, a palace at the top, the city framed by a wall that protrudes with spade-shaped ramparts. A thin rope, the Oreto river, flows into the port, along with what was left of the Papireto (the Kemonia was by now buried). In the bay, a few sailing ships are docked. Fields of agriculture, grain, groves and pastures are arranged around the city like biscuits on a baking tray.

Even in this map we see the city's ancient spine, il Cassaro, running from the palace at the foot of the mountains and out to the sea, which came in where via Roma intersects. It was forged by the Arabs, and its name comes from the Arabic *qasr*, castle. For the Normans, it was via Marmorea, Marble Street, so named for the flint that paved its surface. The Spanish named it via Toledo in 1564, and it remained that way until Italian unification, when it became via Vittorio Emanuele. Once, when it was the most important road in the city, it was lined with shops and cathedrals or mosques and palaces. Processions came through this street, ending at the sea.

Via Vittorio Emanuele was pedestrianised a few years ago, in 2017. Before, the street was clogged by motor traffic. It was lined with antiquarian bookshops, but one passed hardly any people walking down it. Now, the bookshops are gone. One walks down these streets amidst waves of people. It is lined with places to buy souvenirs, such as painted ceramic plates and Sicily-shaped magnets, gelato shops and kiosks selling granita and *limonata al sale*, a tart drink of salted, ice-cold lemonade.

Throughout all these changes, however, it has always and still remains il Cassaro for Palermitans, who have the tendency to refer to streets and landmarks by their ancient names, even when giving directions to foreigners or newcomers. This temporal muddle is an essential part of the language of the city, by which I don't necessarily mean its dialect. By language I mean manners of speaking, knowing the special terms for things, knowing what certain gestures mean, or what is implied by the invocation of certain names. I mean sharing in the collective knowledge of the city, and its particular way of seeing the world.

On il Cassaro is a small museum that has opened up in the few years since the road became pedestrianised. Over the entrance there is a rainbow banner announcing the No Mafia Memorial. Inside, a few trestle tables are stacked with books for sale, and a person at a desk accepts donations and directs the visitor up the short flight of stairs behind them, to a tight, white-walled courtyard. The courtyard opens onto two rooms, which themselves open onto two more rooms, walls all filled with photos taken from the archives of the newspaper *l'Ora*. Along with the photos, plaques tell the story of the bandits in Sicily and the mafia in Palermo.

The bloodshed began in the sixties, when one mafia clan was at war with another. These were silent wars in which most Palermitans were bystanders. Bodies were their only discernible symptom. It was in the seventies that the mafia began to assassinate members of the public. They murdered journalists who were planning investigative stories and prosecutors who investigated their activities of building speculation, drug trafficking and cigarette smuggling. They killed magistrates and police detectives.

My mother had told me that when she lived here, it was said that a fresh cadaver turned up every morning. The city stank of rot. The photos in the memorial show the backseats of cars sticky with blood and shattered glass, veiled widows in mourning, funeral gatherings and bodies slumped back, mouths agape in car seats, prone corpses outlined in chalk, photos of the dead alive with their family, mutilated cadavers, bloodied bodies on stretchers, and the eventual mayor and reformer of the city, Leoluca Orlando, speaking to a crowd in what must be the late eighties. These were photographs that littered the newspapers over decades, photographs to which readers inevitably became somewhat hardened, confronted as they were each morning by the fragility of the human body, gruesome death, the pain on the faces of loved ones.

The photographs of the murder scenes are artfully framed. In one, the lens of the camera peers through a car window to a lifeless slumped head. In another, a group of men carry Piersanti Mattarella's body away from the crime scene, attempting to cover his face with a blanket. The camera focuses on his face, just at the moment that the blanket has half-fallen away. In these photos, no detail is spared. We see the blood, the shattered glass, the terror in the crowd, the limpness of the limbs, the face of the dead, emptied and slack.

In her book *Regarding the Pain of Others,* Susan Sontag outlines Leonardo da Vinci's rules for battle painting, which is to be unsparing in its depiction, to show all the pain of war and the agony of death in detail, so that the image is upsetting enough to look at. She writes: 'The image should appal and in that *terribilità* lies a challenging kind of beauty.' Because, even though an image of atrocity displays an atrocity, it is still an aesthetic image that pays attention to aesthetic constructs such as composition and focus. While the thing photographed – the murder scene or the death-stricken battlefield – may have nothing beautiful about it, the photograph transforms it into an image, which may, in and of itself, be beautiful, at the same time as being terrifying or horror-inducing. This provokes confusion about what the photograph is saying: 'The photograph gives mixed signals. Stop this, it urges. But it also exclaims, What a spectacle!'

Alongside the assassinations of anyone who attempted to investigate or stop them, the mafia entered into another clan war in the eighties. The magistrate Rocco Chinnici created the famed Antimafia Pool of magistrates, which had the goal of dismantling organised crime in Italy. The Pool resulted in the Maxi Trials of the 1980s and 1990s, when an entire generation of mafia bosses was incarcerated.

This was not before a generation of antimafia figures were taken out. The photos gradually cover the vast web of men who went against the mafia in the seventies and eighties and early nineties. A few snapshots show the men in life, along with one that shows them in their untimely death. There, on the walls of the exhibition, are Giuseppe Russo, the ex-*carabiniere* Colonel, murdered along with his friend, Filippo Costa, in 1977. There is Boris Giuliano, the Deputy Police Quaestor assassinated in 1979 a few days after discovering a mafia lair. There is Piersanti Mattarella, president of the Sicilian region. In 1980, Mattarella had been in the process of cleaning up government contracts, blocking those in which the mafia was interested. He was shot and assassinated on his way to Mass, just after getting into his car with his wife, children and mother-in-law. This was on via della Libertà in front of his family home, in which his brother, the President of Italy, Sergio Mattarella, is still said to reside when he is in Palermo. There are photos of Piersanti Mattarella smiling in professional shots, next to photos of his body being taken away. There are Giovanni Falcone and Paolo Borsellino, magistrates who brought down an entire generation of mafia bosses in the eighties and nineties, the former assassinated by a bomb on his way from the airport to the city in 1992, the latter by a bomb at the door of his mother's apartment building a few months later.

These photographs attempt to relay the mood of the city during that time, one of many efforts in the city to keep Palermitans from forgetting the past. This brutality was once a daily occurrence, they say. They shock in their graphic portrayal of death, in the vast number of deaths, they centre not the murderers but the murdered. To the tourist seeking a Sicily straight out of *The Godfather*, they pose a question, or a challenge: is this what you were looking for?

In Italy, the reaction to Falcone's murder was, Alexander Stille writes in his book *Excellent Cadavers*, 'as if a head of state had been shot'. It was reported by all the major networks, and it was one of those events that people remembered where they were when they heard it for the first time. Stille writes that Ucciardone prison resounded with applause. On the day of Falcone's funeral, all shops and businesses took a day of mourning, and thousands of Palermitans showed up at the funeral. They hung bedsheets out their windows with messages of mourning or protest scrawled on them. The same was repeated at Borsellino's funeral a few months later, and four thousand police officers were required to contain the crowd.

These assassinations were what Leoluca Orlando was referring to, when he later told me that 'the mafia went overboard, which forced to the blind to see, the mute to speak, the deaf to hear'. We were sitting in his study in Villa Niscemi. He was chewing thoughtfully on the end of an unlit Toscanello, which he had placed in his mouth at the beginning of our meeting, assuring me he would not light it, but just keep it in his mouth as we talked. On the floor-to-ceiling bookshelves behind his head, propped up against some leather-bound tomes, were photos of Orlando with the Dalai Lama, the Pope, and Sergio Mattarella, in their younger days, laughing like old friends. He kept the Toscanello between his teeth or in his hand for the rest of the interview, gesticulating with it or chewing on it thoughtfully. He was wearing a double-breasted suit and tie, his dark floppy hair pushed back off his face. In photos of him when he first became mayor, he is handsome, but now, at the same age as my father, and after decades of work, of having survived a mafia death warrant, his face betrays a weariness.

Orlando, once the protégé of Piersanti Mattarella, is synonymous with Palermo, by now a symbol of the city, and perhaps Italy's best-known mayor. At the time of our meeting, he was on his sixth non-consecutive mandate since first stepping into the role in 1985. He is famed for having been the first mayor of Palermo to not only utter the word *mafia*, but also to take a stand against it. His candidacy brought about what was referred to in the media as the 'Palermo Spring', *la primavera di Palermo*. Accordingly, his name peppers the many books that deal with Palermo in the eighties and nineties.

I met Orlando at Villa Niscemi, once the residence of Corrado Valguarnera and his wife Maria Favara, the couple who are thought to be the inspiration for the characters of Tancredi and Angelica in Giuseppe Tomasi di Lampedusa's novel

The Leopard. Tancredi's hereditary seat, the half-ruined palace bursting with bougainvillea, Villa Falconeri, is likewise said to be Villa Niscemi's literary likeness. In 1987 the New York-based, Sicilian-American daughters of the Prince of Niscemi needed to sell the villa, and offered it to the municipality for a modest cost so that it wouldn't be bought by someone who might demolish it. The villa is situated in the middle of la Favorita parkland, loomed over by the rocky promontory of Mount Pellegrino, and is now open to the public as the seat of the local government. At the gate, I was waved down a white gravel path surrounded by verdant gardens. The palace in question is a large, sand-coloured villa surrounded by palms and centred around a lavish courtyard.

Orlando tends to speak as though he is delivering a theatrical monologue, in quotable aphorisms, his Palermitan accent hugging the consonants and resting in the vowels, placing emphasis on words to deliver his point. For example: Palermo is 'not multicultural, but *intercultural*'. Or: 'we are a city that is more *living* than liveable. Cities that are liveable don't *live*.' Tying his declaration of Palermo as a sanctuary for migrants to Palermitans' attitude towards COVID restrictions: 'legality is not always respectful of rights . . . We are not a city that respects prohibitions, but we are a city that respects *life*' and 'laws should not be respected, *life* should be respected.' On migrants: 'visibility means recognition of the dignity of the person. An invisible person has no dignity of person.' They're the kinds of pull-quotes one sees in bold and enlarged in newspaper articles.

Making the (I venture to say tenuous) link between the mafia's assassinations with Palermo's history of foreign rulers, he says that 'the change came about when we discovered that the mafia was our enemy. It was our enemy and I think we perceived this when we discovered that the mafia was killing the good kings. The Palermitans have never killed a king . . . And when it became clear that the mafia was killing the good king – and the good kings are everyone from Scaglione to Don Pino Puglisi – there was an awareness.'

When listening back to the recording of our interview, I am struck by all the names he mentioned without explaining them to me, in a tacit acknowledgement that I knew what they meant. It occurs to me that Orlando was speaking a language that is unique to this city and those who know about this city. He assumes, if I am interviewing him, that I know it too. Knowing this language requires knowing, for example, about Palermo's ancient history, and about its more recent history. It requires knowing who 'the good kings' were: 'because Peppino Impastato opposed his father and mother. Piersanti Mattarella opposed his party.' These were the men whose photos covered the walls of the No Mafia Memorial, and almost countless others. There was Pietro Scaglione, chief magistrate of Palermo, killed in 1971, and Puglisi, a priest who worked with youths in Palermo's impoverished Brancaccio district, steering them away from crime, who was shot in front of his home in 1993; there was Peppino Impastato, who defied his mafioso family by becoming a public antimafia activist. He had been campaigning to be elected to his local council when he was murdered in 1978. These are names that now represent different stars in the constellation that is Palermo mythology, one of martyrs and mafia, of a struggle over the city and what it means.

Map of Palermo circa 1800

The city reverts back to its old core, a small cluster of buildings to the north the only clue of the growth that the coming centuries will bring. North of this growth is a green patch, a park. Wedged between the park and the Borgo Vecchio fishing village is a field. The park has yet to become the grid of streets on which my mother was raised, and the field, about a fifteen-minute walk away from via la Farina, still has not been overtaken by what will be Ucciardone, the prison where a generation of mafiosi would be prosecuted and put away.

I am on via della Libertà, retreading the same path that I often make from the old centre to my mother's childhood home. Until studying the many maps of Palermo, I had never taken notice of Ucciardone's proximity, even though I have driven past its high stone walls many times before. The map makes it seem so close to my current location, and yet an invisible veil seems to separate the prison from the rest of the city. There are veils throughout the city, separating bourgeois areas like the streets surrounding via della Libertà from the working-class district of Borgo Vecchio between the former and the sea.

These veils are impossible to perceive on paper. They are felt rather than seen, a near-silent murmur which encourages one to favour a certain street over another. The map offers freedom from obstructions and barriers, such as walls, time, and the body. But, as I've said before, the alternate viewpoint it offers is not true to the experience of *being* in the city, which is fragmentary. We are drawn through it by whims, scents, desires and recollections.

I deviate off via della Libertà, and head towards via la Farina, which cuts across it. I stand outside, across the street from the butter-coloured building. The air of the sirocco gums up my mind, and I cannot muster any of my own memories of the building, though I can still recall some interiors: walking down a long, cool hallway with many doors, playing with my mother's old toys in her bedroom, skidding on the hallway tiles in socks with my cousins.

In the years between arriving in Palermo and Annalisa's marriage, my great-grandparents had organised a cooperative with a few other families and petitioned the government for a low-interest loan that would allow them to build a new block of flats on via la Farina. The block, which still stands, is five storeys, with three apartments on each floor and extra apartments for the doorman and *garagista* (the doorman for the palazzo's underground parking lot). This was where my grandmother had her twenty-first birthday and where she took refuge with her children after fleeing from Alimena. My mother was four. My aunt, the youngest, was seven months old. The last time I spoke to my mother about this, a new detail emerged. Apparently, my grandmother told her husband that he could come to the city any time he wanted to see the children. She said she was going to look for a job, and once he found one too, they could live together again in the city. This never came to be.

My mother tells me she recalls feeling desperate for her father, and clinging to her mother, who now spent her days applying for jobs or working. Annalisa worked in the administrative office of, my mother tells me, a politician named La Loggia, which a Google search tells me may have been Giuseppe La Loggia, ex-president of the Sicilian Region and regional councillor for tourism at the time when she may have worked for him. She later found another job in public administration. A nanny named Mariane was hired, though this didn't curb my mother's clinginess. A therapist recommended that my mother be sent to her father in Alimena for a period, which she recalls as being a long time, but was most likely only a week.

This was the sixties: Sicily was still very Catholic, and divorce was not yet legal. Once she started school, my mother says, she was alone in a sea of children with both a mother and a father. While my grandmother's single parenthood seemed to be socially accepted, she reminded her children constantly, throughout their lives, that they were being observed. Any mistake made on the part of my mother and her siblings would be blamed on my grandmother. They were different from other families, she would remind them.

As my mother grew up, her father's presence mainly manifested itself through the debt collectors knocking on the door, demanding the antiques that he had pledged as collateral. My grandmother added her surname onto her children's surnames. Salvatore, my mother said, became the siblings' father figure. In 1970, the year divorce was legalised in Italy, Annalisa divorced Rosario. In the preceding years, in between moving in with them and divorcing, both her parents died. My mother told me that by 1968, when my grandmother was thirty-seven, she was totally alone in the world, a feeling that had probably chased her since she had left Benghazi, and a state she had been running from her entire adult life. She said to my mother that both her parents dying was the worst thing that had ever happened to her.

Perhaps she spent her life running from aloneness only to find that life would conspire to leave her alone, or perhaps that is my mother's interpretation of her own mother's life, a manifestation of my mother's own lifelong evasion of loneliness. I recall something my aunt said once, that my mother would spend days listless in the house alone, reading books and smoking.

In the decades in which my mother lived there, the city streets emptied out right after the shops shuttered their doors. Families like my mother's, who lived around Libertà, did not often go out at night, preferring to entertain at home. Whenever I encounter family friends, those of my mother's generation never fail to recollect with pleasure the dance parties that my grandmother threw. I imagine made-up women and men in collared shirts driving through desolate streets before coming to a halt near my mother's building. The women bundle their handbags to their chests like babies, and once buzzed in, inside the entrance, they proceed to adorn themselves: from a bag slinks a mink stole for the shoulders, pearl earrings are hooked through earlobes, a gold necklace is clasped around a neck, rings are slipped on fingers.

My mother still struggles with my grandmother's death. She tells me that though they had a fierce attachment to one another, they always fought. My grandmother was decisive. She always knew what to do, no matter the situation. If you came to her with a problem, she would immediately tell you what you needed to do. My mother is the opposite. She takes her time and struggled to find her way.

It's interesting that, living lives defined by migrations, our stories tend to fixate not on movement but on the places that we left. For my mother, migration was not as outwardly traumatic as migration often is. She simply went to Australia on holiday and decided to remain. At the time, so she tells me, she was feeling adrift, another state she had spent her life walking with. This was the late eighties. She had dropped out of university a few years earlier and, after an unhappy stint of living in Milan, had recently moved back to her family home in Palermo. She and her boyfriend at the time were on-off, and she still didn't feel like she had any direction in life. A few weeks after she arrived in Sydney, she met my father, a Sicilian who had migrated to Australia two decades before. In my interpretation of events, he was her anchor. They married three months later. The next time she was in Palermo was three years later with me in tow.

Perhaps it is for this reason that I felt so comfortable with the narrative structure that embodied my childhood, in which the past had remained in the repository of a fixed Palermo, while Australia encapsulated the ever-shifting present. In the stories, the motherland remains in stasis, as though, fractured by our migration journeys, we need to fix a part of ourselves to something stable and unchanging.

In this part of the city, the newer buildings mix with the older, nicer ones that were spared in the Sack, and here and there, amongst the apartments, is a gated villa with an overgrown garden. The new buildings seem to me like towering tombstones, vestiges of the corruption that slapped them together, containers of the corpses between their walls and in their foundations, but also like markers of an urban burial ground, haunted by its ghosts. This isn't only true of the new palazzi and the groves and green and villas that they blanketed and replaced, but also of the razed mosques on top of which Christian churches were consecrated, the ancient synagogue, of which only sparse remnants remain, the heretics' drawings on the walls of their cells in Palazzo Steri, the Koranic plaques strewn throughout the Christian churches.

The past haunts the streetscape. Not just the great past of official history, but also that of individual city dwellers. Our stories play out in and affect the city. This may be through deliberate markings, such as carving our initials onto a tree or tagging a wall with spray paint. It may be correlative to our actions. Perhaps we argue with our partner in the street, and it affects someone who witnesses us, like a couple I once saw with a baby in a pram. I still recall how the man picked up the crying baby and shoved it into the arms of the crying woman and pushed the empty pram away, down the street. This happened in Berlin, and the scene returns to my mind every time I think of that city. It is as though they are now frozen there forever, ghosts destined to repeat the same action over and over.

And yet, while the couple continues to repeat that same motion in my head, each has gone on to live their lives. Perhaps they are still together, perhaps not. Maybe they don't even recall the incident, are not even in Berlin anymore.

Later I paid a visit to the city's official burial ground – the catacombs beneath it. I do not like cemeteries, and yet I have visited the catacombs twice. My aunt recalls being taken there on a school trip. The class of children was led into the tunnels burrowed underground by a sinister Capuchin monk carrying a lantern. Then, there were no guard rails. The children made a game of snatching relics. Femurs were the most popular, as they could be used for mock sword fights.

When I visited, first with two Australian friends and a couple of years later with my cousin and uncle, no monk led our way. Now there were museum spotlights and glass flooring. There were rope barriers and signs prohibiting the taking of pictures. As we descended the concrete steps, the air grew cool and hollow. The ceiling was covered in faded frescoes. Like a carnival of death, the walls were lined with corpses hooked by their shoulders so that their heads lolled.

Back when the catacombs were in use, cadavers were embalmed and desiccated. Once desiccation was complete, the skeleton would be dressed in their best clothes from life and hung up in a section dedicated to their social class or age group. Walking around, I noted sections for monks, priests, women, men, children, a chapel for virgins. Some bore all their teeth, others one or two. Some still had skin, and moustaches. Heads hung in armpits, as though bashful. Some of these gone Palermitans were dressed in smart suits with waistcoats, others donned burlap sacks, women wore matronly lace bonnets. In the children's section, babies in baby coffins wore frilly suits, bloomers, white leather gloves and shoes. Women lay down behind cages in ruffled lace or floral dresses and bonnets and gloves with their shoes on.

Buying nice clothing, clothing meant to be worn in nice places, for nice occasions, is a gesture of hope for the future. Laying the dead in their best clothes extends this gesture of hope into the afterlife. It is a tender wish to prepare our loved one for what awaits them, a hope that it is something worth dressing up for.

In those cool corridors, I also observed how time affects what is gone: moths had eaten away at lace collars, velvet was worn, cuffs had frayed or disintegrated. The straw used to stuff hollow bodies exploded between the buttons of collared shirts, skulls had cracked.

In a way, Palermo's cityscape – what remains of the historic structures, the ghostly absent-presence of that which was razed, along with the tombstones that replaced it, strangled rivers, and the fetid roots of torn-up citrus groves, whose dust I imagine rests under the paved ground like decomposing bodies – is a testament to the irrevocability of time. With each step forward into the future, something is lost, and this loss, the void created by it, travels with us. It is there to remind us that there is no such thing as returning.

Palermo after the cutting of via Maqueda, after 1620

A birds-eye view of the Spanish city, the newly cut via Maqueda creating the cross that splits the old centre into four sections. There, away from the city in the bottom, are the few scattered dwellings that mark out the Borgo Vecchio fishing village, there above, next to the city, are the sparse beginnings of the city's expansion, as via Maqueda forges northward. Surrounding the centre, like a moat, the absence of the old rivers becomes empty space, and beyond are scattered constructions amidst farmland.

The map, however, tricks us into thinking we can always return. It freezes place in time, like a snapshot. But it is in the nature of cities to be forever unfinished, forever changing, and they are just as much made up of encounters and events and memories as they are the physical elements that constitute them.

In this map, we travel back in time. It shows the city after the Spanish paved via Maqueda, effectively quartering Palermo into what the Spanish referred to as *mandamenti*. It was named after Bernardino de Cardines, Duke of Maqueda, Sicily's viceroy for three brief years, from 1598 to 1601. The street, which runs from the train station and on to Teatro Massimo, before it turns into via Ruggero Settimo and then via della Libertà, constitutes one axis in the cross. The rivers have disappeared. The map focuses on what is there now.

There was no way of telling, however, that this much-recorded city would one day be abandoned and left to decay. From the beginning of the Sack in the fifties to its end in the eighties, a mass exodus occurred from the old city. Two-thirds of its inhabitants abandoned it, despite the fact that the larger population of the city itself doubled. Allied bombing during the war had destroyed about a third of the historic centre, and no effort had been made to restore it, leaving it overcrowded and strewn with rubble. Over the decades, parts of it were deprived of gas, electricity and water for months at a time. Families moved to the new neighbourhoods. The Renaissance fountains, the pink domes of Arab-Norman cathedrals and Baroque churches, and the old noble palaces were surrounded by dilapidated buildings with broken or boarded-up windows, stripped paint and crumbling balconies.

The neglect was deliberate. In one of his many books, Orlando writes of discovering documents in the municipal files that outline the never-fulfilled stage two of the mafia's 'Town Plan': the demolition and razing of the entire historic centre. He quotes one of the documents, which says: 'It is necessary to eliminate the abomination of these buildings of the past.' These 'buildings of the past' included the Baroque churches and the Arab architecture of La Kalsa, which had been standing over a millennium, and the centuries-old palazzi. The decay had a purpose: once the edifices were declared unfit for use, the mafia would be able to buy up the land for little money and fill it with the concrete blocks they had such a predilection for.

I am fascinated by this designation of 'buildings of the past' as abominations. Were the mafia men so coarse-minded that they could not distinguish between what was pleasing to the eye and what was not? Perhaps it was an attack on the city's nobility, many of whom owned palazzi in la Kalsa that were totally or half destroyed in the war, like Giuseppe Tomasi di Lampedusa, who spent his final years living in a palace without running water and a ballroom with a caved-in ceiling. Or maybe it was the natural conclusion to centuries of exploitation.

As the inhabitants of the city scrambled to find lodgings, who occupied those once-lavish rooms? When I walk past an abandoned or seemingly abandoned palazzo in the old city, most likely owned by some descendent or businessman who cannot afford restoration, I try to peek through the boarded-up windows. These are spaces of wilderness in the middle of the city, in the sense that they are void of regulations. Inside, families reside in secret, drug deals are made, bodies are dumped, teenagers break in to explore rooms perhaps still covered in regal portraits and gilt-framed landscapes, rich rugs and antique furniture. The interior lives of a whole class of people, wiped out.

The mafia were unable to complete their plan of razing the old city, but they did carry out an attack of neglect. While before it seemed as though the city centre was a massive, lived-in ruin, a government subsidy along with a decades-long push by the municipal government has facilitated this city-wide restoration project. Peach and pink and yellow facades that still stink of fresh paint circle piazzas in the old centre, the wrought iron of their balconies gleaming. It is almost comical: the peach-coloured paint ends in straight line, precisely measured so as not to coincide with the unrestored palazzo beside it, whose own front is mottled and rough, its balconies gobbled up by red rust, the wooden door and the shutters splintered. I wonder whether, in losing those lawless spaces, some kind of magic, perhaps of possibility, is lost. One can no longer go on imagining what they might look like were they complete.

Touring Club Italiano map of Palermo, 1919

One of the Touring Club's tourist maps of cities. Here, the old city is still visible amidst the larger shapeless growth of the peach-pink city. Despite the expansions, the city is still manageable, a place where it is possible to orient oneself. Surrounding it, the fields are yellow; below, the port is pale blue.

The map is the place in which we plot our stories, which tricks us into believing that it is simply a static background against which our actions play out. In her book *For Space*, Doreen Massey writes that maps propagate the illusion that space is a complete surface, immutable and resistant to the effects of time. She suggests that if we are to accept the nature of time and space as interrelated, then space is therefore a sphere of assorted 'practices and *processes* . . . it will always be unfinished and open'.

In his book, *Midnight in Sicily*, Peter Robb paces via della Libertà in the mid-nineties during the evening, 'at the height of its frenzied saunter'. He notes the furriers, the authorised Rolex dealers, the shops specialised in expensive wedding gifts. As closing time approaches, and the shops begin to turn out their lights, turn on their alarm systems and roll down their shutters, the streets suddenly empty. The strollers evaporate, retreating to the privacy of their homes. He reasons that the emptiness of the streets is connected to the thousand or so corpses that have been made in Palermo over the last decade and a half: nobody wants to be a witness.

In the loss or paucity or inadequacy of my own memories, I turn to those of others. What I noticed, visiting when I was young, or at least what I kept in my mind seems to say nothing substantial or revealing regarding the city. Of those decades, my aunt told me that the assassinations and the bodies, at least for her, were just events that played in the background on the nightly news. My mother, in high school at the time, remembers differently. You were either on the right or on the left, she told me: there was no in-between. The school students held constant rallies, chanting *governo fascista, governo ladro* (government of fascists, government of thieves). She recalls an article that came out one January, counting the assassinations of the previous year: 365 deaths for 365 days. She recalls an incident in which a car parked for three days at the train station was discovered to have a decomposing body inside. The roads were filled with car chases. *We didn't pay attention to them*, she said, *but occasionally there would be an accident, and someone would die, or someone would never return home from school*. I read the writing of travellers and novels by Italians set in Palermo, and allow their recollections and observations to colour my own.

I wonder what one can hold on to of a homeland, or a place we imagine to be our homeland, if it changes so much so that it no longer matches our image of it. In travelling to such significant sites of ancestral history, the eye confronts the city as it is, while the mind reconstructs what was or what we have been told was there before. What was there before becomes what *should be* there.

If I were really interested in returning, or attempting to return, to the Palermo in which my mother grew up, I would have returned here, rather than staying in il Capo. Invisible lines, constituted by via Cavour, down the centre of the map, and via Roma running horizontal on the lower left half, divided the Palermo of the bourgeois city of my mother's youth from the decadent wild west of the old city. When I ask my mother for her memories of what the city was like, she focuses solely on the everyday, on how the tenor of the city at that time affected her. When walking down via Maqueda to university, for example, she recalls that she would purposely wear torn jeans so as to not garner attention, and would clip a bum bag around her waist with her wallet inside. Men would ride past on motor scooters and rip the handbags off women's shoulders, or tear the necklaces from their necks, she tells me.

Now, the steps of the Teatro Massimo, one of the city's two opera houses located almost in the centre of this map, and the piazza before it, is a meeting place perpetually brimming with energy: families shopping and walking, businessmen on their way to work, bustling office workers, delivery men, couriers, guides leading tourists with tall poles from which dangle flags, young backpackers licking gelato out of brioche for breakfast on the steps to the Teatro. As it's located in the centre of the city, I often recline here to either people-watch or wait for a friend. Here are families downing gelato, tourists hunched over guidebooks, leather-jacketed adolescents smoking cigarettes. Street vendors pedal gaudy Palermo tourist magnets and keychains of Sicilian horses and the like on large white perforated boards that hang around their necks. At the piazza's edge, there is always a line around the turreted red-and-lavender Liberty-style kiosk, which, unlike the vacant newsstands of other cities, still sells newspapers and cigarettes and lottery tickets.

When I ask myself what draws me to the old city, I think it is more a case of what repels me from the blocks around via della Libertà, which seem saturated with my mother's memories, or perhaps with my preoccupation with my family's past. It seems lodged in my personal history, and yet it is also inaccessible to me.

Via Libertà does not look now how it did when my mother lived here, nor is it what I recall from my childhood. Then, it was lined with elegant coffee bars and *pasticcerie*. Then, Libertà was the spot for Palermitans to enjoy their *passìo*, the evening stroll which has long been an element of daily Sicilian life. One could sit at an outdoor table and sip espresso while watching the city take a turn. The concentration of this activity has now moved further south to via Maqueda, and the streets are no longer empty after dark. Now, most of the historic bars and *pasticcerie* along Libertà have shut up shop, and the street has been overtaken by designer shops and expensive boutiques. There are no longer crowds, particularly since via Maqueda became pedestrianised. Rather, the traffic roars up and down this main artery, while a steady trickle of women and men walk to their cars carrying their purchases of luxury goods.

Palermo has not been considered a rich city probably since unification. The gap between rich and poor is also thought to be wider in Palermo than in the rest of Italy. But there has always been enough money to justify the high-end shops on via della Libertà. The palm tree-lined avenue is home to the flagship stores of Max Mara, Hermes, Prada, Gucci, and Louis Vuitton. There is a vintage shop that deals solely in Louis Vuitton, Prada and Gucci handbags. There are stores in which one needs an appointment to enter, which display nothing or a single thing in their windows, where heavy velvet curtains hide what is sold inside, where the people who shop there are driven there by their drivers.

Two days before Christmas 2020, Italian newspapers reported that a twenty-three-year-old had been Christmas shopping with some friends. As he was walking out of Gucci with his purchases, some handbags and accessories, he was assaulted by a pickpocket, who punched him in the face and took his wallet. Inside his wallet, he told the police, was twenty-five thousand euro, in cash. None of the articles address why a twenty-three-year-old might have a wad of twenty-five thousand euro in his wallet. I can't help but feel that this is an article a Palermitan might know how to decode. Someone from this city would know what the cash means, whether it means everything or nothing.

Perhaps the present city obscures the one that lives in the mind. I question how much these two Palermos have to do with one another.

Diagrammatic map of 'Arab Palermo', between 800 and 1500

The original Phoenician foot atop which the city's kasbah was erected lies beneath the borders of the expanded area. Fainter lines depict the rivers after they were interred. The port pokes into the land, meeting the tip of the foot.

There, at the bottom of the map, is the deep curve of la Cala, the ancient port into which ships once sailed, before entering one of the two rivers that encircled the city. Now, these entry points have been replaced by roads, and the new port, up north, welcomes all new ships to Palermo. Here, a mob of docked yachts gently bobs in the water. There, in the curve of road, is the man selling barrelfuls of watermelon, a bar, a bookshop dedicated to aquatic-themed books, and behind that building is the giant mural recreation of the famous photo of Giovanni Falcone and Paolo Borsellino seemingly sharing a joke with one another. La Cala was where the Arabs and the Phoenicians entered the navigable rivers of Palermo before staking their claims to the city, laying down the foundations and constructing their churches and mosques and palaces, etching their roads into the ground.

Directly behind the curl of the port is the rectangular square of Piazza Marina. I am back in la Kalsa, where restored buildings recall the glamour of life as it once was. In the centre of the rectangle is a leafy garden circled by a boardwalk, and on weekends a flea market blooms on the boardwalk. It must be the weekend, because I am parsing over the stalls, my eyes panning the arrays without resting on anything in particular.

Antique items are littered across the white tablecloths that are draped over tables, or blankets on the ground, or rough white shelving. There are antique cameras in stiff leather cases, carved wooden cigar boxes, stout vases. There are old records and dusty encyclopaedias and movies on VHS. There are moustachioed Sicilian marionettes, miniature recreations of colourful Sicilian carts being pulled by a plumed Sicilian horse. There are gramophones and rusted antique coffee grinders. There are oil landscapes and gilt-framed portraits and porcelain teapots and chipped espresso cups. There are war medals and the glossy ceramic artichoke finials that Sicilians like to put on pillars in front of their homes. A hundred Madonnas of different heights are corralled together on a table. There are vintage clocks and ugly rococo ceramic things and unidentifiable rusted things and faded newspapers from decades ago. An African man sells carved wooden tribal statues and masks, an elderly woman sells her trousseau, another man sells his own watercolours, yet another sells items perhaps stolen from the dusty and cluttered homes of Palermo's ageing rich.

During the Holy Inquisition, heretics were burned here at the stake. Dacia Maraini's novel, *The Silent Duchess*, begins with the hanging of a young bandit in Piazza Marina. The square is thronged with spectators, carriages and horses. Faces bulge out of windows and the surrounding balconies are packed. The crowd has dressed for the occasion. Street vendors bearing toffee and offal and prickly pears elbow their way through. An adolescent boy, his wrists bound by a rope, is slowly paraded through the crowd, followed by an assortment of trumpeters and drummers and priests, to a platform at the square's centre, where gallows and the executioner await him. As the boy's body swings from the noose, the crowd is jubilant, the air above them punctuated with flung caps.

A massive Moreton Bay fig tree looms over the market. Introduced here from Australia in the nineteenth century, its thick trunk and strangling roots pour into the earth. Circling the piazza are historic palazzi, a palace now in possession of the university, an ancient jail, a theatre, a church. A few years ago, one didn't generally walk aimlessly around here. Now, many of the facades have been restored. Palazzo Fatta is robin's egg blue and white instead of grey, the piazza is mostly pedestrianised, and out the front of the two new restaurants sweaty tourists lean back in their chairs and stare at laminated menus. They place their elbows on the tables and sip spritzes through straws and twirl pasta into their spoons and sip cappuccinos. Later they'll circle the market, snapping photos of the stalls and their owners, as though they are zebras at the zoo. It is July 2020 and Palermo is full of tourists. This is partly because of the cheap flights offered by airlines and Italy's lack of a required quarantine. But Palermo has been a prime holiday destination ever since Europeans decided that North Africa had become too dangerous for holidays, and Palermo was just safe and exotic enough.

Now it's Piazza Marina on a weekday in August. I have a bloody blister on my heel and I'm limping. I sit down on a bench out the front of a municipal office to gather my energy in the heat. An elderly woman sits down next to me. She is wearing Sunday clothes: a matching blue skirt and jacket two-piece, a blouse, tan pantyhose, court shoes, a large leather handbag that she sits on her lap. Her hair is bottle black. It's combed back, and something has been combed through it, so that the waves have stiffened. As we both fan ourselves, we lock eyes and laugh at the futility of our attempts to cool down. She asks where I'm from. I don't want to talk about myself, so I neglect to mention Australia, simply telling her I live in Trieste. 'Ahh,' she says. 'I knew you were Triestine. I could tell by your cadence.'

All the women in her family, she tells me, are unlucky in love. I don't recall how we get to this topic – although I am inclined to believe that it is because she is telling me how great a book her family's story would make. Her great-grandmother, a baroness, made a bad match with a man who squandered her family inheritance. This interloper condemned the family to being middle-class. The woman herself had a bad marriage. Her husband had not been an affectionate man. She tells me that she is a passionate person, that she is someone made to love and be loved with furious affection. Being married to her husband was therefore like some inner part of her was being starved. Her daughters, too, she says, all three of them have found themselves in unhappy marriages. 'Every one of us,' she tells me, 'we're all unlucky in love.' The misstep of the baroness condemned them all. The woman says: 'I've told my daughters, there is no hope. It's a curse.'

More than a few Palermitans, I have noticed, tell stories like mine: stories of squandered fortunes, of titled ancestors, people bitter at having been reduced to bourgeois lifestyles and wistful for a past of having money they didn't have to work for, or count. As though the island is full of Tancredis, the Prince of Salina's nephew in *The Leopard*, whose reckless father managed to fritter away the family fortune before dying. Tancredi's father ate away at their wealth so thoroughly that 'it was one of those total ruins which engulfed even the silver braid on liveries'. The use of 'one of those' suggests that this kind of case is not uncommon. Tancredi, whose mother is also dead, is left with his family villa, which is in a state of ruin.

In her novel, Maraini writes that:

The greatness of the nobility lies in scorning accounts and bills, whatever they may be. A nobleman never calculates, cannot add or subtract and does not know arithmetic. For there are administrators, major-domos, secretaries, servants. A nobleman does not sell and he does not buy . . . Seeing that everything that grows and multiplies in the beautiful Sicilian earth belongs to them by birth, by blood, by divine grace, what sense is there in calculating profit and loss? That is a matter for tradespeople and the rising bourgeoisie.

These are people incapable of squaring their credit with their debts (in fairness, for a long time they haven't been required to).

Their real-life counterparts are, to this day, people who recall with fondness the Kingdom of the Two Sicilies, when the island and southern Italy were under Bourbon rule. They are people who still place stock in noble titles. Even today, when titles have not been recognised in Italy since it became a republic, Roberto Alajmo writes that there are more princes in Sicily, concentrated in Palermo, than in the rest of Italy. 'We saw *la principessa* at the theatre last night,' a certain friend of my family's will mention out of nowhere. This is a woman who reassures me, as though I need to be reassured, of the 'importance' of my grandfather's family, even though the estate no longer exists, and in any case, I never saw it and I barely saw him. Another relative, who hails from a branch of the family who retained their money, once informed me: 'Your grandfather was charming, smart. He could talk about anything. And so rich. Oh, he was *so rich*. Richer than all of us.' (It took him twenty years to gamble it all away.) I wouldn't know, I wanted to say.

Yet I am not immune to the seductive glamour of the past. An old Palermitan flatmate and I once commiserated over riches lost long before we were born, riches that I am perhaps so seduced by because they seem so unreal, and because, in Palermo, I am constantly reminded of their loss. Our commiserations are representative of a certain mood that grips the city, one of regretful sighs and snobbery, of the conviction, at once bitter and nostalgic, that we were somehow cheated out of our due, or born in the wrong time. Palermitans are the human personification of Palermo itself: a city that was once the centre of the Mediterranean, the confluence of the East and West, and is now on Europe's periphery, a city that can't get over its past greatness, and agonises over its present inconsequence.

When my mother speaks of *The Leopard*, for example, she lionises the morose Prince of Salina, the last aristocrat of his kind. His feudal Sicily is romantic in her vision of the book, the Prince the last of a species and a way of life that is on the brink of being extinguished. I feel as though my mother and I read two different books. What I remember of *The Leopard* is that on the walls of the Prince's home in Palermo hang portraits of the family's distant and various estates. The landscapes are described as 'masterpieces', but they are also abstractions of the real thing. Diminished to ornaments, they fail to convey the reality of life on the land. They are 'useless . . . at showing boundaries, or detailing areas or tenancies; such things remain obscure'. Their presence in Villa Salina seems to highlight the obscured connection between the Prince's wealth and the land that produces it. Later, two tenants of one of the Prince's landholdings come to his estate office. They bear customary gifts of *caciocavallo*, a traditional Sicilian cheese (the narrator notes that the Prince gives the cheese 'a careless glance; he loathed that particular cheese') and six slaughtered lambs, the fruits of their labour. The men themselves are the fruits of the land they live off; their skin tanned by the sun, they 'smell of flocks and herds'. Along with the gifts, for which they have probably toiled a great deal, they are there to pay the rent for use of land which the Prince knows only from his framed landscapes.

Leonardo Sciascia wrote, in his novel *Open Doors*, that in the eighteenth century, there were around two thousand aristocratic families in Palermo. What else, he asks, could the rest of the population be but serfs? The social structure was one in which a landowning privileged class lived off the spoils of their tenant farmers. It was an old story that had been ingrained through centuries of colonisation. Sicily had been feudal since the Romans conquered Greek-speaking Sicily. Despite peasant uprisings and the official abolishment of feudalism in 1812, the island remained one of vast ancestral estates.

We are cursed with having been born too late. Of course, during this golden time, most Sicilians lived in servitude to a small ruling class, which is perhaps why we like to recall or imagine that we have claim to the former.

Palermo, from Italia: Meriodonale e Insulare - Libya, Guida Breve Volume III, Consociazione Turistica Italiana, 1940

A scale topographical street map of the city before the Sack. The city is a complex concentration of roads cut through horizontally by via Maqueda and via della Libertà. The roads veer off from the central knot, so that it all looks like a molecule. Line shading in the bottom right corner signals Mount Pellegrino.

Sontag wrote that 'photographs actively promote nostalgia', and I think the same thing can be said about maps. Both photographs and maps distil a scene or a place in a moment in time, preparing for a future in which what was captured – the youthful smile, the city limits – no longer exists. In this way, photographs and maps memorialise what is there and eventually what was there, acting as witnesses to the relentless effects of time. Both seduce us into thinking that the past can somehow be revisited, but all that they really offer is a half-knowing, a shadow half-world for our imaginations. In the end, both photographs and maps remind us of how little we know of the past, how little is knowable, and furthermore, how little of our own lives will be knowable to anyone but ourselves.

When I am in Palermo, I am constantly looking back to past iterations of it, comparing those iterations with the present, attempting to square them with one another, trying to locate my family through the years and generations between arrivals and departures. I would like to travel, for example, to the Palermo my mother was born in, in 1957. Then, the historic centre was like Chernobyl. Plant life grew where kitchens once stood. The absence of a façade might reveal all relics of life before: blackened couches and beds and tables topped with the crumbs of crockery. Or else everything but the façade had been destroyed, so that birds now rested on glassless windowsills.

Perhaps people were no longer living in grottoes when she brought me back from Australia in 1990, but the historic centre remained half in ruins. Parts were still half in ruins when I was in Palermo in 2013, having a drink with my cousins and mother and aunt in la Vucciria, a small, stone piazzetta in the middle of a dense tangle of intertwining alleys. In this 1940 map, the centre was yet to crumble, but I can still locate where I would be within it, decades later. There, off via Roma, a main artery parallel and at a slight angle to via Maqueda, before it intersects with il Cassaro, down some worn stone stairs to the left of the street, is la Vucciria.

My cousin took us there one night, and I recall how we sat at one of the plastic tables in its centre, the piazzetta empty but for a table of drunk, red-faced, and fair-haired Irish girls on holiday. Then, the little square consisted of a few dank dive bars emblazoned with Coca Cola signs and selling one-euro shots of spirits that burned the throat like lighter fluid. Around us were ancient three-storey palazzi, mostly boarded up and covered with graffiti. I remember no music, just the trills of the Irish girls and our own conversation.

A vaguely post-apocalyptic feeling pervaded our silent surroundings. Above us, the upper storeys of a palazzo were missing their façade. It was like a diorama: on display was a dining table strewn with crockery and some chairs, the kitchen counter to one side, and a dust-caked couch on the other. I asked my cousin whether it was a result of Second World War bombings, and she replied that it couldn't be – it must simply be age, that one day the wall collapsed. From her response, it was evident that question had never occurred to her. She is a person who values immediacy – the *why* behind how things are is irrelevant to her. She is more occupied by how things actually *are*. For this reason, I don't know how much stock to place in her answer, although it is true that by that point, the damage done by warfare was inextricable from the ruin wrought by decades of mafia-infested councils allowing the historic architecture of the city to crumble.

La Vucciria had once been one of the city's four main markets. All that is left of its centuries as a throbbing market is a 1974 painting by the Sicilian Neorealist Expressionist painter Renato Guttuso. I went to see this painting one afternoon, at Palazzo

Steri, where it was displayed in a white stone chapel. I remember it being tall, as tall as, taller than I am. It is large enough that one feels one could step into it, so vivid that one can almost smell the scene. In one corner a fish vendor grips the sharp nose of a large swordfish, holding a cleaver with the other as though he is about to slice through its leathery skin and cut off a wheel of pink flesh. A basket of silvery sardines, a crate of crimson prawns, the squiggly tentacles of squid cut up on a table. Fruit at the top of the frame: the red and greens of apples, mottled pears, sunset-coloured melons and green-yellow bananas. On the next stall over, chubby links of purple sausage, the large pink circles of mortadella and cured meats, salamis. The cheesemonger: different shades of yellow cut in chunks of varying sizes and the creamy white of ricotta in a bowl. And then, olives: deep grassy green and glossy black and spiced in different-sized jars. And near us, the viewer, the vegetable stand, with crates of plump red tomatoes and bundles of green leeks and white fennel bulbs. Behind them, hundreds of white eggs cradled together. On one side, a butchered cow strung up by its feet. The butcher carves into it, its interior visible: its spine, bluish muscles and yellow organs, and the rest of it in various blood and flesh shades.

And then the people of the market. Return to the fish vendor who grips a cleaver; he stares menacingly across his stall and the market goers to the cheesemonger, a small dark man with a monk's bowl cut. The cheesemonger stares back, his arms crossed, his expression stormy. A woman makes her way through the market, only her back visible to the viewer. She carries a yellow shopping bag and wears sandals and a dress that clings to her ripe figure. An olive-skinned man before her, wearing a yellow turtleneck and a blazer, fixes her with his gaze. Because we can't see her expression, it is impossible to tell whether the man is leering, or whether it is a look of recognition, or whether she returns his gaze happily. Behind them, the fruit vendor helps a woman select her purchases, and a grey-haired woman, presumably a widow judging by her black dress, clutches a sack of something, a frown of disapproval etched into her face.

The painting is an expression of a myth that surrounds the island from the outside: that it is a sort of fertile Eden, with its abundant bounty. An almost vicious, taut sensuality, the woman with the clinging dress, the menace stemming from the woman's ripeness, ready like fruit for plucking and the intense gaze of the man before her. Likewise, the island's violence lurking beneath the abundance and the sensuality: the stare between the cheese and fishmongers, the butchered body of the cow.

In the nineties, the market began to dwindle, and the neighbourhood became one of the city's main spots for drug dealing. I returned to la Vucciria in 2019. Six years had rendered it unrecognisable from what I recalled. Now, la Vucciria is a nightlife hotspot. The laneways that siphon off into the cramped piazzetta were pulsing with music from the bars that have proliferated in recent years, street food spots and souvenir shops. A human mass choked the narrow streets, sitting at side tables or standing in groups, all drinking beers or mixed drinks, and the collective din of their conversation competed with the music. Many of the facades were now covered with the scaffolding of restoration, by now a common sight in the historic centre.

The piazzetta itself was packed full of tables assembled around the fountain in the centre. It is now filled with street food places. Dark-haired or balding men wearing white aprons cut up offal for *stigghiola*, the trestle tables around the piazza were piled high with bread rolls ready to be filled. They thrust fish into breadcrumbs before flinging it into oil. Octopus was lowered into boiling vats and served with squeezed lemon. Steam and sweet-smelling smoke billowed out of the grills upon which skewers of prawn and meat were charred. Tubs of *milza* (chopped veal lung and spleen) were churned by hand, ladled into panini and sprinkled with salted ricotta. Whiting and *panelle* were lowered into frying oil.

The number of people, both at the tables, which were full, and those anxiously waiting, was what one might expect at a hot restaurant. Dark, olive-skinned, skinny-armed young boys, with rags tucked into their pockets or over their shoulders, zipped from table to table, running orders and choreographing the crowd. In between taking the orders of those seated and clearing tables, they kept an eye on new arrivals into the piazzetta. They would note the number of the group, and somehow memorise the order in which people had arrived. It was late at night and the boys were young and I wondered if they were in school. When an appropriate table opened up, they knew exactly which group to beckon. Considering how busy it was, we asked the couple waiting behind us if they wanted like to join our table.

The couple was Spanish, from Barcelona. They had taken the ferry over to Italy, along with their golden retriever, who lay at our feet. We chatted as we consumed our orders and shared them with one another. I can't recall our conversation. I remember now that the couple spoke only Spanish, although I don't recall having any trouble understanding them. I believe we got by speaking our own tongues, Italian and Spanish, slowly, and peppering our speech with a word or two from the others' tongue. My boyfriend at the time, who spoke some Spanish, must have also translated. I don't recall what they thought of Palermo. They had just arrived. Mostly, when I return to the meal in my mind, our conversation bleeds into the din of the conversations taking place around us, the regular hisses of vapour rising from the stalls, the music seeping into the square from the bars that lined the alleys around it, and the occasional whines of the dog at our feet.

In my memory, I look up and note that the diorama is no longer there and wonder if it ever was. I cannot believe how much change six years can wreak. How did it happen? A part of me wonders whether it was not already like this when I came the first time, and perhaps I was just here on an off night, though it seems impossible. While la Vucciria began as a vibrant market, for me its original is as a silent, empty, and ominous square. There is a part of me that misses how it was when I first saw it – misses the absent façade, the sullen bartenders, the drunk Irish girls, our voices echoing and carrying up from the piazza and into the night.

Blueprint: Marshes of Mondello by R. Pareto, 1870

A blueprint sketch for a proposal to develop the swamp on the other side of Mount Pellegrino with a drainage system of canals.

My boyfriend and I are going to dinner at the Charleston, a Mondello institution. For decades, the restaurant occupied the iconic home of the *Antico Stabilimento Balneare*. Built on pylons over the water, the lido is a huge custard-coloured structure in the Liberty style, set in the middle of the seafront. Reached by a boardwalk, it is a confection of cornices, colonnades and friezes, topped with iron lightning conductors. A few years ago, family friends told me as we were driving past, that, inexplicably, the company that owned the structure refused to renew the restaurant's lease, instead giving it to someone who, it had been said, had a connection to Mondello's management company. But locals still refer to the building as the Charleston, despite the fact that it is occupied by a new restaurant. The actual Charleston has moved down the promenade, a five-minute walk away from its prior location.

It is the summer before the pandemic, August. A time when Palermo is infernal, filled with tourists, and those who haven't retreated from the city turn nocturnal, or sweat in front of fans, or roast by the sea at Mondello. Mondello, a sandy bay on the other side of Mount Pellegrino, is flanked by it and Monte Gallo. Its geographical positioning in a gulf means that the water collects heat. During the months of May, June, even July, and September, the turquoise water is temperate. In August, it becomes a human broth. It is so full that one can't move, and plastic bags and chocolate wrappers and empty soft drink bottles bob between the bathers. Men amble over the browning bodies on the yellow sand, hawking cotton sundresses or corn on the cob or bottles of Moretti beer.

We get off the sand-strewn bus at Piazza Mondello and walk along the promenade, past the small amusement park, where sticky children blub beside creaky rollercoasters. They jam dodgems and throw up over the Ferris wheel. In the summer, entire families who don't have holiday villas make the beach their seasonal home. They arrive early in the morning lugging containers of pasta, panini, and eggplant parmigiana. Some bring a portable grill. These families leave only after the sun sets.

The free part of the beach is a mosaic of towels. The sand, cleared each night, is cigarette studded. There are old men with leathery chests and gold chains, bronzed youths, corpulent mothers, swarms of children. Coloured beach huts line the sand, which families who can't afford a holiday residence treat like a home; inside, they store barbecues and rafts and towels and umbrellas and folding tables and chairs, and come sundown groups will gather around small campfires among the huts. The young drink beer and smoke joints and perhaps one will be strumming a guitar. The old play cards while smoking cigars in their skimpy bathing suits.

We are a little early for our dinner reservation, and we decide to go searching for my grandmother's old house. We pace the streets, passing the high white walls of the great Liberty villas of the very rich, with their many romantic bay windows and airy turrets and porticoes and arches and wrought iron balconies and colourful majolica tiles, on to the more modest summer bungalows. I had recalled that my grandmother's house had been in the Greek island style: a stone white flat-roofed structure tumbling with explosions of bougainvillea.

In truth, I had hoped that we might be early, so that we could do just this. Something had always kept me from looking for that house, from planning to look for it, as though I was afraid I might not find it, or that if I did find it, the materiality of it would tear through my memory. Perhaps I was afraid that, like so many other structures, it had been knocked down. In any case, my return to it always seemed better left to fate. Superstition told me that it was better to stumble across the past, reach it through a side door. Stalking it seemed like looking for trouble.

The sun is slowly setting and people are returning from a day under its rays, ready to shower, change and return to Piazza

Mondello for *aperitivo* hour. Children haul boogie boards and the spray of outdoor showers can be heard, along with the sundown sounds of clanking plates and mothers calling to their kids, the low growl of ignitions and the jangle of keys turning in locks. The usual smells of brine and jasmine and citrus fruit.

The walls of our home were lined with beach scenes of Mondello – my grandmother in her twenties posing against a wall with bare feet, svelte in her black one-piece and coyly gazing away from the camera in black shades; my mother and her siblings playing in the sand wearing metal helmets; majestic Mount Pellegrino, that ragged hunk of sombre rock, constant in the backgrounds.

Mondello as it is now was dreamed up by a Milanese engineer named Luigi Scaglia. One day in 1902, he was standing at the peak of Mount Pellegrino, surveying all that lay below. What he was looking at, at the time, was a small fishing village on a seaside swamp, between the feet of two promontories, Mount Pellegrino and Monte Gallo. Scaglia saw an opportunity. What this seaside city was missing was a seaside. He put together a plan for reclamation and subdivision, and presented it to the city.

While he waited for the city to approve his project, Scaglia sought a foreign lender to help fund it. He found Jules Morand, a Belgian businessman, who, once he had Scaglia's drawings and accounts in his possession, stole the project away from him. Morand formed a company called *Les Tramways de Palerme* (which later became *Mondello Immobiliare Italo Belga*), which took over the project once it was accepted and pushed Scaglia out. The latter later killed himself and the former's company still oversees Mondello.

The swamp was drained and the land was reclaimed and subdivided. Water and sewage systems were constructed. Streets were carved. Tracks were laid down for a tram that ran from the city, through the grounds of the massive Parco della Favorita, to Mondello and back. Carbide lamps were installed and houses with double-pitched roofs were built in the style of those from the Flemish city of Ostend.

Mondello filled up with Palermitans on weekends and in the summer months, who came to sit at the tables in the piazza overlooking the sea, to walk along the promenade and to eat gelato. Although Mondello is only a short distance from the city, families bought or built their summer houses here, and it became custom to reside in Mondello from June to August each year.

Gradually over the decades, people started to move to Mondello full time. My aunt and grandmother moved here when I was a child, a move my mother regretted. Nevertheless, my memories of it are populated by sun and cream-coloured villas, sweet-smelling jasmine and bougainvillea growing in their private gardens and hanging over their walls into the street. The smell of the flowers almost overpowered the stench of the household rubbish that was deposited in the gutters: broken furniture and soiled mattresses, clumps of no-longer-identifiable things and sloppy things, empty packets of pasta and dirty nappies festering in the harsh sun.

Some of my most enduring memories are those hot nights when, well past my Australian bedtime, we'd stroll down to Piazza Mondello, thronging with street food carts, and we'd slurp gelato perched on the low stone wall separating the promenade from the beach, surrounded by other families, groups of adolescents, old couples, kissing lovers, and lone strollers.

I didn't realize it at the time, but that trip must have been a catalyst of great change in my mother's life. I had assumed that my mother had left Palermo behind when she moved to Australia, however I believe this trip was when she truly processed her departure fourteen years earlier. For years after the trip, whenever the apartment on via la Farina was mentioned, she declared that it never should have been sold. *It's such a shame,* she would say. *I told her it was a mistake, but my mother never listens.* During that visit, something shifted in my mother, and I think it was the first time she took stock of what she had given up. She realised that she no longer had something to return to, or else that what she had returned to no longer existed.

My mother is not nostalgic. When I was growing up, everything was periodically thrown out, and throughout these spring evacuations I would assume the role of memory's defender. Clutching onto clothes that no longer fit, toys I was too old for, books I no longer read, I would make the case for each item, explaining the way in which it had enriched our lives and could still if we let it. Perhaps my nostalgia is a response to my mother's lack of it. In his book *Alibis*, André Aciman describes the sense of leaving and remembering place as feeling the pain of a phantom limb – once we've left, returning to the place we once were is impossible: 'part of me didn't come with me. Part of me isn't with me, is never with me.'

As my boyfriend and I walked, my mind called back: waking up in the middle of the night and creeping to the kitchen, where my mother and aunt were whispering under a halo of cigarette smoke; eating rounds of *panelle* and fingers of *crocchè* in the lush, walled garden of a relative. My only memory of my grandfather drifted back into my mind, and then I was transported to meeting my half-uncle over a decade later.

After my grandmother divorced him, my grandfather had met another woman, and had three more children with her. At an outdoor table on a windy afternoon in Venice, my mother and her half-brother, who looked so much like my own, reminisced about their father. I cannot recall whether he was still alive then. They swapped stories of their separate childhoods, and the stories painted a portrait of a proud, selfish man, who told nostalgic stories that were half fiction. My half-uncle, like my mother, had a distant relationship with their father. My mother and her half-brother laughed over their father's pretensions, his obsessions with heraldry. My half-uncle recalled a time when he was young, and an acquaintance dropped by. He had made the faux pas of copying my grandfather's pose of resting his feet on the coffee table. Once he had gone, my grandfather flew into a rage. *Only a Tedesco (himself) could permit themselves such a thing!* However, this self-importance did not extend to his children. Another time, my half-uncle bitterly recalled, he complained to my grandfather than he was on his way to eating up his entire fortune. My grandfather sneered: 'Better to eat it than to leave it to you.'

My grandfather did not say anything as memorable as this when I met him. I was eleven, and I can't remember him saying anything much at all, or taking any interest in me. He was sat at a table on the terrace of my grandmother's villa, a silent, fat old man.

Shadows lengthen, a reminder that we are nearing our reservation. We have found many white villas, but none that are a match for the one in my mind. When I am in this city, my memories seem as fantastical as dreams, my dreams as solid as memories. Perhaps it is a function of return, or the experience of physically being in a place that I usually visit somewhere between my memory and imagination.

Turning around and beginning to retrace our steps, I kick myself for not coming sooner and allowing more time. Next time, I think. Whenever I am not in Palermo, I am planning new itineraries for my next visit, itineraries which invariably fall by the wayside each time I return. Inertia sets in, something else comes up, or the sirocco makes it impossible for me to drag myself anywhere. Perhaps I am afraid of being confronted with my inevitable failures or disappointments in locating the past.

Palermo Mondello Concessione, ca. 1906

Plans for the concession of the area between the Municipality of Palermo and the company Les Tramways de Palerme. The curve of Mondello's bay wedged between Monte Gallo and Mount Pellegrino. Behind it, the area to be developed is outlined in red.

As we walk back down to the promenade, I recall another meal there, a few summers ago. I was with a friend, having lunch at one of the seafood restaurants that line the seafront, where the waiters wear tuxedoes. We chatted to our waiter, and he asked if we were from Palermo. My friend replied yes, she was, though she was now studying in England, and I explained that I was from Australia, but my father is from Agrigento and my mother is a *Palermitana*. At this, the waiter turned to me and replied *bentornata* rather than *benvenuta*, and that suffix, probably used intentionally, filled me with warmth. The choice in suffix marks a distinct difference. While *benvenuta* can be literally translated to the English 'welcome', *bentornata* has no literal equivalent. *Tornata* literally means 'returned', which would render the accurate translation of *bentornata* as 'welcome back'. That suffix designation contains within it the difference between foreigner and family, between tourist and native.

Looking back on that moment with the waiter, a kind of whiplash occurs, with all the moments in which I feel a heart-bursting sense of being at home and the moments in which I feel an alienating dislocation. At what point, I wonder, is one's claim on returning lost? There were just as many realities and misunderstandings that left me feeling unmoored as there were moments when I felt embraced by the city.

Another time, I was pushed out. I was in the main piazza of the mountain town of Monreale with my boyfriend and the teenage daughter of a cousin. We ducked into a small newsagent/bookshop so that he could buy a newspaper. An ancient, spindly, suspendered man had been sitting out the front in a deck chair, and he followed us in. After a few minutes of my cousin and

I leafing through the books on display, the man approached my boyfriend and told him to get us away from the books. 'Books,' he told my boyfriend in a low voice, 'are not to be touched.' Now I noticed that his wife, the ancient, stooped woman behind the counter was staring at us too. When my boyfriend protested, she squawked, 'I don't know where you're from, but around here, in *civilisation*, we don't touch books.' The situation ended with the man banging his cane on the ground and the woman screeching, 'Animals! Get out, get out, get out!'

It is in moments like this that I feel coming to any understanding with this city is an impossible task. To suture the chasm that opens in those moments, I search for the subtext, the explanation, the hidden reason.

Map of Communities, Palermo Atlas, OMA for Manifesta 12, 2018

Overlaid onto the x-axis are new areas or suburbs that divide the city into its various cultural communities, a multicoloured jigsaw puzzle. Here, one category of the invisible borders and zones that divide and comprise the city are shown. Over half the districts in the historic centre, following the routes of the UNESCO areas, are the tourist communities. BANGLADESH and TAMIL communities are puzzle pieces that take up half of la Kalsa, bordering the southern section of via Maqueda. They each also take up a large portion of il Capo in the area around Teatro Massimo. Around here there is also another UNESCO area, along with SRI LANKA and GHANA, which extends out into via della Libertà. On the opposite side of via Maqueda, the market area of Ballarò is a mixed zone surrounded by TUNISIA and GHANA. CHINA is next to the botanical gardens, where all the fabric shops are. The seaside, along la Kalsa and the Gardens, is a free port. On il Cassaro, after the cathedral, there are pieces of CHINA and the UNIVERSITY communities, each surrounded by ITALY. To the north of the city, a TOURIST island sits bordering both the BOURGEOIS community that occupies most of the Libertà zone and the LITTLE SICILY neighbourhood of Borgo Vecchio. Surrounding these central communities are the suburbs, marked ITALY.

A decade ago, Maqueda was so choked with traffic that the pollution blackened the disintegrating Baroque palazzi that lined it. In Susanna Bellafiore's 2014 guide to the city, she writes, shifting from the aloof tone of the travel guide narrator to the disgruntled Palermitan, that 'the former unified sense of the street has been severely mutilated by haphazard demolitions, neglect, and badly reconstructed old palaces; the main impression is one of chaos due to the many tiny little shops with overfilled windows and unattractive signs'.

And it's true that many of the once-noble palazzi that line it are in disrepair. Windows are patched with wooden boards or else left glassless like empty eye sockets. The peeling facades and splintering doors look like sunburned skin. But one by one, the dilapidated and boarded-up buildings on via Maqueda are being restored. A tract of the street, from Piazza Verdi to the Quattro Canti, was pedestrianised in 2014. Since then, souvenir shops and boutiques and Indian clothing bazaars and vintage stores have opened up along it. On the street, tables spill out of the small bars and Sicilian street food places, artists sell oil paintings and postcards, musicians strum guitars, designers sell jewellery and African men sell leather handbags laid out on white sheets. Down the side streets of via Maqueda, one can buy saris and phone cases and embroidered tea towels, clothing and underwear, and fabric and an array of plastic toys and gadgets.

When it was pedestrianised, the shop owners protested, convinced that it would bankrupt them. They argued that Palermitans would refuse to go anywhere they couldn't park their cars directly at the front door. But Maqueda became the most foot-trafficked area of the city. In the summer, a constant throng of tourists and Palermitans marches up and down. Tourists and locals form a human river, and every evening leading up to Christmas, the rugged-up residents take their *passìo* along it.

I am cutting through Quattro Canti, the centre of the x-axis, up past Piazza della Vergogna and the Town Hall. I can never recall the real name of Piazza della Vergogna. It constitutes a large square, with the sumptuous town hall, Palazzo dell'Aquile, on one side, and on the other a decadent palazzo with a peeling façade and boarded-up windows. The square revolves around a massive fountain circled by steps on which sixteen nude sculptures stand. It is said that when the work was unveiled in 1581, the pious city was so scandalised that the people rechristened it the Piazza of Shame. Another theory is that it wasn't impiety that shocked the Palermitans – they were directing their disgust towards the municipal government for spending so much money on follies rather than taking care of more important things, like the roads. On the opposite side of the road is the Baroque building of the University of Palermo's jurisprudence faculty. On the road, men from the countryside smoke cigarettes leaning against horse-drawn carriages with their skinny young sons in the carriage seat, awaiting tourists to ask for a ride. The horses are ridiculously adorned with pompoms and small straw hats with holes cut out for their ears.

The crowd thins out as I walk further down the street. In 2019, they pedestrianised the rest of via Maqueda, from Quattro Canti to corso Tukory near the train station, although pedestrians still tend to loop back before the street ends, stopping at Piazza della Vergogna. Some of the locals continue, but most of the tourists, when they see that the colourful souvenir shops and *arancina* stands have petered off – that the city has stopped performing itself – tend not to venture further.

I come across the narrow shopfront of the agency. Inside, the man I am meeting is speaking to a customer, and he beckons me in through the glass. We have spoken numerous times on the phone. He tells me to go for a walk up via Maqueda, to where it ends at the train station, while I wait for him to finish up. Obliging, I see why he made the suggestion. Here, the businesses are mostly migrant-owned: Bengalese fast-food cafés, Pakistani shops selling phone cases, stores displaying West African-style clothing. The street is populated by black and brown mothers pushing prams, men in tunics, and Sicilian women taking their time strolling in heels. Austere apartment buildings are guarded by heavy wooden doors, which, when left open, reveal lush garden courtyards, with internal balconies looking out onto cobblestone interiors.

Behind them, I know, is what the maps call Albergheria. I have only ever heard it be called Ballarò, the name of the market that it revolves around. Each afternoon, I go to visit my aunt in her artisan workshop there, a quarter of narrow alleys where old men in singlets smoke cigarettes on folding chairs with one hand on their paunch, manning junk shops operating out of garages, and children weave around cars doubled up and helmetless on bikes, or ride electric motor scooters in bare feet. My aunt's workshop is on the edge of a dusty piazza, where a group of old men drags a plastic patio table each day to smoke cigarettes and play cards and drink beers from the tiny *panelleria*, whose constant frying makes the hot air greasy. Next to it there is a doorway around which are clustered mannequins wearing dresses and skirts in bright African prints, the small shop owned by a designer from the Côte d'Ivoire.

When I reach the travel agency, the imam is finishing up work on the phone, and we sit on a bench in front. Imam Macaluso is not what you would expect a Sicilian nor an imam to look like. He has blue eyes. His skin is light, lighter than most Sicilians. His hair is white and uncovered by a *takiyah*. The green and blue stripes on his collared shirt match his eyes. His proper Muslim name is Ahmad Abd al Majid, but his birth name is Francesco Macaluso, and I have read and heard him referred to primarily as Imam Macaluso. Born in New York, his parents were Catholics who reversed their migration and returned to Palermo. When he converted to Islam he was already married, and eventually his wife converted too.

He is the Palermo representative of COREIS, the *Comunità Religiosa Islamica Italiana*, a national association of Italian Muslims that was founded in the early nineties with, he tells me, 'the priority of witnessing and protecting the spiritual and intellectual heritage of the Islamic religion in the West'. The group works with local authorities and state institutions, Christian and Jewish associations, and both national and international Muslim associations, barring those that veer towards 'ideological and fundamentalist tendencies'.

There are 1.6 million Muslims in Italy, and of these only a hundred and fifty thousand are 'native' Italian. Likewise, most of Imam Macaluso's congregation are migrants. COREIS therefore organises religious events and performs outreach to migrants and refugees, including in prisons and migrant reception centres. COREIS has a particular focus on 'inter-religious dialogue', and it has long participated in 'Christian-Islamic Dialogue Day', Holocaust Remembrance Day and Hanukkah feasts with the Jewish community.

As we talk, mothers wearing patterned *gele* push their children in prams, motor scooters whizz past, a group of children gather on the church steps opposite us with a soccer ball and sticks. One kicks their ball into the street and a passing African man kicks it back, the game extending for a minute until he continues on his way.

Palermitans, and Sicilians more generally have a welcoming spirit, he tells me, which can be traced back to their Islamic heritage. He refers to what many consider to be Palermo's golden age under Norman rule. The Normans were descendants of Vikings, Gallo-Romans and Franks from Normandy. When they arrived, the Arabs were ruling Palermo, and the city was filled with hundreds of mosques, some of which had been converted from churches, and many of which were turned back into churches.

Despite the pink cupolas and Moorish arches and Arabic tilework and the labyrinthine topography of la Kalsa, there is actually very little architecture left from Arab Palermo. When the Christian Normans arrived and took the city, they razed all the mosques to the ground. But all those cupolas and mosaics and Moorish arches and secret courtyard gardens are the work of Arab architects who, soon after the arrival of the Normans, were welcomed at Norman court along with Arab poets, and artists and scientists and functionaries. The Normans had the Arabs build them palaces outside the city walls, of which a couple remain, filled with muqarnas and mosaics and lush gardens. They designed new Christian churches, which is why many look like mosques, and some even have quotations from the Koran etched into marble plaques. This was the Middle Ages. While the rest of Europe shivered from disease in dark, dank castles and villages, the sun shone on Palermo, where green gardens flourished and the inhabitants enjoyed fresh, clean water courtesy of the Arab-designed pipelines. While the Normans were western Christians, they oversaw a multicultural, multifaith, multilingual society of Christians, Jews, Arabs and Byzantines, where divorce was legal, rapists were prosecuted, freedom of speech and literacy were considered rights, and slavery was abolished.

The story of Palermo's centuries as a multifaith and multi-ethnic paradise is one that the city has only recently begun to tell. In the past few years, Palermo has pushed its tourism by highlighting the Arab-Norman architecture, an itinerary which was listed as a UNESCO heritage site in 2015. Orlando was credited by the *Guardian* for turning Palermo 'from a mafia city into a haven for refugees'. He often states that borders between East and West don't exist in the city, which he pithily refers to in the same article as a 'Middle Eastern city in Europe, and a Norman city in the Mediterranean'. According to Orlando, it is thanks to Palermo's influx of refugees (before the pandemic, I was told that about a thousand arrived in the city's port each week), that mafia control is diminishing, and the city is returning to its Middle Eastern roots.

As Imam Macaluso and I talk, a man walks past carrying a cloth sack of handbags hitched over his shoulder to sell on the street in Maqueda – one of those ones where they can scoop everything up if the police happen by. More kids show up, one on one of those electric, pedal-generated motor scooters, which many of the children around here seem to have. Imam Macaluso gestures to them and says to me that the kids are 'indigenous Palermitans and new indigenous Palermitans', meaning Sicilian children and second-generation children of Maghrebi, West African, Senegalese and Moroccan parents.

The kids are running around, kicking their ball, yelling excitedly to one another. Leaving, I walk past them, and I overhear that they are speaking in Sicilian, in heavy Palermo accents. I don't speak Sicilian, let alone *Palermitano*. I don't speak it because my great-grandmother spoke Piedmontese, and not Sicilian, and the rule in my grandmother's home growing up was that Italian was lingua franca. Not speaking Sicilian is not exactly a hindrance in getting around Palermo, but it does mark one as an outsider. My cousin sometimes teaches me a few words, the bad ones. A real Palermitan speaks *Palermitano*. This lack and my accent, which is always mistaken for northern when I'm in the South, and southern when I'm in the North, betray me. I think about how those Palermitan kids, all born or raised here, all speak *Palermitano*, and I think about something that Orlando had said to me when I spoke to him: 'I am not a *Palermitano* because my father and mother were from Palermo, I am not a *Palermitano* because I was born in Palermo. I am a *Palermitano* because I decided to remain a *Palermitano*.'

Modern topographic map of the Gulf of Palermo, no date

Here, the craggy coastline juts out into the sea, Mount Pellegrino at its pinnacle. Contour lines trace the intricate network of roads, so dense at the city centre that it is a thick, black mass. Shading relief forms the deep mountain peaks and ridges surrounding the city. Palermo is below Mount Pellegrino, on the right, and on the Mount's left peeks another, smaller bluff, backed by the serpentine tops of a mountain range.

The sun casts its rays directly onto the island, making the mountains glint and the sea glimmer with phosphorescence. The plane sweeps over fishing villages flanked around gulfs and rough, wind-swept red cliffs. Looming behind the airport are Montagna Longa and Mount Pecoraro, and behind them the mountain ranges of Palermo fan out, mythic, majestic as though they are sandcastle monoliths that the wind has gradually shifted over time, or cruel, indifferent gods, unmoved by the difficulty with which the island's inhabitants clamber over them or toil to make things grow on them. Once, this land was heavily forested. It coursed with rivers. Volcanic soil and the Mediterranean climate made the island ideal for growing crops of wheat, olives for oil, vineyards for wine, and fruit groves. When the Romans colonised Sicily, they stripped the island of its trees so that the land could be used to harvest grain for the empire. Rainfall diminished. The water sources, once rich, dried up, and droughts began. The lack of running water caused malaria to spike and the once-lush terrain to become lunar.

As it lands, the plane creeps so close to the sea that the shoreline appears in detail. The water is an ink and turquoise-coloured mosaic, and one can make out the individual pebbles that comprise the beach. The plane glides along the runway, the sea still near enough that were someone to open the emergency door, they could make a clean dive. On the other side, the grey chiselled slope of the mountains, carpeted in swaths of sun-bleached scrub and grass.

Move closer to the city, into the thick, indistinguishable black mass. The mountains become hulking barriers partially seen at the end of a street, in the distance. The sea is invisible behind the city blocks and the traffic roar. Pathways no longer seem so clear-cut, now that the realities of traversing them have become apparent, like getting stuck in traffic, for example, or shoving one's way through a crowded street. Space becomes unwieldy just as the life that inhabits it comes into view, becomes real.

From the balcony of the rented apartment, I spy a Chinese family's cramped kitchen across the street. I see the grandfather in the morning, smoking in his singlet, I see the mother cooking in her nightgown. I see the children sitting at the table eating from steaming bowls. I try not to look, but their apartment window is so close to our balcony that it is difficult not to. When the mother notices me glance in their direction, she pulls down the shutters.

The quarter we are in is il Capo, the area that surrounds the long, tangled market that winds through it, southwest of the Teatro Massimo. The area itself is tangled, made up of tight, winding streets. The palazzi, more rudimentary here than in places like la Kalsa, are all three or four storeys, warm-coloured, each with a simple iron balcony. Il Capo is inhabited by working-class Palermitans who either couldn't afford or chose not to leave during the Sack of Palermo, and by migrants, like the Chinese family, Tunisians and Bengalis.

The Chinese family owns a shop below their house. I see one of their children sitting behind the register, doing homework during a lull. There are many Chinese and Indian shopkeepers in the street below. They sell shoes or homewares or stretchy clothes that smell like plastic wrap. On another hot morning, a Sunday maybe, the streets are silent and empty except for Muslim men walking the street, alone or in groups of two or three, and wearing pale-coloured tunics and *takiyah* or kufi caps, perhaps on their way to mosque.

Our balcony looks out over this narrow alley, but we enter the building on the opposite side, via a piazza. Although the historic centre has become a tourist hotspot, the area's historic residents still live here. Even though via Maqueda is one block away, the piazza through which we enter our building is still populated by mean-looking adolescent boys, broken glass, empty chip packets and used condoms, graffiti, dog shit smeared over the cobblestones, and an overflowing rubbish container.

After the war, this area was a slum. In the early 1950s the Italian sociologist and social activist who Aldous Huxley would dub the 'Gandhi of Sicily', Danilo Dolci, surveyed a hundred families living in the area, chosen at random. Dolci notes that in one alley, he sees a naked child squatting on the ground pass a twenty-five-inch tapeworm. The apartments are so cramped that at bedtime, mattresses are laid down, covering most of the floor space. Ninety-one rooms provide accommodation for 576 people. Of the hundred families he surveys, only one has a toilet, and fourteen have water taps, which are cut off during the summer to direct water to the public gardens. Forty-nine of the families have electricity. Most of the floors of the dwellings are broken tile, a few are packed dirt or coarse cement. Most children don't go to school. Dolci records twenty past cases of typhus and adds that 'forty-one children have suffered from various chest diseases, nearly all of which were diagnosed as tubercular. Infant mortality is due largely to some form of blood poisoning.'

Slowly, the apartments in il Capo are being bought up, renovated, and rented as Airbnbs. Tourists prefer to stay here than around via della Liberta, because it has the exoticism that tourists seek in coming to Palermo. Here, you can smell the intensifying smell of fish from the market, can hear the hissing of *panelle* being fried, can hear the howls and yelps of the market vendors calling to customers and one another. You can also see the underwear and linens and dresses flapping like flags from the lines above your head and boys riding scooters without helmets. In the Capo market, some restaurants have opened up amongst the stalls, so that tourists can sit at the outdoor tables cooling themselves with crisp white wine and perch their feet on the table legs, in nervous fear that the water being hosed away from the seafood stalls will seep into their sandals.

Around the corner from the churches are mosques. In some streets, warehouses have been turned into shops, fronted with tables filled with an assortment of paper fans, plastic tennis rackets, fabric bags, stickers, phone cases, clocks, calculators, glue, straw hats, hair rollers. Inside, oriental rugs and leather bags are strung from the ceiling. Other shops have been assembled using corrugated iron sheets, selling magnets and aprons with Sicilian lemons or a map of the island, and patterned lengths of cotton.

Deviating from the market and heading further west into the thick of the quarter, domestic life becomes more and more evident. There are pot plants and small gardens outside front doors which are open, covered only by a fringe of hanging beads through which kitchens are visible. Next to the entrances are plastic bags of household refuse. The women sweep the footpaths around their doors and chat to one another from their doorways, old people sit on chairs in front of their homes in the tight alleys, and speak to their neighbours. Men convene to smoke cigarettes. They live their lives outside, the distinction between the threshold of their homes and the street indistinct.

Walking back through to via Maqueda, a stout, broad-bodied woman wearing a stained cotton house dress clutching a broom in one hand and a cigarette in the other returns my gaze, eyes narrowed. All eye me off with the suspicion that one would lend an intruder into their Palermo, a break-and-enterer, which is what I am.

According to G. Malcolm Lewis, Homo sapiens developed a sense of 'spatialization' early in their evolution as a response to a pressing need. Forty thousand years ago, early Homo sapiens were constantly on the move. They sought out food and water sources and avoided danger, such as larger animals or threatening weather. Constantly coming upon new surroundings meant constantly scanning those new surroundings. They developed sharp eyesight, which allowed them to understand spatial elements such as distance, orientation and area, elements with which we are still preoccupied. They developed language, which enabled the transmitting of information, and the ability to abstract space into a visual form followed on from this.

Most maps tend to be neutral in their representation of space, but the spaces in which we live are not neutral. Within them are boundaries, different zones with different customs and different rules. The borders of maps – like the limits of our language – constitute the boundaries of our known worlds. There is only so much you can know of a place without coming up against the limits of your own abilities.

La Via dei Frati by Santo Mazzarisi, 2017

A meandering route traced through the hinterland of le Madonie mountain range, from Caltanissetta in the island's centre out towards Cefalù on the coast near Palermo. The route, according to laviadeifrati. wordpress.com, was conceived by Santo Mazzarisi after he had undertaken the pilgrimages of Santiago de Compostela, Cammino di Assisi, and Cammino di San Benedetto. In 2016, he walked the 166-kilometre tract from Caltanissetta to Cefalù, traced along ancient communication trails and the passages of friars who tackled the terrain on foot or on the backs of mules.

We tend to think of, or perhaps feel, migration as an aberration, an anomaly, a rupture, but this is not actually so. The history of the world is defined by movements, by the mass passage of migrants and refugees, by the shifting of borders themselves, moved and stretched and cut up by wars and colonisations and invasions. In fact, maps, although they present places as static, are themselves driven by movements, in the sense that their purpose is to assist us in moving through the world, and they are based on previously taken paths. The static lines on maps that denote roads, paths and routes, after all, are all derived from an initial recorded movement through space. Both mapping and movement through space are attempts to orient oneself within space. Once plotted, sea becomes navigable, land routes become clear. It is here, in the map, that the routes stamped out by others are immortalised in the landscape.

Later, my boyfriend and I returned to the Madonie. We spent a weekend there, staying in a *masseria*, a fortified farmhouse. We rode on the backs of horses that clambered up and down rocky slopes, among vineyards and through olive groves. Goats bleated and jumped atop sheds and cars, making the whole place smell of tart cheese. Cannons periodically fired shots to scatter the wild hogs that roamed the forestland. From the open terrace, where our meals were served, dotted with wine barrels and trellised with wisteria, we could see past the thickly wooded mountain slopes through to the sea of Cefalù. We didn't return to Alimena.

The manager prepared simple meals for us, local wine and meats and seasonal vegetables and fresh bread, cuts of cheese and bowls of glistening olives, and baskets of pastries and pots of homemade jams for breakfast. We were the only people staying there and as we sat in the afternoons, drinking red wine and extricating olive pits from our mouths, he would sit at another table, smoking rolled cigarettes and chatting to us. He showed us photos of peasants from a nearby town, gathered in the piazza for a mass wedding before a war. 'See their faces?' he said. 'The lines in them, the tiredness. It's the work that aged them. They're only eighteen, twenty – kids – but they're already old.'

These were people who lived in poverty, haunted by the magnificence of the past, or perhaps it wasn't magnificence they saw, but merely proof of their timeworn servitude to foreign rulers. Perhaps this is why some Sicilians see their monuments in such an ambivalent way, and why, up until not too long ago, I heard somewhere, it was normal to take a wheelbarrow to ancient places like the Ancient Greek temples of Agrigento and wheel away a cart of limestone to build one's home.

In Palermo, there are seven ancient statues of a king known as *il Genio*, the *genius loci* of the city. Of these, two date back to an unknown pre-Roman date and origin. In each iteration, *il Genio* is a statue of a king cradling a thick serpent who is either devouring the king's heart or suckling at his breast. There is an inscription in Latin on the statue that reads: *Panormus conca aurea suos devorat alienos nutrit*. In Italian: *Palermo conca d'oro divora i suoi e nutre gli stranieri*. Palermo, the golden shell, devours its own and nourishes its visitors. If a Sicilian feels a tie to the island – which, in my anecdotal experience, all do – it is one characterised by heartbreak. In most cases, this tie is not to history, or monuments – most Sicilians I spoke to, outside the city, felt this tie most strongly to the earth, to owning a piece of it, to making things grow from it and possessing this produce, something which they were denied for millennia.

This relationship to the land as a basis of cultural identity is one that echoes the beliefs and religions of native peoples all over the world. There is something attractive, comforting, about having a relationship to land that I can call my own birthright. Perhaps this is a symptom of growing up a migrant, an invader, in a colonised country. In Rebecca Solnit's *Book of Migrations*, she writes of how the presence of indigenous people in North America creates questions for Americans who are the product of migrations, 'questions of what it means to be and whether it's possible to become native; about what kind of a relationship to a landscape and what kind of rootedness it might entail; and about what we can lay claim to at all as the ground of our identity if we are only visitors, travellers, invaders in someone else's homeland'. Sicily is, for me, a place where history is on my side, and it was once a place where I felt as though I did not have to ask questions about being or becoming native, questions that arose and arise the more time I spend there.

Telling the man about the book I was writing, I explained my family history. He told us that he had lived in Rome for ten years, but that as the years went by, he became too homesick for the island. Something inside him had to be rooted here, toiling to make things grow from the arid earth, fruits that tasted of their labour. You're like this too, he said. It doesn't matter that you weren't born here. Your blood ties you to this earth, and you too feel the need to make something grow from it.

The thrill of being welcomed into the fold, much like the slippery satisfaction of being mistaken for an Italian who never left. A kind of confirmation.

What he was describing was the concept of homeland, the idea that we have an origin in this world, a place where we unquestionably belong, and that this place is passed down through bloodlines. What does that even mean? Even though I am sceptical about notions of blood, when I am in Sicily, something inside of me uncoils. It is the red, rugged crags, the villages crowning mountain tops, the smell of churning coffee beans outside bars, the crystalline sea a reminder of the clear borders of the island, the whips of the sirocco wind against my cheeks. Perhaps it is the knowledge of being on land or among people with whom I share a history.

What are we talking about when we talk about homeland? In her essay, 'The New Nomads', Eva Hoffman suggests that every individual feels themselves an exile. 'We feel ejected from our first homes and landscapes, from childhood,' she writes, 'from our first family romance, from our authentic self. We feel there is an ideal sense of belonging, of community, of attunement with others and at-homeness with ourselves, that keeps eluding us.' Often our creation stories begin with such an expulsion from an original home. Abrahamic religions follow the story of humankind's expulsion from the Garden of Eden, while the Aztecs originated from the Seven Caves (*Chicomoztoc*), from which humanity crawled out of and onto the earth. The Pueblo tribes that follow a matrilineal kinship system originally dwelt in a dark underground, from which they emerged into the world of daylight.

Once, when I went to my father's village in the province of Agrigento, I paid a visit to my father's ancient aunt. She hobbled from room to room, sweeping a hand over the matching bedroom set (the mahogany bed with the looming headboard, above which hung a framed picture of Christ, and the heavy four-door wardrobe, and the bedside tables topped with an Evangelical Bible and white lace) and the dining set (an oval mahogany table that took up almost an entire, barely used room, with its matching high-backed chairs, along with a long mahogany sideboard loaded with porcelain) that her late husband had bought her, *a good hard-working man.* We settled in the kitchen and she tried to make me eat one of the sweets off the tray she had bought from the *pasticceria*. She told me that my paternal grandfather had worked for relations of my maternal great-grandfather, Salvatore, who also happened to be from that same town. She told me: 'Your father didn't have to leave. He had it good here. It would have been better if he'd stayed.' Her daughter piped up, admonishing her mother, reminding her that my parents met in Australia. 'So what?' she replied. 'They could have met anyway and had children here!'

As much as I did not enjoy being carted around Palermo and then my father's village on the island's southern edge as a child, there was a part of me that was wistful for what I sensed was an absence, something that my parents had neglected to pass down to me. The fact was that my mother had been and still was so connected to Palermo. Our family had a network of countless friends and family, and it made our aloneness in Australia starker, more obvious.

Perhaps this is where the rupture is, a rupture that sits within children of migrants, who share a past with one place and a future with another. Or, as in my case, they are uncertain of where their future lies, and so they parse the past, looking for clues, searching for the lost future in which they never left. I am, of course, a product of migration – my parents met far away from their origins in Australia. And yet I stalk the streets of Palermo looking for that other version of me.

Map of Palermo by Marquis de Villabianca, 1778

The map was drawn by the Marquis of Villabianca, a famous scholar of Palermo history. It is a Wonderland-style Palermo, with chequerboard fields and stained-glass city blocks. On the left, a road runs parallel to the city: via Lincoln, where the botanical gardens are to be laid down. In his map, the Kemonia and the Papireto, long smothered by the city, are visible beneath the buildings, shaded in a lighter colour, as though he is saying that in their absence they still maintain a ghostly presence. Like all relics, they remind us that while they no longer exist in their prior forms, here they once were. Nothing ever truly leaves us, and no river can ever truly be smothered. The rains can be relied on for resurrection, just as the past comes back to haunt in unexpected moments.

This is a map that seeks to solve the problem of time. Villabianca's map includes the past as a subterranean entity, visible only to the viewer of the map but nonetheless real. Just because we cannot see the past, the underground city beneath our feet, doesn't mean it is not there.

As we walked through the streets one summer, my boyfriend kept pronouncing the streetscape as '*decadente*'. Usually, we use the English equivalent of this word to mean rich, indulgent or luxurious, but the Italian is connected solely to its other meaning, which means to be in a state of decay. But I like how these two meanings, together, encapsulate Palermo, the way the crumbling buildings echo the past, both that of history and my own, narrower family past, and how the echo, once it reaches my ears, has lost its form, so that what is discernible are only abstract sounds of feeling. Rust sprays, crumbling plaster, rotted beams, the suggestion of what was there, but also the inconsequentiality of what was there. Does it matter anymore? It is so unreachable and yet it reaches its way to us here in the present, it edges into our lives the way the strangling roots of a Moreton Bay fig might, uprooting the plumbing of our house.

In one of the Melbourne houses I lived in, great cracks branched off on all the walls like an egg about to hatch, and in another, the floor of the house was on a diagonal, so that we could set a tennis ball down at the back door and watch it roll to the front. A friend of mine told me that this was because the earth of the northern suburb we lived in was clay, and so all the houses were slowly sinking. In that suburb, the weatherboard and brick homes were all being bought up for millions of dollars, and being knocked down so that shoddy townhouses could be built in their wake. These, too, would sink.

The word *haunt* is rooted in the Old French *hanter*, 'to frequent, visit regularly; have to do with, be familiar with; indulge in, cultivate'. We are only ever haunted by ghosts, synonyms of the past. To be haunted is to be visited by the past, like the resurrection of an ancient river in the rain, but also to indulge the past, to cultivate a haunting by making ourselves more attractive to ghosts, like obsessing ourselves with the cities of our mothers, begging to be haunted.

And I suppose this is what I do in Palermo: haunt the city in the hope that it haunts me back. Later, in Trieste, during months of confinement, I researched and wrote lists of haunting sites I had missed on my last trip, bemoaning how I was bound from now visiting and also, in a small sense, enjoying this imposed limitation, because it meant that I would not need to come up against my own innate limitations. One day, when researching what I could online about Alimena and our Tedesco relatives, I found a record of a potential ancestor, Stefano Tedeschi-Oddo, who was born in Alimena in 1836 and died in Palermo in 1882. There was, it was written, a bust of him in the *Giardino Inglese* in Palermo, erected due to his service as a battlefield medic in the Expedition of the Thousand, Garibaldi's project in liberating (some would argue conquering) Sicily and unifying the island with Italy in 1860.

Asking my mother about it over the phone, she said, 'Yes, of course he's our ancestor. Everyone knows that. Your uncle took your cousins to his bust when they were last in Palermo.' She was indifferent when I mentioned that she had never bothered to point this out or take me. *We had people to visit.* My uncle sent me photos of the bust, of he and my cousin, looking a bit bored, standing beside it, behind a pruned rosebush and marigolds. The bust, mounted on a column which reads *Stefano Tedeschi-Oddo dei Mille*, is twice as tall as they are. There he is, on top of the column, possessor of a thick horseshoe moustache that reaches to his jawline and a broken-off nose. My uncle explained to me that the family surname was Tedeschi up until the cusp of the twentieth century, when a clerical error changed it to Tedesco. Our ancestor also changed his surname to Oddo, his mother's surname, because he wanted nothing to do with the colonising power of Austria (*tedesco* is Italian for 'German').

There is a thrill in unearthing some kind of permanence in regards to my family's presence in the city. Gazing at the photograph, I am tempted to observe a resemblance, but I tell myself that this is ridiculous – marble faces all look the same. Severe, uncanny, lifeless, or cut off from life. I hear a whisper, my mother in my childhood telling me about some great-great-uncle who had plotted and battled for Italian unification. I know nothing other than these scant facts, cannot begin to know where to slot him if I were to attempt a family tree. My mind cannot seem to intellectually connect this marble face with my mother's stories or with the deserted streets of Alimena. What is the point of commemorating people when in the span of four or five generations they will be strangers to all those living, including their descendants?

But of course, Stefano's bust is on my list of sites to tour the next time I am in Palermo, and he will be on my list if I have my own children. I oscillate between indulging in the comfort of old photos and places, of longing to be in Palermo, and examining that comfort further, poking holes in its flimsy ramparts. It is a kind of ambivalent nostalgia, one that turns and folds constantly in on itself before spinning out again.

Why does it comfort me to look at photos and visit the places of my ancestors? Our gazing and touring is much more about us than it is about these strangers with whom we may share a nose. David Berry writes in his book, *On Nostalgia*, that even Hofer knew that nostalgia for one's native land was more about 'the strength of the imagination alone' than it was about the land missed, more about memory, and the way it moulds the past, than material circumstance. But nostalgia was still homesickness, remedied only with returning to the homeland in question. Perhaps it was that a return to the homeland settled the yearning in the sufferer's heart, or perhaps Hofer recognised that when we speak of home, we are often speaking of a place located in a past time. In returning to the homeland, perhaps the sufferer saw how such a place as they yearned for no longer existed, or only existed fleetingly.

Nostalgia, Hofer maintained in his 1688 medical dissertation, was like the German *heimweh* or the French term *maladie du pays* (literally sickness of the homeland). He denoted specific embodiments of this sickness, such as *pothopatridalgia*, to describe the feeling of pain derived from yearning for one's parents' home. While Hofer held fast to the belief that nostalgia was recurring memories and thoughts, one Swiss physician suggested in 1705 that nostalgia was actually caused by the 'increase in atmospheric pressure' produced when the Swiss soldiers descended to ground level from the mountains.

Later, in the twentieth century, theory surrounding nostalgia was infiltrated by psychoanalytic thought. It became, according to H. Kaplan, 'a variant of depression, an acute yearning for a union with the preoedipal mother, a saddening farewell to childhood, a defence against mourning, or a longing for a past forever lost'. Nostalgia could be a fleeting moment of sorrow, or a persistent gnawing ache, not for a tangible home or terrain, but for a place that was merely a symbol of an idealised past.

The yearning had also to be bittersweet: sweet because in remembering and longing, the nostalgic recovers some of the pleasure of the original memory, bitter because the nostalgic recognises that the pleasurable moment is in the past and therefore irretrievable, but also because the memory of the moment is more pleasurable than the moment itself. In fact, it is perhaps more pleasurable precisely *because* it is irretrievable. We mourn the past and the irreversibility of time, while simultaneously knowing that this is what makes both the past and the present so beguiling to begin with.

Master plan for City of Palermo by engineer Luigi Castiglia, 1884

Here is a plan for a future Palermo that never came to be. This plan features fewer expansions, with major building on a grid merging via della Libertà with Borgo Vecchio. The next year, the new plan by Felice Giarrusso would be produced and chosen for the city.

I find myself gazing at this map and longing for the lost Palermo it depicts. It represents a potential, another path, a city in which everything may have turned out differently. Perhaps, if the expansion had not already begun, then more attention would have been paid to reconstructing the old centre, or perhaps without the expansions, the old centre would have been levelled. Perhaps this is why we look to the past rather than the future: the past is all potential. It contains all possible futures and versions of the present. It's what gives us lust for youth. Back then, we might say to ourselves, anything was possible. As time passes and we move through our lives, possible futures are driven out by the present. The lost future suggested by Castiglia's plan is a ghost narrative that haunts the streets.

It is always sunset when the ship leaves Palermo's port for Naples, and what seems like the entire population of the vessel rises to the stern to watch the city recede. Pink clouds tumble over the darkening mountains. Below, in the port, are commercial vessels and shipping containers and construction. Smoke billows from the ship and the air is sticky. Palermo is a gargantuan entity, impossible to decipher. That miniscule peninsula rounded by two rivers has bloated into a monolith that envelops everything in its path and clings to mountain sides. Lights flicker on, creating constellations. It's hard to describe how it feels, looking out over Palermo's endless rooftops, the pink cupolas and the palm trees, the rising Madonna from the Column of the Immaculate Conception, the mountains looming over it all, a frenetic jumble of ongoing lives, an ongoing city that will be changed by the time I return.

Palermo has its back turned to the rest of the island, making it an island of a sort itself. The valley in which Palermo rests faces seawards. When readying to sail away I always try to put myself in the minds of the city's first settlers, foreign seafarers who, I imagine, spotted from their ships a green valley crowned by mountains, overrun by plant life flourishing under the sun and criss-crossed by rivers. They drew their ships closer, sailing them straight into the mouth at which the many rivers met, and up along their banks.

Each new ruler came not from the island, but outwards, from the sea, and each left its mark on the city. Palermitans spoke Phoenician then Latin then Greek then Arabic. The history of many of these colonisers and the arrivals and departures that define the city can be read in Palermo's streetscape. The first people of Sicily were Sicels, ancients whose stone tombs have remained, and Sicans. Then came the Greeks in the eighth century BCE, who left temples and open-air theatres and olive trees. The Romans then came, making Sicily their empire's first province and logging the island's forests. The Arabs brought oranges and lemons, almonds and pistachios. The Normans then took over, erecting cathedrals and castles and leaving their genetic mark, visible in today's blue-eyed Sicilians. The Spanish and the French and the Austrians kept palaces in Palermo, from which they exploited the countryside and its people. Temples turned to mosques turned to churches. They left their architecture, their roads, their gardens. Each loan word, each dish, each architectural hallmark a reminder of their existence and their demise, the temporality and impermanent permanence of everything.

Perhaps this is why Sicilians so distrust talk of the future – because they have learned that it is out of their hands, that life is a series of ruptures. Sicilians, Orlando had said, do not respect time. In their language, there is no future tense – there is only an eternal present. He had demonstrated, speaking in Sicilian basic enough for me to understand: '*Io vaio a Roma oggi. Io vaio a Roma tra un anno. Io vaio a Roma fra dieci anni. Vaio. Cosi.*' I go to

Rome today. I go to Rome in a year. I go to Rome in ten years. Go. Like that.

I recall my mother, when I was a child, would refuse to make promises for the future. If I asked, for example, if we could go to the park the next day, she would only ever say 'maybe'. After I begged her for a definitive answer, she would always reply that she couldn't promise me that we would go to the park the next day, because what if we died before then? Then she wouldn't be able to keep her promise.

Similarly, I worry that every time I leave Palermo will be the last. As the ship leaves port, I gaze back at the city, making plans and wondering whether I will ever carry them out, attempting to ward off bad luck by worrying. My English student had told me that at a certain point when leaving Palermo by ship, the cross-cut by il Cassaro and via Maqueda is visible in the canopy of rooftops. I had never taken note of this, and I kicked myself for not noticing. I promised myself that next time I left Palermo by ship again, I would look out for the moment, but I cannot count on returning again, and I don't know when or if I will ever leave by ship again.

As the ship gradually pulls away, the blue sea dazzles in the fading light, and the windows of the houses all built up along the coast of the mainland slowly glow under the fall of dusk. There is a haze of shimmering particles in the air, and through the fog blown up by the ship's ducts, it feels like a smoky dream. I always cry when I leave Palermo, and I always wonder why I am crying. More experiences have been relegated to the faulty faculty of memory. Although I spend much of my time outside Palermo wishing I were there, each time I leave I feel a nag of regret. Regret at not having seen enough, regret at having gone at all. Each time I return, my own memory supplants the myth that I was nourished on as a child. With each return, Palermo is yanked further from the island of the past, towards that of the present. Progressively, more and more of the nostalgic sheen is rubbed off, so that the old places lose some of their magic.

But even as the old magic wears off, the pull of the city remains, strengthens, even. Attempting to articulate, even to myself, my feeling towards Palermo triggers a state of inner aphasia. I simply cannot draw the necessary words to describe a relationship which to me feels crude, innate, irrational. I know only the flush of emotion that floods my body when I am there, or when I see it in a film or hear about it in a story. I close my eyes and I can feel the fierce embrace of the sun's rays, can feel the melted ice from the fishmonger's stall seeping into my sandals as I wind through a tight-packed market, can sense the hot sizzle in the air at the port as I wolf down *panelle e crocchè* at a food truck, the very roots of my hair greasy from the steam that billows from the grill.

My own body is made up of migrations, a past which contributes to a sense of being unmoored. Palermo is a place onto which I can project this feeling, the last stop on a series of them, itself a product of settlements and trade and invasions and, in the last century, of exoduses to the north and arrivals from the south. Despite this sense of being unmoored, I never felt the desire to cease my family's pattern of movement, of failing to put down generational roots. Likewise, I never felt the need, when I was a child, to return. I always assumed that one day, I would leave the place where I grew up, and leave Australia more generally. I thought it was normal that when people grew up, they left their familiar surroundings and found a new place to call their own, and I was certain that this was what I would do. It actually came as a surprise to me when, after that first trip to Palermo in my twenties, I began to feel an itch for the cities of my family's past.

The hopeful, rubble-strewn city my grandmother first arrived in is just as vanished as the troubled city my mother grew up in, just as lost as the ancient cities of the Normans or the Arabs. The city I visited in my childhood, too, is gone. I want to reconstruct or reverse the destruction of the palazzo my grandmother and her parents first stayed in, the palazzo in Alimena. I want my grandmother to visit me from beyond and take me on a tour of these places. I want their lives to play out before me like a film on screen. I want to be in the film. I want to see my mother and siblings as children. I want to return to my own childhood visits to Palermo with the knowledge that I have now, that it would all end, so that I would know to remember it or record it or live it better. I want to do-over all my visits to Palermo. I want to reverse time, back to before my grandmother had her first stroke, to ask her about the past. I want to walk the streets of her cities, Benghazi and Turin and Rome and Palermo, and run into her, see her as a stranger might. I want to hear her voice again.

Acknowledgements

[TK]

A Note on the Author

Amaryllis Gacioppo is a journalist and author with a Joint PhD in Creative Writing from Monash University and the University of Bologna. In 2015 her story 'Dreams' won the Lord Mayor of Melbourne Award for Short Story. Her writing has been shortlisted for a number of awards, including the Bristol Short Story Prize and the Scribe Nonfiction Prize. Her stories and essays have appeared in Award Winning Australian Writing, Catapult, 3:AM, and elsewhere. This is her first book.

A Note on the Type

The text of this book is set in Bembo, which was first used in 1495 by the Venetian printer Aldus Manutius for Cardinal Bembo's De Aetna. The original types were cut for Manutius by Francesco Griffo. Bembo was one of the types used by Claude Garamond (1480–1561) as a model for his Romain de l'Université, and so it was a forerunner of what became the standard European type for the following two centuries. Its modern form follows the original types and was designed for Monotype in 1929.